MUTINY AND REBELLION IN THE OTTOMAN EMPIRE

EDITED BY JANE HATHAWAY

A Publication from the University of Wisconsin-Madison
MADISON, WISCONSIN
2002

CONTENTS

Jane Hathaway: Introduction ... 1

Part I: Rethinking the Historiography of Seventeenth-Century Ottoman Mutinies

Gabriel Piterberg: The Alleged Rebellion of Abaza Mehmed Paşa: Historiography and the Ottoman State in the Seventeenth Century ... 13

Baki Tezcan: The 1622 Military Rebellion in Istanbul: A Historiographical Journey ... 25

Palmira Brummett: The River Crossing: Breaking Points (Metaphorical and "Real") in Ottoman Mutiny ... 45

Part II: Mutiny and Rebellion in the Ottoman Provinces

Virginia H. Aksan: Manning a Black Sea Garrison in the 18th Century: Ochakov and Concepts of Mutiny and Rebellion in the Ottoman Context ... 63

Antonis Anastasopoulos: Lighting the Flame of Disorder: Ayan Infighting and State Intervention in Ottoman Karaferye, 1758-59 ... 73

Robert Zens: Pasvanoğlu Osman Paşa and the Paşalık of Belgrade, 1791-1807 ... 89

Jane Hathaway: Ottoman Responses to Çerkes Mehmed Bey's Rebellion in Egypt, 1730 ... 105

Part III: Mehmed Ali Paşa of Egypt: Both Mutineer and Mutinied Against

Judith Mendelsohn Rood: Mehmed Ali as Mutinous Khedive: The Roots of Rebellion ... 115

Khaled Fahmy: Mutiny in Mehmed Ali's New Nizamî Army, April-May 1824 ... 129

Select Bibliography ... 139
Index ... 149

Maps

The Ottoman Empire, showing locations of mutinies ... 12
The Ottoman Balkans in the 18th and 19th centuries ... 61
Egypt in the 19th century ... 62

CONTRIBUTORS

Virginia H. Aksan is associate professor and chair in the history department at McMaster University, Hamilton, Ontario, Canada.

Antonis Anastasopoulos is assistant professor of history at the University of Crete.

Palmira Brummett is professor of history at the University of Tennessee-Knoxville.

Khaled Fahmy is assistant professor of Near Eastern Studies at New York University.

Jane Hathaway is associate professor of history at Ohio State University.

Gabriel Piterberg is assistant professor of history at the University of California, Los Angeles.

Judith Mendelsohn Rood is associate professor of history and Middle Eastern studies at William Tyndale College, Walled Lake, Michigan.

Baki Tezcan is assistant professor of history at the University of Wisconsin-Milwaukee.

Robert Zens is a doctoral candidate at the University of Wisconsin-Madison.

The articles in this volume were submitted originally to the *International Journal of Turkish Studies*, published at the University of Wisconsin, 4255 Humanities Building, Madison, Wisconsin 53706, USA.

Jane Hathaway

INTRODUCTION

This collection is the first collaborative volume devoted to the subject of military rebellion, and more particularly mutiny, in the Ottoman Empire. In the course of its more than 600-year history, the Ottoman Empire weathered rebellions and threats of rebellion from every quarter, both within the imperial capital and in its far-flung provinces; mutinies and threats of mutiny were likewise not infrequent occurrences. Perhaps the most famous mutiny, the 1730 revolt of the low-level naval officer known as Patrona Halil that brought down Ahmed III, is the subject of a well-known book.[1] The infamous *Edirne vak'ası* of 1703, which had helped bring that sultan to the throne, has provided fodder for at least one major monograph and one Ph.D. thesis.[2] Meanwhile, the widespread Celali rebellions of dispossessed *reaya* and discharged soldiers of *reaya* origin, which traumatized Anatolia in particular at the end of the sixteenth and the beginning of the seventeenth centuries, are well represented in the secondary literature,[3] and smaller revolts have received due treatment in articles and within the context of larger studies.[4] Recently, Palmira Brummett has set the standard for a systematic appraisal of the empire's many military rebellions in a path-breaking article that attempts to construct a model of

---

1. M. Münir Aktepe, *Patrona İsyanı, 1730,* İstanbul Üniversitesi Edebiyat Fakültesi Yayınları No. 808 (Istanbul, 1958).
2. Rifaat A. Abou-El-Haj, *The 1703 Rebellion and the Structure of Ottoman Politics* (Istanbul, 1984); Sabra F. Meservey, "Feyzullah Efendi: An Ottoman Şeyhülislâm," Ph.D. thesis, Princeton University, 1965.
3. Mustafa Akdağ, *Celali İsyanları* (Ankara, 1963); William Griswold, *The Great Anatolian Rebellion, 1591-1611* (Berlin, 1983); idem, "Djalālī," *Encyclopaedia of Islam*, 2nd ed.; Halil İnalcık, "The Socio-Political Effects of the Diffusion of Fire-Arms in the Middle East," in V.J. Parry and Malcolm Yapp, eds., *War, Technology, and Society in the Middle East* (London, 1975), pp. 195-217; Karen Barkey, *Bandits and Bureaucrats: The Ottoman Route to State Centralization* (Ithaca and London, 1994). This is not taking into account the many works on socio-economic circumstances related to the Celali rebellions, notably population pressure and inflation.
4. For example, Robert Dankoff, trans., *The Intimate Life of an Ottoman Statesman: Melek Ahmed Pasha (1588-1662)* (Albany, 1991), pp. 125-35; Abdul-Karim Rafeq, *The Province of Damascus, 1723-1783* (Beirut, 1966), pp. 208-84; André Raymond, "Une 'Révolution' au Caire sous les Mamelouks: La Crise de 1123/1711," *Annales Islamologiques* 1 (1966): 95-120; Daniel N. Crecelius, *The Roots of Modern Egypt: A Study of the Regimes of Ali Bey al-Kabir and Muhammad Bey Abu al-Dhahab, 1760-1775* (Minneapolis and Chicago, 1981), pp. 46-103; John W. Livingston, "The Rise of Shaykh al-Balad ʿAli Bey al-Kabir: A Study in the Accuracy of the Chronicle of al-Jabarti," *Bulletin of the School of Oriental and African Studies* 33 (1970): 283-94.

2   Introduction

Ottoman mutiny.[5] This collection hopes to carry forward this promising and long-overdue line of inquiry while pointing it in a new, comparative direction.

The original inspiration for this collection was a panel on mutiny in the Ottoman Empire organized by Professor Brummett for the 1996 meeting of the Middle East Studies Association of North America. Four of the contributors to this volume participated in that panel. Our discussant, my colleague Professor John F. Guilmartin, afterward suggested a much broader, indeed global, project comparing mutinies in all societies and at all periods. We eventually launched a call for papers that yielded thirty-six essays on mutinies of every conceivable type in societies ranging from ancient Rome to the People's Republic of China. Fourteen of these essays, including one by Professor Brummett on the motif of river-crossing in Ottoman mutiny narratives, appeared in a volume entitled *Rebellion, Repression, Reinvention: Mutiny in Comparative Perspective*, published in 2001 by Praeger, a subsidiary of the Greenwood Publishing Group.

The nine papers assembled here, including Professor Brummett's "The River Crossing," reprinted with Praeger's permission, constitute a self-contained unit on Ottoman mutiny that merits separate publication. They seek not so much to define Ottoman mutiny or to construct an analytical framework for it as to use specific instances of military revolt as keys to the political, social, and territorial tensions pervading the societies in which they occurred. By examining rebellions in different parts of the empire at different periods, moreover, the contributors reveal patterns that rebellion tended to take within an Ottoman context, patterns of Ottoman response to rebellion, and patterns of narrative treatment of these rebellions in contemporary and later sources.

The contributions fall into three distinct sections. Gabriel Piterberg's and Baki Tezcan's essays offer sometimes conflicting yet uncannily complementary historiographical analyses of the events surrounding the 1622 regicide of Sultan Osman II, popularly known as Genç Osman. This incident was a critical turning point for the empire that has troubled historians from that day to this. Together with Palmira Brummett's provocative reading of mutiny narratives, the articles offer a vision of the seventeenth century as an era not only of battles over state authority but of struggles for the official narrative of these conflicts. Judith Mendelsohn Rood's and Khaled Fahmy's contributions provide similarly complementary, occasionally conflicting, appraisals of Mehmed Ali Paşa. The rebellion of that Albanian notable against Sultan Mahmud II arguably laid the groundwork for the emergence of modern Egypt, but, viewed from another standpoint, he can be seen as the most successful in a long line of ambitious provincial *ayan*. The four remaining essays address specific instances of provincial rebellion that help to set in context the mutinies of both Mehmed Ali Paşa and Abaza Mehmed Paşa, the self-styled avenger of Genç Osman. Virginia Aksan examines the mutinies that plagued the Ottoman garrison at the critical Black Sea fortress of Özü (modern Ochakov, Ukraine) during the eighteenth century. Ochakov's garrison included a surprisingly large number of

---

5. Palmira Brummett, "Classifying Ottoman Mutiny: The Act and Vision of Rebellion," *Turkish Studies Association Bulletin* 22:1 (1998): 91-107.

Albanians, as well as Bosnians and Kurds, who illustrate the territorial, ethnic, and social dislocations resulting from continuous warfare on three different fronts during the eighteenth century. At the same time that Albanian *reaya*-turned-soldiers were far away in the east, trying to hold Ochakov against the Russians, the *ayan* of their native region were extorting illegal taxes from the populace left behind. Antonis Anastasopoulos' essay scrutinizes the rebellious behavior of one such group of Albanian *ayan* in what is today eastern Greece--the homeland of the future Mehmed Ali Paşa of Egypt. Robert Zens focuses on one extraordinary *ayan* leader near the Ottomans' border with the Hapsburg Empire, their other chief European enemy. Pasvanoğlu Osman Paşa led a brigand band that attracted opponents of Sultan Selim III's westernizing military reforms; his raids over some fifteen years ultimately triggered the Serbian national uprising of 1804. My own paper follows the exploits of Çerkes (Circassian) Mehmed Bey of Egypt, who, in 1730, committed the greatest act of mutiny of any of the rebels examined here: not simply challenging the sultan or disobeying his orders but blatantly betraying him by seeking Hapsburg support. His ignominious fate served as a warning to later rebellious Egyptian grandees, including Mehmed Ali, of the limits beyond which provincial *ayan* dare not go.

Were all of these rebellions mutinies? This question is impossible to answer satisfactorily, particularly given the ambiguous vocabulary employed by the Ottoman sources themselves. Various instances of military revolt are termed *fitne*, *fesad* (*fesat*), or *isyan* in these sources. As Brummett points out, *fitne* seems to carry the connotation of overturning social and political order--a connotation that no doubt stems from its earliest use in Islamic sources to denote a disruption of the Muslim *umma*'s unity.[6] *Fesad* in Ottoman parlance seems a more generic term for disloyalty or disobedience. *İsyan* is more generic still, denoting rebellion in general, perhaps more widespread than *fesad*. None of the three needs to be limited to military populations, although military revolt is often implied. At the same time, any of them could carry the conventional dictionary definition of mutiny: refusal, often violent, by military personnel to obey the commands of their superiors. Regardless, as Aksan observes, Ottoman sources not infrequently use all three almost interchangeably. Their choice of words is sometimes calculated to achieve a certain rhetorical effect: *fitne ü fesad*, as Piterberg, Tezcan, and Anastasopoulos confirm, is veritable code for seditious wrongdoing that undermines political authority and civic order. On the other hand, serious rebellions and even near revolutions, such as the 1703 outbreak, receive the cryptic, understated label *vak^{c}a* ("incident") for different rhetorical reasons. The ambiguity of the sources' own vocabulary underlines the fact that in Ottoman society, the boundary between military revolt and social protest was exceptionally fluid. Military revolts, particularly among rank-and-file soldiers, often adopted the rituals and strategies of popular protest and, indeed, sometimes dovetailed with wider social protest, drawing in members of the ulema and the craft guilds--to which soldiers, particularly Janissaries, often belonged.[7]

---

6. See Hathaway, "Ottoman Responses to Çerkes Mehmed Bey's Rebellion in Egypt, 1730," n. 22, in this volume.
7. On popular protest, see, for example, Gabriel Baer, "Popular Revolt in Ottoman Cairo,"

The causes that triggered Ottoman military revolts were not unlike the causes that led to mutiny in other societies. Stereotypical incitements to mutiny were unquestionably present: chronically delayed pay, poor food, corrupt or brutal commanders, long months of service in exhausting wars far from home. Tension between the officer elite and the rank-and-file was endemic throughout the empire, as attested by the Patrona rebellion and by the frequent appearance of Janissary "bosses" from the lower officer cadre in Egypt and other provinces.[8] As in other societies, these incitements typically reflected more profound grievances within the society at large: inflation and currency debasement, a particular hazard for Janissaries on fixed salaries from the state;[9] artificial shortages resulting from hoarding by corrupt officials; wars needlessly prolonged by the agendas of particular palace factions;[10] or the more abstract notion that the sultan had violated a "contract" to protect and provide justice to his subjects.[11] Such grievances resonate throughout most societies and offer a basis for comparing Ottoman mutinies to those in other polities.

As Brummett has noted, however, the category of Ottoman mutiny includes a phenomenon that, while not uniquely Ottoman, is a hallmark of Ottoman rebellion. A provincial governor or grandee, after building up a regional power base, would rebel against the sultan--seeking, in most cases, not outright independence from Ottoman rule but an autonomous sphere of operation free from the interference of the central authorities. The provincial rebel Abaza Mehmed Paşa, who claimed to be avenging a martyred sultan and carrying forward his reforming policies, was an exception. More typical were Çerkes Mehmed Bey, Mehmed Ali Paşa, the *ayan* of Karaferye, and even Pasvanoğlu, who for all that he defied Selim's military reorganization, seemed to desire material gain and personal aggrandizement. These provincial grandees are readily comparable to the warlords who dominated China during interregnums or to the *caudillos* of nineteenth-century Latin America.[12] What perhaps distinguishes them is their place in the Ottoman administrative hierarchy and in the imperial web of household politics. They were government officials, and many of them had started out as clients in the households of provincial

---

Der Islam, 54 (1977): 213-42; Afaf Lutfi al-Sayyid Marsot, "The Ulama of Cairo in the Eighteenth and Nineteenth Centuries," in Nikki R. Keddie, ed., *Scholars, Saints, and Sufis: Muslim Religious Institutions since 1500* (Berkeley and Los Angeles, 1972); Jane Hathaway, "The Role of the Ulema in Social Protest in Late Eighteenth-Century Cairo," unpublished M.A. thesis, University of Texas, 1986.

8. See, for example, P.M. Holt, "The Career of Kuchuk Muhammad (1676-94)," *Bulletin of the School of Oriental and African Studies* 26 (1963): 269-87; Raymond, "Une 'revolution'".

9. On this point, see especially Şevket Pamuk, *A Monetary History of the Ottoman Empire* (Cambridge, 2000), pp. 56-58, 141-42, 198, 227-28.

10. See Virginia H. Aksan, *An Ottoman Statesman in War and Peace: Ahmed Resmî Efendi (1700-1783)* (Leiden, 1984), pp. xii, xv-xviii, 104-05, 120-22, 154, 162-63, 184ff.

11. See Baki Tezcan's and Palmira Brummett's essays in this volume.

12. On the latter, see Seth Meisel, "The Politics of Seduction: Mutiny and Desertion in Early Nineteenth-Century Córdoba, Argentina," in Hathaway, ed., *Rebellion, Repression, Reinvention: Mutiny in Comparative Perspective* (Westport, CT, 2001).

governors or vezirs, or perhaps in the household of the sultan himself.[13] Establishing a power base in a province meant building a household that could rival the sultan's own, to say nothing of the households of competing provincial grandees and officials in other provinces. The duties of provincial governors and grandees, furthermore, included providing troops for the imperial armies and, not infrequently, leading them into battle. Often, the opportunity for a governor or grandee to rebel occurred in the course of an imperial campaign, when his provincial army was mobilized and on the march. In such circumstances, his revolt entailed removing troops from the sultan's service to his own, or even turning them against the sultan, and thus constituted mutiny in the conventional sense.

In responding to mutiny, the Ottoman central authority showed a certain consistency. When Janissaries or *sipahi*s in the imperial capital demanded the heads of specific officials, they typically received them. There was little else the palace elite could do when the mutineers were right there in the capital--and sometimes right there on the palace grounds--and no alternative military force was at hand to counter them. When mutinies occurred far off in the provinces, by contrast, the central authority's response was initially, and sometimes entirely, rhetorical. To mask the state's inability or unwillingness to take forceful action, we see instead a flurry of indignant sultanic orders, demanding that the mutiny cease or, in the case of the Karaferye Albanians and Çerkes Mehmed Bey, that the unruly *ayan* be exiled from the province and never allowed to return alive. Anastasopoulos laments the state's inefficacy in quashing Karaferye's mutineers, but perhaps this lack of concrete action was in some respects calculated, much like the Ottoman punitive expedition's mysterious failure to encounter Abaza Mehmed Paşa, noted by Piterberg. If a provincial grandee raised a large army and started conquering territory in his own name, as Mehmed Ali Paşa did, that was a threat to the empire. On the other hand, if he simply extorted taxes and harassed the peasantry, fomenting disorder, the annoyance and loss of revenue could perhaps be constrained by imperial directives. When the state imposed a fundamental institutional change, however, as in the case of Selim III's *Nizam-i Cedid*, the opposition of a rebellious grandee such as Pasvanoğlu could no longer be countenanced, even rhetorically; the labels that the *ferman*s attach to Pasvanoğlu are harsher even than those directed at Çerkes Mehmed, and they accurately reflect a new determination to stamp out opposition.

Even before the *Nizam-i Cedid*, the imperial directives were more than just empty words. The rhetoric of loyalty to the sultan meant something to the grandees; every *ferman* that arrived reconfirmed their identities and positions, from the names to whom the order was addressed to the epithets directed against the wrongdoers. It was typically sent in response to the written complaint of a loyal grandee, who was

---

13. On this phenomenon, see Rifaat Abou-El-Haj, "The Ottoman Vezir and Paşa Households, 1683-1703: A Preliminary Report," *Journal of the American Oriental Society* 94 (1974): 438-47; Metin Kunt, *The Sultan's Servants: The Transformation of Ottoman Provincial Government, 1550-1650* (New York, 1983); Jane Hathaway, "The Military Household in Ottoman Egypt," *International Journal of Middle East Studies* 27 (1995): 39-52.

cited in the prologomena. A public ceremony entailed welcoming the sultan's *kapıcıbaşı*, who came to deliver the order and perhaps to investigate the complaint, as well as receiving the order and reading it. The directive was subsequently recorded in the local *kadı*'s *sicil* and perhaps summarized in local chronicles. Thus, flurries of orders served to proclaim publicly who was loyal and who was mutinous or, worse, treasonous. Mutiny itself sometimes took the form of a ritualistic public display,[14] as when Janissaries overturned their soup kettles, and so could the government's response. In the latter case, a highly formulaic, rhetorical proclamation would label the event and the participants, perhaps without doing much to stop or punish them--either because the state could not do much or because it preferred to let warring *ayan* "bleed each other white."

As the essays included here attest, such proclamations and court records comprise a vital part of the source base for studies of Ottoman mutiny. Indeed, the records of *şeriat* courts are probably the closest Ottomanists can come to proceedings of official enquiries or courts-martial, major sources for studies of mutiny in other societies that do not exist in the Ottoman field before the nineteenth century. The court records also give some indication of popular reaction to mutiny, for the court was the arena in which townspeople and peasants might accuse the perpetrators of theft or injury, or where the rebels' estates might be sorted out. Even these records barely hint at such critical features as the motivation or self-perception of the rebel or mutineer. As far as the events of a revolt or mutiny are concerned, on the other hand, the *şeriat* court records of a region where rebellion occurred, such as those of Karaferye, Vidin, Cairo, or Jerusalem under Egyptian occupation, often prove a gold mine, providing a blow-by-blow account of the revolt's progress and resolution (or lack thereof). *Fermans* or records of *fermans* listed in *mühimme defterleri* can serve a similar function, as in the case of Pasvanoğlu and Çerkes Mehmed Bey.

Analyses of the Genç Osman affair, on the other hand, rely overwhelmingly on chronicles. As Piterberg's and Tezcan's essays make abundantly clear, our perception of the events of the affair, to say nothing of its import and ramifications, depends on which chronicles we consult, and even on which manuscripts of a particular chronicle. In the case of Çerkes Mehmed Bey's revolt, a chronicler such as al-Damurdashi, writing only a few decades after the fact, embroiders his account of Çerkes' exploits with tropes from parallel tales of upheaval and flight to enemy territory. In this case, archival documents can serve to "correct" the chronicler's fabrications, although the fancies to be glimpsed in the chronicles give us a window into popular perceptions of rebellion and mutiny that may have been circulating in that time and place.

---

14. On this point, see David J.B. Trim, "Ideology, Greed, and Social Discontent in Early Modern Europe: Mercenaries and Mutinies in the Rebellious Netherlands, 1568-1609," in Hathaway, ed., *Rebellion, Repression, Reinvention.*

CENTRALIZATION AND DECENTRALIZATION/EAST vs. WEST

Quite apart from the light they shed on patterns of Ottoman mutiny, the essays in this book engage, explicitly or implicitly, with key issues reshaping the Ottoman field. To begin with, the mutinies and revolts that the contributors investigate occurred during the Ottoman Empire's "middle years," after the so-called "Golden Age" of Süleyman I (1520-1566) but before the westernizing reforms of the mid-nineteenth century, known collectively as the Tanzimat. The conception of this period as one of "decline" has by now been discredited, thanks to the revisionist publications of Suraiya Faroqhi, Linda Darling, and numerous others.[15] Instead, this period is now recognized as one of, to use Faroqhi's term, "crisis and adaptation." Yet it is still regarded as an era of empire-wide decentralization, during which the Ottoman provinces achieved substantial autonomy from the central government. In fact, these rebellions can easily be regarded as symptoms or products of this decentralization.

It is almost too easy, however, to substitute decentralization for "decline," positing weakening central control, rather than institutional decay, as the root cause of the empire's accumulating territorial losses and ultimate collapse. In such a context, decentralization is no more satisfying a historiographical construct than decline, as historians of the Ottoman Empire are beginning to acknowledge. We might rather suggest that the Ottoman Empire, like most empires and, indeed, like most modern polities, underwent alternating cycles of centralization and decentralization. These cycles, in turn, depended on the economic, political, and military circumstances of the empire's different parts, as well as on the economic, political, and military goals of the empire's leadership. Decentralization, in this context, was not necessarily an unstoppable, wholly negative force but the sum total of rational choices made by different elements of Ottoman society in the capital and in the provinces. Furthermore, different episodes of centralization and decentralization varied according to the circumstances in which they occurred and the agents who contributed to them. Within this less value-laden framework, mutiny and rebellion can be interpreted not as inherently decentralizing (and therefore inherently negative) but as the result of conflicting trajectories of either centralization or decentralization.

No rebellion better illustrates the ambiguities of centralization and decentralization than the Genç Osman affair, the subject of Gabriel Piterberg's and

---

15. For example, Suraiya Faroqhi, Part 2 of Halil İnalcık, ed., with Donald Quataert, *An Economic and Social History of the Ottoman Empire* (Cambridge, 1994), pp. 413-14, 468-70, 572-3; Linda T. Darling, *Revenue-Raising and Legitimacy: Tax Collection and Finance Administration in the Ottoman Empire, 1560-1660* (Leiden, 1996), Introduction; Leslie P. Peirce, *The Imperial Harem: Women and Sovereignty in the Ottoman Empire* (New York and Oxford, 1993), pp. 153-85; Douglas A. Howard, "Ottoman Historiography and the Literature of 'Decline' of the Sixteenth and Seventeenth Centuries," *Journal of Asian History* 22 (1988): 52-77; Jane Hathaway, "Problems of Periodization in Ottoman History: The Fifteenth through the Eighteenth Centuries," *Turkish Studies Association Bulletin* 20:2 (1996): 25-31.

Baki Tezcan's papers. The young sultan Osman II (reigned 1618-1622) was murdered at the behest of rebellious Janissaries of largely *kul* origin. In other words, the murderers had been recruited as boys from the subject Christian population of the Ottoman Balkans and Anatolia in the process known as *devşirme*, or "collection," converted to Islam, and taken into palace service. The *kul* system is typically regarded as the quintessence of centralized rule, for all palace pages, Janissaries, governors, and vezirs who rose through it were servants of the sultan who reinforced his centralizing authority. Yet elements of this *kul* population formed an entrenched interest group in the imperial capital, contributing to a process that could justifiably be termed decentralization at the center or, perhaps more appropriately, a competing vision of how central power should be apportioned. Osman's goal was to augment, if not to replace, these *kul* with recruits from the empire's eastern provinces. Was Osman therefore seeking to recentralize his authority by depriving the *kul* of their unprecedented political clout and by expanding the base of recruitment? Or was he seeking to decentralize the empire by bringing personnel from far-flung provinces into the military machine? Here, "centralization" and "decentralization" are of limited utility in analyzing Osman's own political agenda, as opposed to the agendas of late Ottoman and Republican historians--incisively analyzed by Tezcan--who equated "centralization" with progress and attributed both to Osman's venture.

The centralization-decentralization dichotomy obscures a more profound geographical and ethnic spasm that seemed to be wrenching the empire during and after the Genç Osman affair. The empire was torn between East and West in a rift that had arguably been in preparation ever since Selim I and Süleyman I conquered the Arab lands in the early sixteenth century. *Devşirme* recruits from the Balkans, western Anatolia, and Hungary, as well as mercenaries of *reaya* origin, were now required to defend an empire that stretched to the borders of Iran, into the Caucasus, and into the Persian Gulf. As a result, the Ottomans began to draw military manpower from the same sources exploited by the defeated Mamluk sultanate and the embattled Safavid and Özbek empires, namely, the Caucasus region, as well as eastern Anatolia, and many *kul*s and other "westerners" regarded these "easterners" as outsiders--*acemi, ecnebi--par excellence*.[16] It was no coincidence that the two provincial governors who rebelled in Osman's posthumous behalf, Abaza Mehmed of Erzurum and Hafız Ahmed Paşa of Diyarbakır, were Abkhazian governors of eastern Anatolian provinces.

The highly ambivalent relationship between the Ottoman central authority and the far-flung, ethnically diverse populations, already visible in the seventeenth century, became pronounced in the eighteenth, when unprecedented three-front warfare brought the battlefield into the very backyards of the populations in question. As Aksan explains, this period of seemingly endless warfare witnessed

---

16. See Gyula Kaldy-Nagy, "The 'Strangers' (*Ecnebiler*) in the Sixteenth-Century Ottoman Military Organization," in Gyula Kara, ed., *Between the Danube and the Caucasus* (Budapest, 1987); Metin Kunt, "Ethnic-Regional (*Cins*) Solidarity in the Seventeenth-Century Ottoman Establishment," *International Journal of Middle East Studies* 5 (1974): 233-39.

the movement, for military purposes, of large populations from their native regions to far corners of the empire, so that Albanians fought on the Dnieper while Kurds and Abkhazians fought on the Danube. Recruitment for war, combined with new opportunities for participation in the Ottoman administration, contributed to social upheaval in the homelands of these various ethnic groups, impelling some to leave for other provinces, encouraging others to exploit the situation at hand for their own gain. The Albanians studied by Antonis Anastasopoulos, and Pasvanoğlu Osman Paşa, as depicted by Robert Zens, clearly used the opportunity to monopolize provincial leadership positions and to extract revenues from the surrounding population. Their resulting entrenched positions in their respective regions gave them undeniable leverage with the central government, possibly helping to explain why directive after directive from Istanbul failed to have any effect, at least initially.

Surely the ceaseless cycle of strife and ineffective "reprisal" formed one of the earliest memories of the future Mehmed Ali Paşa, perhaps encouraging him to flee his native land while, at the same time, alerting him to the power that provincial *ayan* could now wield vis-à-vis the central authority. As a transplanted mutineer himself, Mehmed Ali realized the hazards of relying on recruits from distant locales and launched a bold new experiment by recruiting from the Egyptian *reaya* on the spot. His gamble paid off, for the opportunities for social and economic mobility provided by an army career, as in so many other societies,[17] promoted cohesion among the men and between them and their paşa, arguably outweighing the solidarity they felt with the native populace.

Viewed through the lens of the "east vs. west" paradigm, in fact, Mehmed Ali looks very different from his conventional image. Numerous historians of Egypt, particularly those of a nationalist bent, have noted the parallels between the autonomy-minded Egyptian grandee Bulut Kapan Ali Bey, who rebelled against the sultan in 1768, and Mehmed Ali. None, to my knowledge, has pointed out that in displacing the grandees of the late Qazdağlı household, the leadership of which was by then overwhelmingly Georgian,[18] and by implanting his own corps of Albanians, Mehmed Ali was essentially replacing a cadre of "eastern" *ayan* with "westerners." But he must have been intensely conscious of this fact. As he consolidated his hold over Egypt, he never downplayed his Albanian origins; on the contrary, they formed the cornerstone of the identity he constructed for himself.[19] Had anyone at the time suggested that he was a successor to the Georgian *mamluk* Ali Bey, he would no doubt have rejected the idea out of hand.

---

17. For a parallel phenomenon in the final years of British rule in India, see Raymond Callahan, "The Indian Army, Total War, and the Dog that Didn't Bark in the Night," in Hathaway, ed., *Rebellion, Repression, Reinvention*.
18. Jane Hathaway, *The Politics of Households in Ottoman Egypt: The Rise of the Qazdağlıs* (Cambridge, 1997), pp. 101-06, 169, 170; Daniel N. Crecelius, "Russia's Relations with the Mamluk Beys of Egypt in the Eighteenth Century," in Farhad Kazemi and R.D. McChesney, eds., *A Way Prepared: Essays on Islamic Culture in Honor of Richard Bayly Winder* (New York, 1988).
19. Khaled Fahmy, *All the Pasha's Men: Mehmed Ali, His Army, and the Making of Modern Egypt* (Cambridge, 1997), pp. 1, 6.

Regionalism and ethnic diversity, then, were not simply extraneous details of mutiny and rebellion during the middle period. Rather, if the studies in this volume are any indication, they were key contributing factors. Geographically marginal populations, notably Albanians, Circassians, and Abkhazians, surface time and again as the instigators and chief participants in these incidents. Revolt was, in many respects, their attempt to negotiate or protect a favorable niche for themselves in an empire that they were increasingly helping to administer and defend. Likewise, the manner in which the central and provincial authorities engaged with these diverse rebels--fighting them, co-opting them, bombarding them with paper--provides a key to Ottoman strategies for projecting authority during a period of considerable territorial uncertainty and demographic flux. Nor was the Ottoman Empire alone in facing such challenges during this period. Its major antagonists, the Russians, Hapsburgs, and Safavids, confronted similarly diverse and widespread populations with their own conflicting loyalties. Comparisons of the modes of mutiny and response in these societies would surely reveal unexpected similarities amid the obvious differences.

In all of these empires, and in virtually every other polity, a mutiny or rebellion provides a moment of social stress in which underlying societal tensions, and the state's ability to cope with them, stand out with unusual clarity. We hope that this exercise in comparing intra-Ottoman mutinies will lead to broader comparisons between Ottoman and other societies, helping to break down the historiographical and cultural barriers that sometimes keep us from seeing that, beneath the outward trappings, one mutiny is often much like another.

ACKNOWLEDGMENTS

It is now time to let the contributors' efforts speak for themselves. Before doing so, I wish to thank those whose support made this volume and the larger mutiny project possible. The Mershon Center for Policy Studies, Office of International Studies, and Division of Comparative Studies in the Humanities at Ohio State University generously funded the initial stages of the project. My colleague John F. Guilmartin was instrumental in launching the project and was a source of advice and encouragement throughout. I thank Leah L. Wong for producing the maps in this volume. I also owe a debt of gratitude to Virginia Aksan for taking decisive action to get these papers published in English. My husband, Robert Simkins (known to my Ottomanist colleagues as "Mimar Bob"), has yet to rebel despite enduring much hardship during the editing process. Finally, I thank the contributors themselves for their participation and for cheerfully responding to my queries and requests for modifications. I am obliged only to add that the views expressed in these essays are those of their respective authors and do not necessarily represent those of the editor or the publisher.

NOTE ON TRANSLITERATION

Ottoman Turkish words are rendered in a form as close to modern Turkish as possible, although ʿ*ayn*, *hemze*, and long vowels are typically indicated in manuscript titles. Names of provincial grandees and place names are given in Turkicized form, without diacritical markings. Names of Arabophone writers are rendered in Arabicized form, although without diacriticals, so as to be recognizable to the broadest range of readers, while Arabic manuscript and book titles are transliterated according to the standards of the *International Journal of Middle East Studies*, with full diacritical markings.

12 The Ottoman Empire, showing locations of mutinies

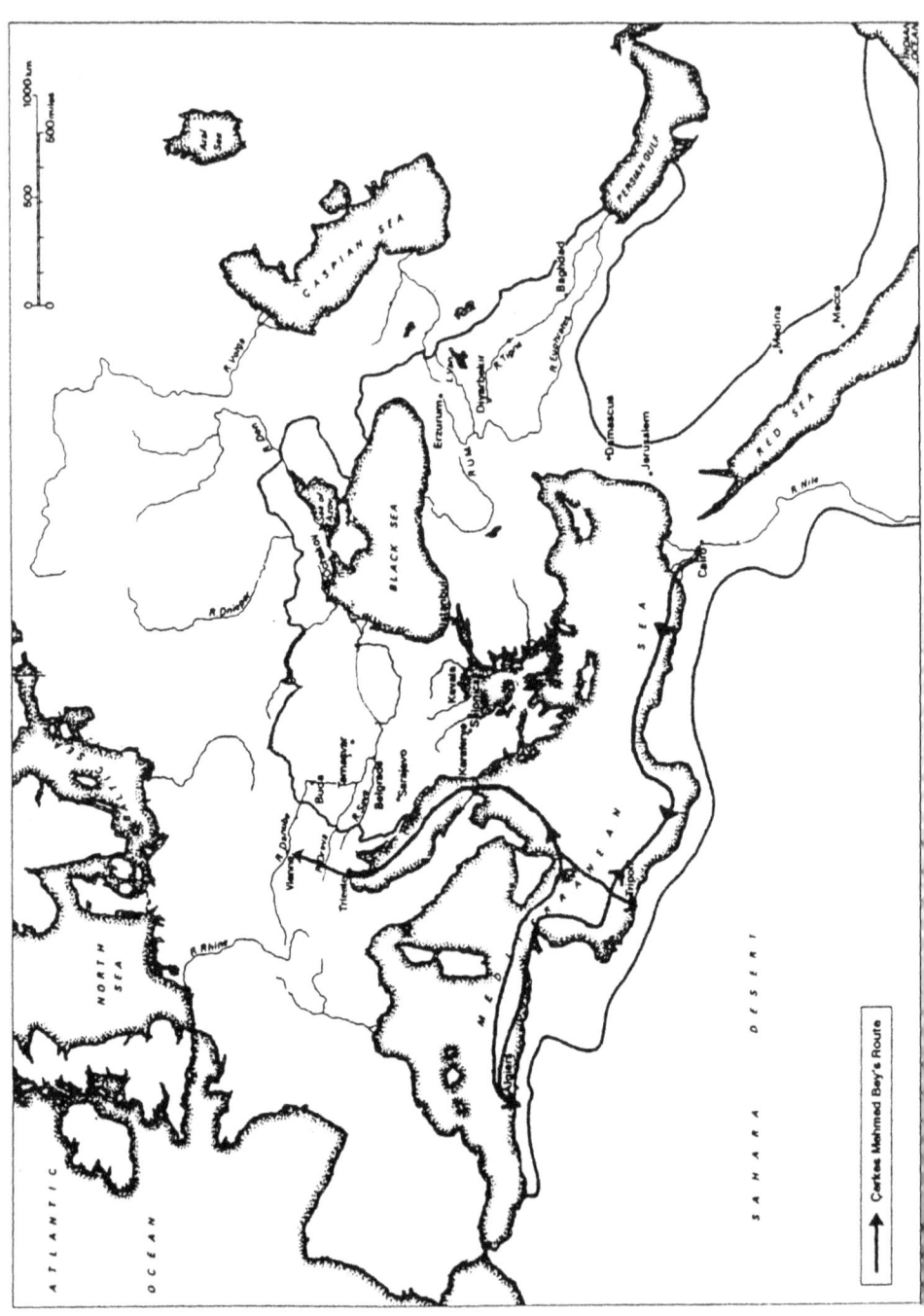

Gabriel Piterberg

THE ALLEGED REBELLION OF ABAZA MEHMED PAŞA: HISTORIOGRAPHY AND THE OTTOMAN STATE IN THE SEVENTEENTH CENTURY

Cümlemiz bir sefine içinde. (We are all in the same boat.)
--from Hatt-ı Humayün issued by Abdülhamid I (1774-89) and Selim III (1789-1807)

The aim of this paper is to interpret the ways in which one layer of an individual's identity was inscribed in contemporary historical texts. (I stress "layer" because the individual in both modern and pre-modern societies never has a single, comprehensive identity.) The paper then relates the micro-case of Abaza Mehmed Paşa's identity to the wider context of seventeenth-century Ottoman history, paying particular attention to scholarly concern with the state's boundaries vis-à-vis society. After unfolding the story of the *Haile-i Osmaniye* (Ottoman Tragedy) of which the Abaza affair was an integral part, the first part of this study takes the historiographical story up to the point when it was sealed as the state's official narrative in *Tarih-i Naima*. The second part then examines the historiographical controversy over Abaza Paşa's sociopolitical identity as a significant key to the interpretation of the Ottoman state and its alleged breakdown in the first half of the seventeenth century. Finally, the essay weighs a few noteworthy interpretations of the Ottoman state in that period and suggests that the contemporary historiographical discourse is a useful guide for understanding the redefinition of the Ottoman state in the seventeenth century.

This paper is based on my extensive research in Ottoman historical texts. Informed by Hayden White and Dominick LaCapra, that work was an attempt to show that such texts constitute narrative discourse that is judgmental and interpretive. Now I wish to take the historiographical discourse beyond the domain of both *Quellenkritik* footwork and literary analysis, bearing in mind Valentine Cunningham's reminder that "[i]t is impossible, then, finally... to distinguish (using the Yeatsian metaphor) the literary and textual dancer from the historical dance."[1]

---

1. Valentine Cunningham, *British Writers of the Thirties* (Oxford, 1988), p. 2.

THE EVENTS

Three turbulent days--18-20 May 1622--were inscribed in Ottoman memory, courtesy of Kâtip Çelebi, as the *Haile-i Osmaniye* (Ottoman Tragedy). Genç Sultan Osman II was deposed by his *kullar* and strangled in Yediküle; then his paternal uncle, Deli Sultan Mustafa I, was re-enthroned. I take the liberty in this history of using Kâtip Çelebi's literary instinct as a trope that captures the period 1617-23 (the reigns of Mustafa I and Osman II), within which Abaza Paşa's alleged rebellion erupted.

In one of the earliest manifestations of the shift from fratricide to seniority in the Osmanlı dynasty, Ahmed I (1603-17) was succeeded by his brother Mustafa I in 1617. After Mustafa's palpable insanity led to his deposition early in 1618, he was replaced by a young, apparently ambitious sultan, Osman II, who seemed to be on a collision course with his *kullar* as soon as he ascended the throne. Following the unsuccessful Polish campaign in 1621, the padişah and his close confidants, headed by the *Kızlar Ağası* (Chief Black Eunuch), reportedly conceived a dramatic venture. They would annihilate the existing body of *kullar*; recruit a new one in Anatolia, Syria, and Egypt; and transfer the capital to Bursa, Damascus, or Cairo. The sultan was supposed to cross over to Anatolia on the pretext of performing the *hacc*.

Osman II's intentions were revealed in early 1622, when a series of communications to his trusted *ümera* in Anatolia were intercepted. In Istanbul the *erkân-i devlet* began a concerted effort to dissuade Sultan Osman from trying to carry out his plan. Once this proved futile, the Janissaries and *sipahi*s took drastic action. Over three days (18-20 May 1622), they staged demonstrations at the Süleymaniye, the At Meydanı, and other sites in Istanbul; assaulted the houses of several officials; and drew up numerous petitions and ultimata, all unheeded. Surging into the Topkapı Palace and its harem, they pulled Sultan Mustafa out of his *kafes* and re-enthroned him. Later, they seized Sultan Osman, who was assassinated in Yediküle at the behest of the new grand vezir, Kara Davud Paşa, and the queen mother, Kösem Sultan.

The trauma did not end with the restoration of Sultan Mustafa. His second reign, from May 1622-September 1623, was marked by unrest and instability, particularly in the eastern provinces and in the capital itself. In the former region, our protagonist assumes center stage. Some accounts allege that Abaza Mehmed Paşa, the *beylerbeyi* of Erzurum, was motivated by his desire to avenge the killing of Sultan Osman, for which he held the *kullar* responsible. He recruited a sizable local army of *sekban* (irregular cavalry troops), extended his rule to adjacent provinces, and persistently harassed both the *kullar* sent from the center and those localized in the Anatolian provinces (*yerliye*). Under severe pressure from the *kullar* in the capital, the sultan's staff ordered Abaza to move to another province. When this order was ignored, they sent out a force that returned to Bursa without having encountered Abaza.

The Abaza affair was to end only under Murad IV (1623-40). Following two serious campaigns in the mid-1620s, the second of which was led by the grand vezir

Hüsrev Paşa, Abaza surrendered. Significantly, the grand vezir treated Abaza and his troops with official pomp and ceremony. Assigned to Bosnia, Abaza continued to persecute the *kullar* and fought on the European front. He later returned to Istanbul and is reported to have been close to Murad IV until the sultan began to reassert his authority. He then was executed in 1632 but, again significantly, he was buried next to Kuyucu Murad Paşa, the grand vezir who had crushed the *celalis* under Ahmed I.

THE HISTORIOGRAPHY

The historiography of the *Haile-i Osmaniye* evolved through five stages or stations. The first historical representation was composed by Hüseyin b. Sefer, better known by his pseudonym Tugi Çelebi, who died sometime during Murad IV's reign. Tugi's text is what I elsewhere call *kul*-centric. The *kullar* were its target audience, and theirs also was the viewpoint from which almost everything was seen. The message conveyed was intended to reassure the *kullar* (and perhaps others in the Ottoman polity) that their role had been a positive one, not because Sultan Osman's plan entailed eliminating the *kullar*, but because the well-being of the Ottoman state was threatened by Genç Osman, a bad sultan whose rule had been rejected by both God and his own subjects. The disastrous potential of the sultan's plan was epitomized in the rebellion of Abaza Paşa. Tugi's text seems to have been an oral address to gatherings of *kullar*; its written version was later used by other Ottoman historians.

Hasan Beyzade (died 1636), the first author of *Tarih-i Al-i Osman*, adopted the prose part of Tugi's account, lock, stock, and barrel, in the first recension of his history. By omitting almost all of the poetry in Tugi's text, as well as the latter part of the *hatime*, Hasan Beyzade avoided disclosing the identity of his source, as Tugi's pseudonym is revealed in the poetry and his real name appears at the end of the epilogue. Hasan Beyzade's only significant addition to Tugi's text was an apocryphal story about the founder of the Sasanian dynasty, Ardeshir, that he admittedly adapted from Ferdowsi's *Shahname*. In the second and third recensions, Tugi remained the main, undisclosed source, but Hasan Beyzade introduced more substantial alterations.

Ibrahim Peçevi (died 1650), who was probably aware of Tugi's work, knew and employed Hasan Beyzade's history but produced a totally different, contradictory version of the *Haile-i Osmaniye*. If Tugi's and Hasan Beyzade's texts are *kul*-centric, Peçevi's gives us the vantage point of the Anatolian *ümera*, most graphically in the account of Abaza Mehmed Paşa. As a consequence, Katip Çelebi (died 1657) could avail himself of two alternative representations in composing the *Fezleke-i Tarih*, which is essentially Katip Çelebi's reading of Tugi and the three recensions of Hasan Beyzade's history. As for *Tarih-i Peçevi*, Katip Çelebi implicitly (yet consciously) rejected Peçevi's overall interpretation but used some of Peçevi's more specific insights without acknowledging Peçevi himself.

Last of all, Naima, the empire's first *vak'anüvis*, adopted the *Fezleke* account with a few significant alterations and additions. The official state narrative of the *Haile-i Osmaniye* is, therefore, the product of a series of readings of Tugi's text by different historians and an implicit rejection of Peçevi's version by two of them, Kâtip Çelebi and Naima.

ABAZA PAŞA'S REBEL IDENTITY

The sociopolitical identity of Abaza Paşa that has come down to us from Ottoman collective memory is that of a rebel (*âsi*) rather than a provincial governor and member of the *ümera* (a collective term for the uppermost echelon of the provincial administration, the *sancak beylerbeyleri*). In other words, Tugi's perspective and judgment, though re-read and rewritten, were adopted by Kâtip Çelebi and consequently by Naima, whose institutional position made his narrative official. Peçevi's were not. As a result, Abaza's identity as a rebel was retrospectively sealed, for Tugi's text deals only with the initial phase of Abaza's activities, not the decade that followed.

The framing of Abaza's alternative sociopolitical identities is to be found in Tugi's (*âsi*/rebel) and Peçevi's (*ümera*-member) texts. Although Tugi's text looks deceptively flat and transparent, the angle from which Abaza's activities are perceived consists of two circles. The wider circle covers the capital in the way that events in the capital are viewed from there; the circle that has a narrower and more significant focus reveals how the Janissaries in the capital perceived the rebellion on the basis of reports from their comrades and envoys. Tugi's account of affairs, along with the rest of the text, is pro-*kul*, anti-Abaza, as well as retrospectively scathing about Sultan Osman's venture. By contrast, Peçevi's representation proceeds from the perspective of the provincial administration, particularly the *ümera*, in some Anatolian provinces.

The most basic constituents of Tugi's angle are verbs that denote motion. They determine the space from which events are seen in this story's two different centers of activity: Erzurum, and the Anatolian provinces in general, and Istanbul. Most frequently used are *gitmek*, *gelmek*, and *varmak*, but *varmak* appears less frequently than the other two and in Ottoman, unlike modern, Turkish, can mean either to go somewhere or to come from somewhere, without indicating the place from which the motion is seen. The other two verbs clearly specify the direction of movement and are abundantly used, so it is possible to identify the position of Tugi's camera and the angle from which events are perceived.

According to Tugi's account, the rebellion in Erzurum erupted when its governor, Abaza, began violently abusing both the Janissaries sent there from the capital and those localized in the province (*yerliye*). After apparently accepting some sort of reconciliation negotiated by the *ayan*, Abaza suddenly seized the fortress of Erzurum, drove out the Janissaries, and detained the *yerliye*. Recruiting a sizable army of *sekban*, he was able to extend his authority to include a neighboring province. His audacity grew to such an extent that he ignored explicit orders from Istanbul to vacate his office and turned away the sultan's envoys.

In the pattern that underlies Tugi's account, the expelled Janissaries always come to Istanbul from Erzurum, and the envoys always go from Istanbul to Erzurum and come back. Clearly, Tugi's camera is always positioned either in Istanbul at large or in specific locales there, such as the Ağa Kapısı (the official residence of the Janissary chief) and the Yeniçeri Odaları (the Janissary barracks). There, complaints and reports from the provinces are digested, reproduced, and translated into forms of action, including meetings or demonstrations and written or oral petitions.

The petitions, in turn, form the basis for Tugi's judgment of Abaza's revolt. Thus, the expelled Janissaries came that day and complained of Abaza Paşa in Istanbul. ("*Yeniçeriler...ol gün gelip, Asıtanede Abaza Paşadan şikayet eylediler.*") Repeatedly, complainants about the governor of Erzurum, Abaza Paşa, came and notified [the authorities], with certainty, that he was a rebel. ("*Erzurum beylerbeyisi olan Abaza Paşadan tekrar şikayetçiler geldiler ve âsi oldugun muhakkak ilam eylediler.*") And the Janissary colonel who had gone against Abaza Paşa in Erzurum came and notified [the authorities] in Istanbul of Abaza's rebellion. ("*Erzurumda Abaza Paşa üzerine giden çorbacı gelip, Asıtanede Abazanın isyanı ilam eyledi.*")

Tugi's interpretive edifice is founded upon the perspective of the Janissaries in the capital, who viewed Abaza's activities through the lens of reports submitted by their expelled comrades and envoys. Consequently, Tugi's interpretation alleges several causal connections, two of which are particularly pertinent.

First, Tugi classifies the state of affairs in the eastern provinces under the trope of *fitne ü fesad* (not literally, civil disorder) and claims that this state was a direct result of Sultan Osman's venture and the sultan's *emirler* (decrees) disclosing it to the *sancakbeyleri* and *beylerbeyleri*. Especially destructive was the effect of a clause that ordered doing away with and replacing the existing *kullar*.

Recalling my contention that Tugi's text was also an oral address, I find that it masterfully lures the audience into following its line of causality. The account of Abaza's rebellion commences by explicitly asserting the causal connection in an objective narrator's voice, as a mere statement of fact: "In what was previously told, it was mentioned that Sultan Osman Han had secretly sent messages everywhere, saying that the Janissary corps would be destroyed. For that reason, sedition appeared in some provinces." Three illustrations of the *fitne ü fesad* immediately follow: a feud in the city of Ayntab (Gaziantep) between an allegedly tyrannical *kadı*, Baki Efendi, and the Janissaries, who, as usual by now, are victimized and act only to restore justice; another feud in Baghdad between the *kullar* and the *beylerbeyi*; and Abaza Paşa's seizing the fortress of Erzurum to launch his revolt.

By linking Abaza's revolt with incidents that occurred elsewhere and might be of a different nature, Tugi's text portrays the revolt as the epitome of a more general state of *fitne ü fesad*, not just a single incident. Put differently, an interpretation made in Tugi's text, not necessarily a relation found in (or among) the events themselves, depicts Abaza's actions as the nadir of a wider pattern of civil disorder indicating the disastrous potential of Sultan Osman's venture. This causal structure is essentially textual in my understanding, but it seems to stem naturally from the order in which things happen as long as the latent *kul*-centric, Istanbul-based viewpoint goes unnoticed.

Tugi's causal connection is reinforced by two additional narrator's statements. Although one follows the three illustrative incidents, the more effective statement is inserted in the conclusion of the prose part of the narrative. There, the narrator asserts that after Sultan Osman had taken a *niyet* (a formal resolution to perform a religious act) to exterminate the current *kullar* and recruit *sekban* in their stead, Abaza began his revolt, and his cause attracted brigands (*eşkıya*) who, according to Tugi, manned his army. The narrative ends on this note, implying that the immediate context shared by Tugi and his audience was the threat posed to the *kullar* by the ascendancy of Abaza Paşa.

Another connection in Tugi's *kul*-centric text is forged by the definition of Abaza's activities as *isyan* (rebellion) and of Abaza himself as an *âsi* (rebel). My contention here is that *isyan* differed from less clear-cut terms, such as *fitne ü fesad* or *hilaf* (contravention). In the political discourse of the seventeenth century, *isyan* specifically meant an official rebellion, or *coup d'état*, against the legitimate sovereign: the reigning padişah and, more generally, the House of Osman. It was also considered an overt attempt to undermine the central authority, and the center's viewpoint typically (with the occasional exception of Peçevi's history) dictated the perception of events in the provinces that we find in the *Tarih-i Al-i Osman*.

Throughout the narration, as well as the alleged speeches and petitions of the *kullar* in Tugi's text, the term *isyan* is reserved exclusively for Abaza's actions. The other incidents in the eastern provinces are described mostly as *fitnes*--indications of *fitne ü fesad*. Tugi seems to follow naturally, as it were, the practice of the *kullar* in Istanbul and their recently expelled comrades from Erzurum, who simply refer to Abaza's actions as *isyan* and to Abaza as an *âsi* without feeling the need to explain why. The numerous ostensible explanations provided by the narrator are actually just statements uttered previously in the *kullar*'s voice but reiterated in the guise of narrative objectivity. Take, for instance, the narrator's conclusion to a digression giving a brief biography of Abaza Paşa. The grammar of that statement encapsulates the way in which language and text transform perspectival logic of causality into an objective state of affairs: "Due to his [Abaza's] spiteful persecution of the Janissary corps, he became a rebel against the blessed padişah" ("*Ve yeniçeri taifesine hüsümet etmekle saadetlu padişaha âsi oldu*").

Peçevi's alternative representation of the Abaza affair is, like Tugi's, the product of his perspective on it. Whereas Tugi's judgment is underpinned by his Istanbul perspective and his *kul*-centrism, Peçevi's is that of an Anatolian province and its *ümera*. That Peçevi had spent much of his career in the provincial administration is revealed with special clarity in the different meaning his representation imparts to the Abaza Paşa affair.

Never applying the term *isyan* to the events, Peçevi intimates that when Abaza Paşa made his first move, he himself was the *defterdar* (director of financial administration) of Diyarbakır under the governorship of Hafız Paşa. Using the first-person voice, Peçevi discloses that he learned at the time that the *ümera* in the provinces around the capital had grown dissatisfied with conditions in Istanbul, especially with the increasing power of the *kullar*. Closer to home, in Diyarbakır, Peçevi noticed more traffic going back and forth between Hafız Paşa and Abaza Paşa: "I realized that an understanding had been established between them." Thus, Abaza Paşa emerges for the first time. Perçevi states further that before killing the Janissaries he had captured, Abaza would often tell them, "You are the slayers of the *halife* of the era and the padişah of the world." Consequently, in Peçevi's reading of the situation, Hafız Paşa intended to unite all the beys in governorship or commanding positions, to secure the approaches to Üsküdar, and to demand the slayers of the padişah.

According to Peçevi's representation, in clear contrast to Tugi's, Sultan Osman's plan did not inflame the *ümera* against the *kullar*; they were already unfavorably inclined toward them. After Osman's deposition and death, the *ümera* became more concerned about the growing influence and power of the *kullar*. Abaza Paşa's initiative was not, in Peçevi's view, the result of Genç Osman's ambitious venture. Rather, this initiative was a concerted effort by the *ümera* to counterbalance the powerful position of the *kullar* at the center. The sultan's assassination did no more than add fuel to the fire and suggest vengeance as an expedient rationale. Contradicting a claim made by Tugi, Peçevi contends from his position on the spot that the Anatolian *ümera* were not coerced into cooperating with Abaza Paşa but supported him wholeheartedly.

THE STATE

For the present discussion, what matters in the historiographical controversy is that the interpretation constructed in Tugi's text won the day. Abaza's sociopolitical identity then became that of a rebel with whom the state had to deal. The acute point at which Tugi's narrative, and not another, became the state's narrative should be sought with Kâtip Çelebi, who was unaware that Naima would esteem his historical writing so highly, and with Naima himself. Elsewhere, I venture explanations for the decisions of these two historians that refer to their own contexts rather than to those of either Tugi or Peçevi. Suffice it to remark here that Naima was not only the official historian of the state but also the unofficial historian of the Köprülüs, and he found it unthinkable to shift the recruitment reservoir of the *kullar* from Rumeli to Anatolia, Syria, and Egypt, let alone to declare this an explicit state ideology.

The record of the past, obviously, often shows how categories of identity were shaped and imposed on individuals by the discourse of power and by the courts of law, the bureaucracy, the *vak'anüvislik* and the other institutions that articulated that discourse. Less clear is what any individual consciously thought and felt about her/his own identity(ies) although imposed identities and consciously shaped ones are inextricably intertwined. Through the *sicil* records, for example, we gain a fairly solid notion of the identitarian categories adopted by the courts (e.g., woman or resident of a given quarter). In order to understand the extent to which those subjected to the court's proceedings accepted or resisted these categories, however, we need to tease the records in speculative ways.

The study of the Ottoman state has made a significant leap in recent years. For decades the field suffered from intellectually stifling and ahistorical concepts such as the Islamic state and the classical state (Hegelian essentialism) or the Oriental-despotic state that reflects the Asiatic mode of production (Marxist essentialism). Now the Ottoman state is being approached in three related, historical ways. First, it is being compared to its contemporaneous dynastic states, not viewed solely as a diachronic evolution of the Islamic state. Also, the leading question has become what did happen and why, replacing an old preoccupation with what did not happen in the Ottoman state. Finally, since the demise of the paradigm of "decline," changes are instinctively felt to have been historically natural features of the state's longevity, not deviations from or corruptions of a classical model.

Stimulating discussions on the state, including the Ottoman state, in the *Journal of Historical Sociology* have tried to rectify several flaws in dogmatic Marxist scholarship in order to offer a more flexible and less Eurocentric Marxist understanding of the state. One such article, by Tosun Arıcanlı and Mara Thomas, "Sidestepping Capitalism: On the Ottoman Road to Elsewhere," proposes a conceptualization that remains within the confines of Marxist thought and terminology yet may constitute an alternative to conventional Marxist and Weberian approaches. In the abstract of their paper Arıcanlı and Thomas state:

> Mapping productivist logic derived from the history of capitalism onto the rest of the world blocks the view of alternative systems and their internal logic. Theories of the capitalist state can capture neither the nature of the non-capitalist state nor those states' social and economic relations. Our alternative formulation of the Ottoman state dissociates class, property, and distribution from the sphere of production and associates them with the state. Thereby, Ottoman history sheds its petrified cloak, and the Ottoman state comes to life: motion, change, and class are things Ottoman once again.[2]

In the Ottoman case, Arıcanlı and Thomas argue, it is in the state as a site that we may find conflict and change. We do not find the dynamics of historical change in the sphere of production as in some European societies. Although the Ottoman Empire was eventually integrated into the capitalist system, that does not impose the presupposition that the capitalist road was an inevitable one. In sum, "The Ottoman Road to Elsewhere" makes a convincing argument, at least at the propositional level, that the Ottoman state in the early modern period was a site of "hot" history.

---

2. Tosun Arıcanlı and Mara Thomas, "Sidestepping Capitalism: On the Ottoman Road to Elsewhere," *Journal of Historical Sociology*, 7:1 (1994): 25-48, quotation p. 25.

The article, however, does not grapple with the state as site of ideology and discourse and does not seriously discuss the pertinent sources and how to approach them, lest we forever remain in the realm of conceptual pondering. While critical and wary of the crude materialist causality of previous generations of Marxist scholars, numerous current scholars still find it difficult to deal with superstructure. One can always sense the unuttered supposition that once things are shown to be valid at the base level, the superstructure of culture, ideology, and politics will take care of itself. Even if it does, the process has to be shown, not presupposed. My preliminary attempt in this paper, therefore, follows the conceptual path opened by Arıcanlı's and Thomas' amended Marxist view, but it addresses both that problem and the matter of sources.

My other inspiration concerning the state is drawn from Timothy Mitchell's concept of the modern state as a universal phenomenon, with particular reference to the Middle East. Employing discourse theory, Mitchell rejects as ahistorical and idealist the attempts to draw a motionless dividing-line between state and society and thus to define the state as a autonomous agency with clearly identifiable intentions.[3] Mitchell sees the modern state as a series of social practices that, through a complex process and a variety of technologies, is made to appear as a coherent structure extrinsic to society. The state/society dividing-line is discursively produced and constantly contested so that trying to come up with an ultimate definition of it is a futile endeavor. In the effort to identify where, how, and by whom this line was marked, I shall argue below that the gist of the historiographical controversy over Abaza Paşa is the contestation over the demarcation of the state's boundaries vis-à-vis society.

Nevertheless, I follow Mitchell's suggestions with a reservation. He assumes that to make some social practices appear to be an extrinsic and coherent structure is a strictly modern and European phenomenon, and then he says that if we identify such a phenomenon, we have a modern European-style state. This identification, moreover, involves the familiar dichotomy between the traditional and the modern. In any case, the Ottoman Empire was from an early stage a highly bureaucratized state with an elaborate and ever-evolving discourse of power, and the passage from tradition to modernity has to be shown historically with regard to concrete issues. It cannot be assumed as given, for the categories themselves--tradition and modernity--are neither simple nor innocent of ideology.

ABAZA, HISTORIOGRAPHY, AND THE STATE

Karen Barkey's thorough study of the Ottoman state in the first half of the seventeenth century fundamentally refutes the view that the state collapsed under external and internal pressures, such as the state response to the so-called bandits in

---

3. Timothy Mitchell, *Colonising Egypt* (Cambridge, 1988).

Anatolia and northern Syria (the *celali*s).[4] Against this view, which emanated from contemporary Ottoman historians, contemporary foreigners (historians and consuls), and modern sociologists, Barkey offers a counter- interpretation in which the intriguing relations between the state and the bandits, or the *celali*s, testify to the strength and flexibility of the former. In fact, the state emerged not only unscathed but *en route* to further centralization by applying a variety of means that ranged from bargaining through co-optation to annihilation. Yet this period, in which the center of government witnessed such strong, shrewd, and resolute men and women as Kösem Sultan, Kuyucu Murad Paşa, Ahmed I, Osman II, and Murad IV has been perceived as one of weakening.

Barkey places the Abaza affair within the second phase of *celali* activity (1623-48). Seeing Osman II's venture as an attempt to continue Ahmed I's centralizing policies. Barkey is adamant that even the deposition and assassination of the young ruler should not be construed as breakdown. Instead, Abaza's revolt exemplified the *modus operandi* of the bandits, who took advantage of the rupture between the central standing army and the provincial units of the *sekban-sarıca*. This second generation of bandits was distinguished by a politicized rhetoric of bargaining, meaning the use of anti-Janissary, pro-*sekban* rhetoric to legitimize demands. This phase ended in 1623 with the steps taken by Murad IV, which, according to Barkey, represented the most ambitious attempt at state consolidation since Kanunî Sultan Süleyman.

In the last part of this paper, I wish to deconstruct Barkey's binary opposition of state/bandits and to suggest an interpretation of the state through contemporary historiography. Barkey's concept of the state seems to emanate from Halil İnalcık's view of the Ottoman state and Theda Skocpol's sociology of the state in general, both of which share the Idealist/Hegelian notion that the state is an autonomous and coherent agency. As a result, Barkey excludes the bandits of the second generation from the state, although even Abaza survived the wrath of the grand vezir Kuyucu Murad Paşa earlier in the century. Many of the bandits were recruited and co-opted into the state via the *kapı*s (households) of high-ranking Ottoman officials following the defeats of the *celali* armies. Aided by their patrons' *intisap* networks, they became officeholders, and some became heads of their own *kapı*s. Barkey herself shows that, regarding the competition over positions in the Ottoman administration, the bandits were not different from governors sent by the palace, and they emulated the state armies in their *modus operandi*.

Abaza Paşa fought in the army of the famous Canbuladoğlu Ali Paşa. Captured in the late 1500s, he might have been executed but was recruited instead into the *kapı* of Halil Paşa, one of the Ottoman commanders in the campaigns against the *celali*s. Halil Paşa's successful career--he was to become grand vezir and *kapudan paşa*--launched Abaza's own career. Later on, Abaza married into the *kapı* of Gürcü Mehmed Paşa, another grand vezir after the death of Osman II. In short, by the time he rebelled, Abaza and many of his colleagues were no longer bandits;

---

4. Karen Barkey, *Bandits and Bureaucrats: The Ottoman Route to State Centralization* (Ithaca, 1994).

they were provincial Osmanlılar. Barkey's idealist concept of the state as a monolithic, autonomous whole, however, leads her to exclude them. The Ottoman state in the first decades of the seventeenth century was a site of both material (Arıcanlı and Thomas) and discursive (Mitchell) contestation, and what Barkey calls politicized rhetoric is, in fact, a declaration of identity by a group that, having acquired an Osmanlı socio-cultural status, is trying to reaffirm its place within the state.

As noted, Barkey takes a positivist approach to the historical texts which form the basis of both her narrative and her interpretation. Sometimes she alludes to them directly but occasionally to their problematic amalgamation by Josef von Hammer-Purgstall.[5] There is, first, a problem at the *Quellenkritik* level, for, as I hope was shown in this paper, these texts constitute an historiographical corpus in which each text is intimately related to another or to others. Even scholars who wish to use this historiography merely as a source for external reconstruction have to grapple with its tangle of interdependencies. Second, and perhaps more important, is the fact that these texts also constitute a discourse whose inscription is part and parcel of the reality it represents. To extract the informational layer that these texts certainly contain with disregard for their ideological layer is to miss the wealth of this type of source.

The Ottoman historiography of the period was caught up in the struggle over the drawing of the state boundaries. Tugi's *kul*-centric text was part of the *kullar*'s effort to exclude the *ümera* of bandit origin and the *sekban* troops from the state. The energy invested to render Abaza an *âsi* (rebel), rather than an *ümera* member, is a cultural signifier whose political significance is that he was not, both as an icon and as a concrete person, part of the state. Peçevi's text, which Barkey uses as yet another purely factual source, gives us what she calls the politicized rhetoric of the bandits' second generation, and what I deem the self-assertion of, in particular, the *ümera* of *celali* origin as Osmanlıs, as fully integrated members of the Ottoman state.

The simultaneously confusing and fascinating facet of seventeenth-century historical discourse, as well as that of the *nasihat*, is that the ideological line articulated in Tugi's text kept winning the day, whereas Peçevi's Anatolian perspective remained aloof. The result is that what were cleavages within the state and constant struggles to redraw its socio-political boundaries are interpreted at worst as decline or breakdown, deviations from a golden age, classical model, and at best as a state/society binary opposition.

The final point is concerned with how the state handled Abaza during the first phase of his rebellion--and what I venture is no more than a preliminary thought. Tugi offers a key insight in this regard precisely because his text is the voice of the *kullar*. When he presents a brief biography of Abaza, this is done for a clear purpose: stressing Abaza's *intisap* to both Gürcü Mehmed Paşa, at that point (mid-1622) the grand vezir, and Halil Paşa, then the *kapudan paşa*. It consequently lends

---

5. Josef von Hammer-Purgstall, *Geschichte des osmanischen Reiches*, 10 vols. (Pest, 1827-35).

credence to the *kullar*'s demand to dismiss the former and to their suspicion that the state was not particularly inclined to suppress Abaza Paşa. The *kullar* were perceptive: what numerous modern scholars interpret as weakness and incompetence actually seems to have been an exercise in the good old Ottoman politics of balance and counterbalance. The palace could not, of course, explicitly endorse Abaza's actions, but it did seem content to dispatch envoys and decrees that were turned away and ignored and to send a military force that, inexplicably, failed to encounter Abaza.

University of California, Los Angeles

Baki Tezcan

THE 1622 MILITARY REBELLION IN ISTANBUL: A HISTORIOGRAPHICAL JOURNEY*

On Wednesday, 18 May 1622, the soldiers of the Ottoman central army stationed in Istanbul gathered in the central square of the city and submitted a number of demands to Osman II, the reigning sultan. The next day, not satisfied with the sultan's answer, they entered the palace, found Prince Mustafa, Osman's uncle, and enthroned him. On Friday evening, Osman was killed in the first regicide in Ottoman history.

According to the prevalent presentation of the event in seventeenth-century historiography, the soldiers made quite justified demands of a sultan who was inexperienced and under the influence of misguided advisers. In modern Turkish historiography, by contrast, this event has been interpreted as a victory of reactionary forces over progressive ones, and Osman II has been portrayed as the ancestor of Turkish reformers, a forerunner of Mustafa Kemal. In this view, had he not been deposed and killed by the military rebellion, Ottoman Turkish reform would have started three centuries earlier.

To place both interpretations in their proper contexts, I will argue that the first resulted from the stakes seventeenth-century authors had in the contemporary system and the second was produced by the needs of a new Ottoman Turkish elite in the early twentieth century. Finally, I will go back to the event and emphasize a central controversy regarding its meaning in the context of the seventeenth century. Let me begin by introducing the major actors and sketching the events that led to the 1622 incident.

Osman, the son of Sultan Ahmed I, was a thirteen-year-old boy when he was enthroned in 1618.[1] He replaced his uncle Mustafa, whose enthronement had been

---

* I would like to thank Professors Rifaat Abou-El-Haj, Molly Greene, Şükrü Hanioğlu, Norman Itzkowitz, and Heath Lowry, as well as Nenad Filipovic, who read the original paper and made numerous suggestions. My research in Istanbul during 1998-99 was made possible through three grants from Princeton University (William Rea '34 fund of the Department of Near Eastern Studies, the Langenberg fund of the Center of International Studies, and a grant from the Council on Regional Studies), as well as a fellowship from the American Research Institute in Turkey. The pleasant study environment provided for me by the Faculty of Arts and Social Sciences of Sabancı University was instrumental in the completion of the final product.
1. Osman was born on 10 Cemaziyül'ahır 1013 (3 November 1604) and was enthroned on 1 Rebiülevvel 1027 (26 February 1618). Mehmed bin Mehmed, called er-Rumi (died after 1639), *Tarih*, Süleymaniye Library, MS Lala Ismail, fol. 9. The date of his enthronement may be verified by the report of Achille de Harlay, baron de Sancy, the French ambassador, to

unusual as he was not the son but the brother of his predecessor.² Mustafa's enthronement and his deposition, as a result of a palace coup after a few months on the throne, are controversial issues but not central to my discussion. Osman's tutor, Ömer Efendi, seems to have had a strong influence on his policy decisions. A man of rather humble origins from the provinces,³ Ömer Efendi was not well entrenched in the web of relations that bound the interests of the Ottoman capital. In addition, Osman's mother had died before he was enthroned, closing one of the channels through which the central elite had influenced policy decisions in the past.⁴ In short, Osman's environment was relatively open to alternative interest groups, such as those of the provinces, or upstarts.

At the level of international politics, the age was ripe for a return to a policy of territorial expansion in the west. The year in which Osman II was enthroned was the first year of the troubles in Central Europe that later spread over the continent to become the Thirty Years' War. Osman and his ministers were indirectly involved in these developments through Bethlen Gábor, the prince of Transylvania, an Ottoman vassal. Gábor was chosen king of Hungary, and a large delegation of the Protestant Union came to Istanbul in 1620 to negotiate Ottoman involvement on the side of the Union against the Catholic League.⁵ Within this context, the decision for a military campaign against Poland was made.

When Osman headed toward Poland in 1621, an Ottoman sultan was personally leading his armies on campaign for the first time in some twenty years.

Louis XIII, king of France, dated 26 February 1618: Bibliothèque nationale, MS Fr. 16148, fol. 281a.
2. Leslie P. Peirce, *The Imperial Harem: Women and Sovereignty in the Ottoman Empire* (New York, 1993), pp. 100, 310, n. 36, referring to Peçevi (died ca. 1649-50), *Tarih-i Peçevi*, 2 vols. (Istanbul, 1281-83 A.H.), II: 360-61, suggests that leading statesmen were hesitant to take the oath of loyalty (*biat*) to Mustafa but were persuaded by the Chief Black Eunuch, Mustafa Ağa, that the sultan's eccentric behavior was attributable to his long confinement and that it would improve once he was in normal contact with society. Yet this suggestion is based on a misreading of the relevant pages in Peçevi, who actually states that Mustafa Ağa opposed the enthronement of Mustafa: "Lâkin ol 'asırda Dârüssa' âde Ağası Mustafâ Ağa 'Bu def'a dahî hakk-gûyulukda taksîr itmeyüb, Sultân Mustafâ Hânın 'aklında hiffet ve re'yinde ve umûrunda kâdir-i isâbet olmadun,' Şeyhülislâm Es'ad Efendiye ve kâimmakâm-ı sadâret bulunan Sofi Mehmed Paşaya ilkâ ve iz'ân itdirdi": Peçevi, *Tarih-i Peçevi*, II: 360.
3. For a biography of Ömer Efendi, see Nevizade Ata'i (died 1635), *Hadâik' ul-hakâik fî tekmîletişş-Şakâik* (İstanbul, 1268 A.H.), reprinted with an index by Abdülkadir Özcan, *Şakaik-ı Nu'maniye ve Zeyilleri*, 5 vols. (İstanbul, 1989), II: 728-29.
4. Peirce, *Imperial Harem*, p. 233, claims that Osman's mother died in 1620. Yet she actually died before he was enthroned. Upon his enthronement, Osman built a tomb over her grave in Eyüp in 1027/1618; see Hafız Hüseyin Ayvansarayi, *Mecmua-i Tevarih*, ed. Fahri Ç. Derin and Vahid Çabuk (Istanbul, 1985), pp. 304-05.
5. See H. Forst, "Der türkische Gesandte in Prag, 1620, und der Briefwechsel des Winterkönigs mit Sultan Osman II," *Mitteilungen des Instituts für Österreichische Geschichtsforschung* 16 (1895): 566-81; Reinhard Rudolf Heinisch, "Habsburg, die Pforte und der Böhmische Aufstand (1618-1620)," *Südost-Forschungen* 33 (1974): 125-65; 34 (1975): 79-124.

The siege of the fortress of Hotin in today's Ukraine, however, proved inconclusive, and the Polish and Cossack forces agreed to evacuate the fort in return for peace.[6] The Ottoman "war party" was frustrated at the performance of the army. An initial decision to winter in Edirne, probably so that a new campaign might be launched in the coming year,[7] seems to have faced strong opposition. Instead, the sultan and the army returned to Istanbul very early in 1622, and the chain of events leading to the regicide began.

The "war party" lobbied for a new central army recruited in the provinces as the current central army seemed too interested in peace. Osman agreed and prepared for a trip to the eastern provinces under the guise of an imperial pilgrimage to Mecca. While most of the central army was to stay in Istanbul, the treasury was to be taken along to finance the new recruitment. For the army and many others whose interests depended on the *status quo*, this was a matter of survival. On 18 May 1622, the day on which the imperial tents were to be transferred to the Anatolian side of the Bosphorus, the central cavalry and infantry troops gathered together and demanded cancellation of the pilgrimage and execution of some of Osman's close associates. Respected scholars of religion and law legitimized their demands, and Osman agreed to give up the trip but refused to execute his ministers. The army corps then entered the palace, enthroned Mustafa, and deposed Osman. Soon afterward, Osman was killed on the orders of the new sultan, Mustafa, his mother, or the new grand vezir, Davud Paşa--or some combination of the three.[8]

In the seventeenth century, a number of short chronicles were specifically devoted to the deposition of Osman II and the ensuing reign of Mustafa. One, which eventually became the most influential source for seventeenth-century Ottoman historiography on the incident,[9] was written by a certain Hüseyin, a retired bodyguard of the sultan.[10] His father, Sefer, was probably a *devşirme* recruit--that

---

6. For a Turkish account of this campaign that presents it as a great victory, see Yaşar Yücel, ed., *Osmanlı Devlet Düzenine Ait Metinler VI: II. Osman Adına Yazılmış Zafer-nâme* (Ankara, 1983). Yücel's facsimile publication and his introduction present quite a number of problems, with which I have dealt in my "Zafername Müellifi Halisi'nin Bilinmeyen bir Eseri Münasebetiyle," *Osmanlı Araştırmaları/The Journal of Ottoman Studies* 19 (1999): 83-98.
7. Mehmed Halisi, *Beşâretnâme-i Sultân Mustafâ Hân*, Austrian National Library, mixt. 21, fols. 171 a-b, presents this idea as the grand vezir's.
8. A more detailed outline of these events appear in my Ph.D. dissertation, "Searching for Osman: A Reassessment of the Deposition of the Ottoman Sultan Osman II (1618-1622)," Princeton University, 2001.
9. Gabriel Piterberg, "A Study of Ottoman Historiography in the Seventeenth Century," Ph.D. dissertation, Oxford University, 1992, deals with this particular chronicle and how it influenced seventeenth-century Ottoman historiography. See also idem, "Speech Acts and Written Texts: A Reading of a Seventeenth-Century Ottoman Historiographic Episode," *Poetics Today*, 14:2 (1993): 387-418. Because Piterberg relies on a single manuscript of this chronicle, some of his assumptions need to be revised. See my "Tarih ile Tarihyazımı İlişkisi Ekseninden *Tugi Tarihi* Metinleri üzerinde bir Deneme," paper presented to the Kuruluşunun 700. Yıldönümünde Bütün Yönleriyle Osmanlı Devleti Uluslararası Kongresi, Selçuk University, Konya, Turkey, April 1999; the proceedings will be published in due course.
10. The information on Hüseyin's life is derived from the last section of his work, in which he

is, a Christian boy recruited for the army and converted to Islam.[11] Hüseyin himself was born in Belgrade and followed his father in entering the Janissary corps. After taking part in a few campaigns in Anatolia against the Celalis and in Iran against the Safavids, Hüseyin was promoted to the *solakân*, the elite corps within the Janissaries charged with the protection of the sultan on campaigns and outings. When he chose to retire from this corps after eight years, his total service in the army had not yet amounted to twenty years.[12] Osman, in the last months of his reign, had decided to cut the lucrative pensions of the Janissaries. Both as a former Janissary and as someone whose retirement salary was at stake, Hüseyin, therefore, had good reason to sympathize with the soldiers who deposed Osman.[13]

Hüseyin, in his chronicle, tries to justify the actions of the soldiers. He blames various personalities around the sultan for encouraging policies detrimental to the central army.[14] He emphasizes, moreover, that Osman was given a chance to avoid the escalation of events yet chose not to comply with the demands of the army on both the first and second days of the rebellion.[15] In addition, he underlines the legitimacy of the soldiers' demands by stressing that the army cooperated with respected men of religion and law.[16] Osman and his supporters are charged with deviating from the Ottoman *kanun*, or sultanic law; the central army is depicted as the guardian of that law.[17] As for the regicide, Hüseyin puts all the blame on Davud Paşa, the grand vezir of the new Sultan Mustafa,[18] thus making a clear distinction between the justified act of deposition and one man's act of regicide.[19]

Among other chronicles devoted to the deposition of Osman and the ensuing

---

tells his own story in verse. Hüseyin bin Sefer, called Tugi, *Tarih-i Tugi* (the author himself does not actually give a title to his work), Austrian National Library, H.O. 74 (hereafter H.O. 74), fols. 60a–61b. A facsimile of this manuscript is provided by Piterberg in Appendix C of his dissertation, but Piterberg himself describes it only as a "long poem."
11. The name of Hüseyin's grandfather appears to have been Abdullah (see the Cambridge University Library manuscript of the same work, Dd. 11.18 [hereafter MS Cambridge], fol. 1 [153]a), a name retrospectively given to the father of a *devşirme* recruit. Hüseyin's own statement "*Kulı oğlı kulıyum pâdişâhın*" ("I am a servant of the sultan for two generations": H.O. 74, fol. 60a, line 14), supports this view.
12. Hüseyin does not tell exactly how long he served in the army. The first grand vezir he mentions is Murad Paşa, who was appointed to this post at the end of 1606.
13. Later on, when Abaza Mehmed Paşa started a movement against the soldiers of the central army, Hüseyin assumed an apologetic role, as well. See "Tarih ile Tarihyazımı."
14. See, for instance, H.O. 74, fols. 3a-4a.
15. Ibid., fols. 7b, 9b-10a.
16. See, for instance, Ibid., fol. 8a-b.
17. See, for instance, Ibid., fols. 19b–20a.
18. Ibid., fol. 24b.
19. Some of these points are not as clearly made in the earlier Tugi texts. That Osman had agreed to comply with some of the demands on the first day was "censored" in later Tugi manuscripts, of which H.O. 74 forms an example; compare H.O. 74, fol. 7b, with MS Cambridge, fol. 9(161)a. Similarly, compare H.O. 74, fols. 19b–20a and 24b with MS Cambridge, fols. 25(177)b-26(178)a, and 32(184)b.

reign of Mustafa, that of Bostanzade Yahya is worth mentioning.[20] In contrast to Hüseyin, Yahya came from what one may call the academic and judicial aristocracy. His grandfather, father, uncle, elder brother, and he held important posts in the academic and judicial hierarchies.[21] In common with Hüseyin, however, Yahya had interests at stake. Those in the higher echelons of the judicial establishment were granted titles of judgeships in small provincial towns for their retirement or for the time between positions when they were not actively employed. The titular judge would send to his post a proxy who would collect the judicial fees on his behalf. This institution, called *arpalık*, which provided a steady source of income for the high-level judges of the empire, was abolished in 1621 on the eve of Osman's Polish

---

20. Bostanzade Yahya (died 1639), *Vak'a-ı Sultân Osmân Hân* (the author himself does not give a title to his work), Topkapı Palace Library, MS Revan 1305; Süleymaniye Library, MS Halet Efendi 611; Bibliothèque nationale, MS Suppl. Turc. 1142. The text is critically edited, based on the manuscripts in Istanbul, by Betül Yazıcı, "Bostan-zâde Yahyâ Efendi ve *Vak'a-ı Sultân Osmân* Adlı Eseri," senior thesis, Istanbul University, 1959. There is also a modern Turkish rendering by Orhan Şaik Gökyay, "II. Sultan Osman'ın Şehadeti," in Erol Güngör, *et al.*, eds., *Atsız Armağanı* (Istanbul, 1976), pp. 187-256.

21. For a biography of the author, see Şeyhî Mehmed Efendi (died 1145/1732-33), *Vakâyi'ül-fudalâ*, Beyazıt Library, MS Veliyüddin Efendi 2361-62; facsimile ed. with an index by Abdülkadir Özcan, *Şakaik-ı Nu'maniye ve Zeyilleri*, III: 45-46. His grandfather was Bostan Mustafa (died 1570), son of a merchant from Tire, *kadı'asker* of Anatolia during the reign of Süleyman I (Nevizade Ata'i, in Özcan, ed., *Şakaik-ı Nu'maniye ve Zeyilleri*, II: 129-32). His father was Bostanzade Mehmed Efendi (died 1598), twice şeyhülislâm during the reigns of Murad III and Mehmed III (ibid., II: 410-13). His uncle was Mustafa (died 1014/1605-06), once *kadı'asker* of Anatolia and twice of Rumelia during the reign of Mehmed III (ibid., II: 506-07). His elder brother was Bostanzade Mehmed Efendi (died 1035/1625-26), twice *kadı'asker* of Anatolia and twice of Rumelia during the reigns of Ahmed I, Mustafa I (second reign), and Murad IV (ibid., II: 697-98). For another brother, see Ibid., II: 449; for other members of the family, see Şeyhî, in Özcan, ed., *Şakaik-ı Nu'maniye ve Zeyilleri*, III: 275-76, 321-22, 388-89, 431-32. He himself (died 1639) was *kadı'asker* of Anatolia during the second reign of Mustafa I, and *kadı'asker* of Rumelia during the reign of Murad IV. There is yet another work of history attributed to him, yet it is a false ascription. Necdet Sakaoğlu, ed., *Duru Tarih* (Istanbul, 1978), argues that the author of the work *Tuhfetü'l-ahbâb*, known as *Tarih-i Saf* (Istanbul, 1287 A.H.), is Bostanzade Yahya. The evidence Sakaoğlu provides from the text, which he published in a modern Turkish rendering, proves that the work belongs to one of the Bostanzade brothers, yet not Yahya but Mehmed. The author of the work states that he was in the service of the *divan*, i.e., a military judge, when Celali Yusuf Paşa arrived in Istanbul (*Duru Tarih*, pp. 14, n. 15, 118). Yusuf Paşa arrived in Istanbul in 1018/1609-10 (Peçevi, *Tarih-i Peçevi*, II: 337-38). Bostanzade Yahya had become the judge of Bursa in Receb 1017/October-November 1608, and in Cemaziyül'ahır 1018/September 1609, he was transferred to Edirne, where he stayed until Rebiülahir 1020/June-July 1611 (Şeyhî, in Özcan, ed., *Şakaik-ı Nu'maniye ve Zeyilleri*, III: 45-46). Bostanzade Mehmed, on the other hand, was Anatolia *kadı'asker* during most of 1018 (his tenure was between Ramazan 1017/December 1608 and Şevval 1018/January 1610: Nevizade Ata'i, in Özcan, ed., *Şakaik-ı Nu'maniye ve Zeyilleri*, II: 698). Mustafa Çarıcı, "Bostanzade Yahya Efendi," *Tarih Diyanet Vakfı İslam Ansiklopedisi*, VI: 311-13, reproduces Sakaoğlu's mistake.

campaign.²² Consequently, Yahyâ's interests, too, were endangered by "Osmanist" policies.²³

In his short chronicle, Yahya displays sympathy for the demands of the soldiers.²⁴ His central argument, like Hüseyin's, blames the inept advisers of the sultan,²⁵ particularly Ömer Efendi, the tutor, whom he sees as the main policy maker.²⁶ Yahya portrays Osman as an inexperienced ruler easily influenced by the ideas of his close associates, and he criticizes Osman's refusal to comply with the demands of the soldiers, especially with regard to the execution of his associates.²⁷ Concerning the regicide, Yahya makes a distinction similar to that made by Hüseyin, holding Davud Paşa responsible.²⁸ In sum, despite the difference in their backgrounds, Yahya's and Hüseyin's depictions of the rebellion are essentially similar.

Of the rest of the contemporary short chronicles dealing with the period,²⁹ only an anonymous account written in Hebrew displays radically different views.³⁰ According to Aryeh Shmuelevitz, the author seems to have been an important personage in the Ottoman capital so that his list of the functionaries of Osman II includes more names than those in Turkish chronicles.³¹ Shmuelovitz states that the author was "an ardent supporter of Sultan Osman II, whom he described as a brilliant and talented young ruler, and of the sultan's officers, believing that Osman's plan to put an end to the corrupt army of Yeniçeris (Janissaries) and Sipahis

---

22. Yahya complains about this decision in his work; see Yazıcı, "Bostan-zâde Yahya Efendi," p. 19; Gökyay, "II. Sultan Osman'ın Şehadeti," p. 204.
23. The Bostanzade brothers seem to have fallen out of favor during the reign of Osman. Yahya held the judgeship of Istanbul in 1613-14 during the reign of Ahmed I; then he had to wait for eight years for his next appointment in December 1622, during the second reign of Mustafa. See Şeyhî, in Özcan, ed., Şakaik-ı Nu'maniye ve Zeyilleri, III: 46. As to his elder brother Mehmed, he was dismissed from the military judgeship (kadıaskerlik) of Rumelia in 1615. His next appointment was right after the deposition of Osman in May 1622: Nevizade Ata'i, in Özcan, ed., Şakaik-ı Nu'maniye ve Zeyilleri, II: 698.
24. See Yazıcı, "Bostan-zâde Yahya Efendi," pp. 16-17; Gökyay, "II. Sultan Osman'ın Şehadeti," pp. 202-03.
25. Yazıcı, "Bostan-zâde Yahya Efendi," pp. 5-9; Gökyay, "II. Sultan Osman'ın Şehadeti," pp. 193-97.
26. Yazıcı, "Bostan-zâde Yahya Efendi," pp. 11, 17-20; Gökyay, "II. Sultan Osman'ın Şehadeti," pp. 198, 203-05.
27. Yazıcı, "Bostan-zâde Yahya Efendi," pp. 27, 30, 32; Gökyay, "II. Sultan Osman'ın Şehadeti," pp. 211-12, 214.
28. Yazıcı, "Bostan-zâde Yahya Efendi," pp. 46-48; Gökyay, "II. Sultan Osman'ın Şehadeti," pp. 227-29.
29. Discussed in my "Searching for Osman," mentioned in n. 8.
30. For this chronicle, I rely on Aryeh Shmuelovitz, "MS Pococke No. 31 as a Source for the Events in the Years 1622-24 in Istanbul," in Graciela de la Lama, ed., Thirtieth International Congress of Human Sciences in Asia and North Africa (Mexico City, 1976): Middle East I (Mexico City, 1982), pp. 33-6.
31. Idem, "MS Pococke No. 31 as a Source for the Events in Istanbul in the Years 1622-1624," International Journal of Turkish Studies 3:2 (1985-86): 107-21, at pp. 107-08.

(cavalry) was essential to bring order and security to the capital."[32] The anonymous author further indicates his "Osmanist" feelings in discussing the major provincial rebellion led by Abaza Mehmed Paşa, the governor of Erzurum, in the aftermath of the 1622 incident; he shows "a certain sympathy" especially toward Abaza's systematic annihilation of the Janissaries and their families in revenge for the deposition and execution of Sultan Osman II.[33] For centuries to come, however, this different interpretation of "Osmanist" policies and the military rebellion that brought them to an end was not the prevalent one.

Osman's deposition and the ensuing regicide were also dealt with in longer chronicles of Ottoman history written in the seventeenth century. An example is that of Hasanbeyzade Ahmed.[34] His father, Küçük Hasan Bey, a graduate of the palace school and hence probably a recruit of Christian origin, reached the highest level of the imperial secretariat shortly before his death.[35] Ahmed himself started a *medrese* education, which would prepare him for an academic or judicial career in the *ilmiye*, but switched to a scribal career after the death of his father, taking part in a few campaigns and holding several posts in the imperial secretariat and the provincial administration.[36]

Gabriel Piterberg claims that Hasanbeyzade's "concluding section--the deposition of Osman II and most of Mustafa I's second reign--is, in fact, a near verbatim and *in toto* transmission of Tugi's [Hüseyin's] text."[37] Being based on a very limited examination of Hasanbeyzade manuscripts, this claim does not stand the test of a more thorough investigation.[38] Hasanbeyzade Ahmed was actually

---

32. Ibid., p. 108.
33. Ibid., p. 112.
34. Nezihi Aykut, ed., "Hasan Bey-zâde Tarihi," 3 vols., Ph.D. dissertation, Istanbul University, 1980.
35. M. Cavid Baysun, "Reis'ül-Küttab Küçük Hasan Bey," *İstanbul Üniversitesi Edebiyat Fakültesi Tarih Dergisi* 2:3-4 (1950-51): 97-102.
36. Idem, "Hasan-beyzade Ahmet Paşa," *Türkiyat Mecmuası* 10 (1951-53): 321-40.
37. Piterberg, "A Study of Ottoman Historiography," p. 189.
38. Piterberg looked at three manuscripts (see ibid., pp. 314-18), whereas Aykut based his critical edition, of which Piterberg was not aware, on the examination of twenty-one manuscripts (Aykut, "Hasan Bey-zâde Tarihi," I: 521-47). The third manuscript used by Piterberg and attributed to Hasanbeyzade is actually a large excerpt from Solakzade's (died 1068/1657-58) chronicle and is not used by Aykut as a Hasanbeyzade manuscript; compare Austrian National Library, H.O. 75 (attributed by Piterberg to Hasanbeyzade) with Solakzade Mehmed Hemdemî Çelebi, *Tarih-i Solakzade* (Istanbul, 1298 A.H.), pp. 622-763. Furthermore, Piterberg claims that the manuscript in which Hasanbeyzade adopts "the prose part of Tuği's account, lock, stock, and barrel" (Piterberg, "Speech Acts and Written Texts," p. 410) represents the first recension of Hasanbeyzade. Yet a careful reading of the relevant part of the manuscript proves otherwise. There are four Hasanbeyzade manuscripts, the concluding parts of which are almost identical with Hüseyin Tugi's text (Austrian National Library, H.O. 19, which was used by Piterberg; H.O. 65; Ragıp Paşa Library 987; and Nuruosmaniye Library 3134), but Aykut, quite rightly, regards the concluding part in these four manuscripts as a later addition, not part of the work of Hasanbeyzade ("Hasan Bey-zâde Tarihi," I: 531-35). Although Aykut does not feel the need to provide any justification for his

unaware of Hüseyin Tugi's chronicle.[39] True, his depiction of the deposition and regicide is not that different in tone from Hüseyin's. Hasanbeyzade is quite hostile toward the close advisers of the sultan,[40] and he portrays the members of the ulema as sympathetic with the demands of the soldiers.[41] As for Osman, his stubbornness is emphasized.[42] Davud Paşa is again named the main actor in the regicide.[43] Nevertheless, Hasanbeyzade Ahmed may have had his own predisposition to adopt a "pro-soldier" and "anti-Osmanist" tone that resembles Hüseyin's. There is strong evidence that in the last year of Osman's reign he had professional trouble under the financial ministry of Baki Paşa, one of the sultan's associates whose heads were demanded on the first day of the rebellion.[44] Besides, Ahmed owed his position in the administrative elite of the empire to the existing system, which now faced the possibility of change.

Another Ottoman historian, Ibrahim Peçevi, came from a paternal family that had produced at least two generations of provincial military commanders in Bosnia

---

claim, the section of transmission from the text of Hasanbeyzade to that of Tugi in these manuscripts is quite explicable. In these manuscripts, Hasanbeyzade's chronicle comes to the end of the first reign of Mustafa in a certain order. But then the text presents a summary of the events since the death of Ahmed I. This repetition disturbs the logic of Hasanbeyzade's chronicle. Furthermore, the four-year-long reign of Osman II is summarized in a single sentence to be followed by the text of Hüseyin Tugi (Austrian National Library, H.O. 19, fol. 303b; Nuruosmaniye 3134, fol. 175a-b; Ragıp Paşa 987, fol. 361a). Thus, this concluding part in which Hüseyin Tugi's text is reproduced must be a later addition to the chronicle of Hasanbeyzade by an anonymous author. Since the copy dates of the four manuscripts are relatively late, it is not possible to determine exactly when this addition was made (the copy date of Austrian National Library, H.O. 65 is 1242/1827; that of Ragıp Paşa 987, 1144/1732; the copy dates of H.O. 19 and Nuruosmaniye 3134 are not given). Therefore, two of Piterberg's three Hasanbeyzade manuscripts are quite problematic: one of them is not a Hasanbeyzade manuscript at all, and the concluding part of the other one, central to Piterberg's argument, is the work of an anonymous author.
39. For instance, Hasanbeyzade asserts that Osman was not brought to the mosque where the soldiers were hosting Mustafa. By contrast, Hüseyin Tugi devotes a few pages to the episode of Osman's stay in the same mosque with Mustafa: Aykut, "Hasan Bey-zâde Tarihi," II: 344; H.O. 74, fols. 22b-24a.
40. He describes the grand vezir Dilaver Paşa as ignorant (*nâdan*) and Ömer Efendi, the tutor of Osman, as "the vehement Turk whose title is ignorant" (*Türk-i sütürg-i cehalet unvan*): Aykut, *Hasan Bey-zâde Tarihi*, II: 342; compare III: 591, for variants in different manuscripts, one of which adds further derogatory adjectives to describe Ömer Efendi.
41. During the rebellion, some of the higher echelons of the religious and judicial establishment reach the presence of Osman and suggest that the heads of the men demanded by the soldiers be given to them. At this point, Hasanbeyzade refers to the people whose heads are demanded as despicable men (*üç nefer le'ım*): Aykut, "Hasan Bey-zâde Tarihi," II: 343.
42. See Osman's response to the demands of the soldiers conveyed by the ulema: Ibid.
43. Ibid., II: 345.
44. Baysun, "Hasan-beyzade Ahmet Paşa," pp. 335-37.

and received income from large "fiefs" (s. *zeamet*).[45] He served in provincial offices of the central military organization as a scribe and administrator and took part in a number of campaigns. Later, he held a number of financial directorates in the provinces. Sometime around 1641, he retired after a long career and wrote his Ottoman history.

Peçevi had recourse to the work of Hasanbeyzade Ahmed,[46] but his own account of the deposition of Osman represents a much different perspective.[47] Although Peçevi does not call the soldiers rebels, he does use the words sedition (*fitne*) and disorder (*fesad*) in describing the actions of the army.[48] Neither Hüseyin Tugi nor Hasanbeyzade Ahmed uses this vocabulary in relation to the soldiers.[49] Peçevi's account, moreover, does not blame the misguided policies of the circle around Osman. Without making any pronounced remarks to suggest that he supports the policies of Osman and his associates, he implies appreciation of Ömer Efendi, a unique attitude among chroniclers.[50]

Two clues further link Peçevi with an "Osmanist" faction. At some points, he uses Baki Paşa as an oral source,[51] and at others he mentions things that happened while he was in the presence of Baki Paşa,[52] indicating that, unlike Hasanbeyzade Ahmed, he was on good terms with Osman's financial minister. After Osman's deposition, Peçevi was appointed to the financial directorate of the province of Diyarbakır, under the governor, Hafız Ahmed Paşa. Hafız Ahmed Paşa had come as far as Maltepe (today a neighborhood in the Asian part of Istanbul) to join Osman with his own provincial forces for the alleged pilgrimage in 1622.[53] Once Osman was deposed, he returned to Diyarbakır and kept in contact with Abaza Mehmed Paşa, another provincial governor who had been planning a move toward Istanbul.[54] Peçevi displays a certain amount of sympathy with their cause.[55] In contrast to

---

45. Şerafeddin Turan, "Peçevî," *İslam Ansiklopedisi*, IX: 543-45.
46. He lists the work of Hasan Beyzade as one of his sources in the introduction of his history: *Tarih-i Peçevi*, I: 3. Yet Piterberg's suggestion that Peçevi was probably also aware of Hüseyin Tugi's chronicle in the form in which it was reproduced by Hasanbeyzade should be revised as Hasanbeyzade was actually unaware of Tugi: Piterberg, "A Study of Ottoman Historiography," pp. 205-06; idem, "Speech Acts and Written Texts," p. 410.
47. See Piterberg, "A Study of Ottoman Historiography," pp. 206-25; idem, "Speech Acts and Written Texts," pp. 403-04, 408-09. Piterberg's comparisons with Hasanbeyzade Ahmed, however, need to be modified as argued above.
48. Peçevi, *Tarih-i Peçevi*, II: 381.
49. Hasanbeyzade Ahmed does use the word *fitne*, yet with reference to Dilaver Paşa's response to the demands of the soldiers: "this speech containing sedition" (*bu makâl-i fitne-isti'mal*): Aykut, ed., "Hasan Bey-zâde Tarihi," II: 342.
50. "Hvâce Efendi rüşvet almamakla": Peçevi, *Tarih-i Peçevi*, II: 372.
51. Ibid., II: 367.
52. Ibid., II: 381.
53. Bostanzade Yahya in Yazıcı, "Bostan-zâde Yahya," p. 41; Gökyay, "II. Sultan Osman'ın Şehadeti," p. 222.
54. Peçevi, *Tarih-i Peçevi*, II: 391.
55. Piterberg, "A Study of Ottoman Historiography," pp. 224-25; idem, "Speech Acts and Written Texts," pp. 408-9.

Hasanbeyzade Ahmed, whose family's political stance would be endangered by "Osmanist" policies.

Another contemporary author of an Ottoman history was Karaçelebizade Abdülaziz (1592-1657), like Yahya from a family of scholars and high-ranking judges.[56] Following his ancestors in due course,[57] Abdülaziz belonged to the central establishment, whose interests could have been endangered had Osman's supporters won the day.

Like Yahya, Abdülaziz is quite critical of the abolition of the pensions of judges and the extraordinary powers of Osman's tutor, Ömer Efendi.[58] He uses *fitne* and *fesad* in reference to the 1622 incident, but in a quite different context from that of Peçevi. Abdülaziz argues that the higher echelons of the state and the close associates of the sultan were the ones who stirred up sedition and disorder by entering a path that was contrary to Ottoman traditions. Implicitly, Osman is once again criticized for being obstinate.[59] Despite equating the incident with sedition and disorder, Abdülaziz is actually reprimanding Osman's ministers for their policies. This view resembles that of Hüseyin Tugi, the Janissary chronicler, who sees "Osmanist" policies as a deviation from the Ottoman tradition.

The last contemporaneous author to be touched upon here is Kâtip Çelebi. Piterberg substantiates Kâtip Çelebi's preference for Hüseyin Tugi's pro-soldier and anti-"Osmanist" approach over Peçevi's implicitly critical stance toward the rebellion.[60] Kâtip Çelebi clearly blames the "tactless and uneducated" associates of Osman for provoking the rebellion with their vicious and perverse ideas. He also holds Osman responsible for subscribing to the advice of those associates.[61] My suggestion is that his background could not let him do otherwise.

Unlike Peçevi, whose family had an independent standing from the palace and

---

56. The father of his grandfather, Hüsameddin, was one of the men of Karamanlı Mehmed Paşa (died 1453), the last grand vezir of Mehmed II. His grandfather, Muhiddin Mehmed (died 965/1557-58), held the judgeship of Istanbul during the reign of Süleyman I: Mecdi Mehmed Efendi, *Hadâ'iku'ş-Şakâ'ik* (Istanbul, 1269 A.H.), reprinted with an introduction by Özcan, *Şakaik-ı Nu'maniye ve Zeyilleri*, I: 495-96. His father, Hüsameddin Hüseyin (died 1598), was *kadı'asker* of Anatolia and then of Rumelia during the reign of Murad III (Nevizade Ata'i, in Özcan, ed., *Şakaik-ı Nu'maniye ve Zeyilleri*, II: 416-17). His elder brother Mehmed (died 1633) held the military judgeship of Anatolia during the reign of Ahmed I. Then, once during the reign of Osman II and twice under Murad IV, Mehmed was appointed to the military judgeship of Rumelia (Ibid., II: 450-52).
57. Abdülaziz was a *medrese* professor in Edirne at the time of Osman's deposition (Şeyhî, in Özcan, ed., *Şakaik-ı Nu'maniye ve Zeyilleri*, III: 252). Later, he would be an influential member of the ulema and play a role in the deposition of Sultan Ibrahim. During the reign of Mehmed IV, he became Şeyhülislâm. For the family as a whole, to which Nedim, the famous poet of the eighteenth century, was related, see Nejat Göyünç, "Kara-çelebi-zâde," *Encyclopaedia of Islam*, new ed. (hereafter *EI²*), IV: 73-74.
58. Karaçelebizade Abdülaziz, *Ravzatü'l-ebrâr* (Bulaq, 1248 A.H.), pp. 536, 541.
59. Ibid., p. 546.
60. Piterberg, "A Study of Ottoman Historiography," pp. 231-69; idem, "Speech Acts and Written Texts," pp. 410-11.
61. Kâtip Çelebi, *Fezleke*, 2 vols. (Istanbul, 1286-87 A.H.), II: 10.

the central army in the provinces, Kâtip Çelebi was the son of a soldier in the central army. His father, Abdullah, apparently a recruit of Christian origin, took the fourteen-year-old Kâtip Çelebi into his own corps, one of the central cavalry units, the *silahdarân*, and then found him a job in one of the financial offices sometime around 1622-23.[62] Thus, Kâtip Çelebi was probably an eyewitness to the whole event as a teenager. His father could have lost his job, or at least his status, if a mainly provincial army had replaced the existing central military organization. Because Kâtip Çelebi's own career also would have been endangered, he has to be read as someone whose interests were in line with the opposition to Osman.

So far, I have tried to argue that the attitude of contemporary chroniclers and historians toward the 1622 military rebellion was shaped by their own standing in the socio-political structure of the empire. Hüseyin the retired Janissary, Yahya the judge, Ahmed the administrator of palace origin, Abdülaziz the professor, and Kâtip Çelebi the secretary offer different opinions on a number of issues. Yet they all agree that the soldiers had good reason to rebel because "Osmanist" policies were a perverse deviation from the Ottoman tradition. The central army in its existing state was part of a much larger socio-economic structure that made it possible for people such as these authors to keep their socially privileged statuses. A new army recruited from the provinces, to be used for an expansionist foreign policy, would bring new strata of secretaries, administrators, professors, and judges ready to legitimize such a move. A new army meant a new exploitive mechanism in the hands of a new elite, as Peçevi and the anonymous Jewish author, despite their differences, both testify.

PRESENTATIONS OF THE EVENT IN THE LATE NINETEENTH AND TWENTIETH CENTURIES

By no means did interpretation of the 1622 incident remain frozen throughout two centuries, but radical change in its depiction occurred only in the late nineteenth and early twentieth centuries. During the latter period, an ever-expanding system of secondary education necessitated the production of textbooks. More important, the new ideologies behind that expansion were entering the political stage and needed to produce new histories.

One textbook was authored by Abdurrahman Şeref (died 1925). After serving as director of the School of Public Administration (*Mekteb-i Mülkiye*), Abdurrahman Şeref became a member of the Senate in the Second Constitutional Period, which began in 1908 after the Young Turk Revolution. In 1909, he was appointed official historian of the empire and held that post until the abolition of the sultanate. The last official historian of the empire, he also became the first president of the

---

62. Orhan Şaik Gökyay, "Kâtip Çelebi: Hayatı, Şahsiyeti, Eserleri," in *Kâtip Çelebi: Hayatı ve Eserleri hakkında İncelemeler* (Ankara, 1957), pp. 3-90, at pp. 3-4.

Ottoman Historical Society.[63]

Abdurrahman Şeref wrote his textbook on Ottoman history in 1895, long before he held his important official positions.[64] His depiction of the 1622 incident is a significant departure from the prevailing seventeenth-century version of the event. The soldiers are called rebels (*yeniçeri ve sipâh zorbaları*),[65] and, as a group, they are given a larger responsibility than ever before for the regicide -- "the first shame that slanders the pages of [Ottoman] history."[66] Osman's advisers are not reproached. The portrayal of Osman as a reformer begins with the assertion that "the state was hoping for important services from the greatness of his zeal."[67] The sole seventeenth-century historian to whom Abdurrahman Şeref refers is Peçevi, the only one whose account of the incident has an "Osmanist" tone.[68] At the turn of the twentieth century, a new political elite of self-identified reformers arose. Unlike the group to which Peçevi belonged in the seventeenth century, this new elite did seize power after the Young Turk Revolution,[69] and Abdurrahman Şeref became the official historian in 1909. Thus, from the early twentieth century on, one could expect the historiographical approach that was initiated by the anonymous Jewish author and Peçevi regarding the 1622 incident to become the prevalent one in a new context with new connotations.

The author of the next work to be examined is Mehmed Murad Bey, known as Mizancı Murad (died 1917). Born in Dağıstan, after an early education in Arabic and Koranic studies, he followed the Russian educational system. In 1873, when he was nineteen, he immigrated to Istanbul. Although he did not know Turkish then, he obtained a post in the Foreign Ministry through his connections and his knowledge of Russian and French. Until 1895, he held various administrative positions, mostly related to education, and published a newspaper called *Mizan*, which was suspended many times. Between 1895 and 1897, Murad stayed in Alexandria and Paris and joined the Committee of Union and Progress, an Ottoman political opposition group based in Europe. In 1896, he was elected its leader, but in 1897, he resigned, mainly because of disputes with Ahmed Rıza, an Ottoman positivist, returned to Istanbul and got a job at the Council of State until the Second Constitutional Period. During this period, when the Committee of Union and Progress was one of the strongest political forces, Murad became a figure of opposition to the organization of which he had once been president. After the incident of 31 March 1909, which was a reaction against the Young Turk Revolution, Murad was sent into exile. He started to write his Ottoman history on

---

63. Franz Babinger, *Die Geschichtsschreiber der Osmanen und Ihre Werke* (Leipzig, 1927), pp. 404-06.
64. Abdurrahman Şeref, *Tarih-i Devlet-i Osmaniye*, 2 vols. (Istanbul, ?-1312 A.H.; 2nd imprint 1315-18).
65. Ibid. (1st imprint), II: 30.
66. Ibid.: "*Sahâif-ta' rîhimizi karalayan birinci leke budur.*"
67. Ibid.: "'*Ulüvv-i himmetinden devlet büyük hidmetler ümîd iderdi.*"
68. Ibid.
69. Ibid.

the Aegean islands of Rhodes and Lesbos in the early 1910s.[70]

Murad recreates the 1622 incident with new connotations.[71] Of Osman, the "greatest şeyh of the Ottoman revolution," Murad writes,

> He is the head of the 'party of renovators' whose other members are Mustafa III, Selim III, and Mahmud II. Our predecessors could not appreciate his value. Let us at least save our successors from this defect. Let us no more be unaware of the identity and character of our own existence.[72]

Murad also discusses at length the possible consequences of Osman's plans:

> The Janissary organization was a tool of execution against the palace in the hands of the higher echelons of the state, the professors, and the judges. The sultan decided to extinguish this organization; if he had been successful, the men of greed would have lost their weapon, because the elements of the country (*'unsur-ı memleket*) who were going to replace the Janissaries were not to become their blind tools. These new elements were going to act in accordance with the feelings of the state, nation, and country, that is to say, in accordance with the local national ideas (*efkâr-i milliye-i mahalliye*).[73]

Here, Murad introduces a totally new element into the historiography. Since the fourteenth century, the central army had been made up of Christian boys recruited by force, converted, and given an appropriate education. I deliberately did not point this out above, as it never was an issue in seventeenth-century historiography and could not really have been one. At least half the men in the higher echelons of the state were of Christian origin; most queen mothers were non-Muslim slaves. In other words, the non-Turk and non-Muslim elements were at the very heart of things Ottoman. Murad's presentation of the soldiers as a foreign element in a national state is strictly an early-twentieth-century phenomenon.[74]

---

70. Michael Ursinus, "Mîzândjı Mehmed Murâd," *EI²*, VII: 205-6.
71. Mehmed Murad, *Ta'rîh-i Ebû'l-Fârûk: Ta'rîh-i Osmânîde Siyâset ve Medeniyet İ'tibâriyle Hikmet-i Asliye Taharrîsine Teşebbüs*, 7 vols. (Istanbul, 1325-32 A.H.).
72. Ibid., V: 63.
73. Ibid., V: 70.
74. A tremendous shift occurred in the meaning of the word "foreign" (*ecnebi*) from the seventeenth century to the early twentieth century. Mehmed Murad describes the Janissaries as "foreign elements imported to the land of Islam from the abode of unbelief." Ibid., V: 25. In the seventeenth century, however, foreign elements among the soldiery referred to the Muslim peasants entering the central army corps. See, for instance, Anonymous, "Kitâb-ı

Ironically, Mehmed Murad himself was not an ethnic Turk. His concept of nation was based on religious and local ties; in the passage quoted above, he does not use the words "Turk" or "Turkish." Later, especially after the foundation of the Turkish Republic, this religious and local understanding of the nation acquired a new meaning. Meanwhile, according to Mehmed Murad, the chief forces frustrating renovation in the seventeenth century were not the soldiers but the higher echelons, such as vezirs, scholars of religion and law, and palace officers. This point likewise would have special significance for historians of the Republic.

Around the turn of the twentieth century, the 1622 incident became the lost opportunity, the missed train that would have taken the Ottoman Empire into a new epoch. The Janissaries and the higher echelons of the state, therefore, were responsible for the Ottoman decay. Because the new elite who identified themselves as reformers had just seized power, they needed a history that would show that their ideas were not foreign to the Ottoman tradition and that their predecessors were to blame for the failures of the past. Mehmed Murad established a prototype in which their own ancestor was Osman, an Ottoman sultan, and the Janissaries and the higher echelons represented the former elite of the empire, whom they were replacing.

In the mid-1920s, the Ministry of Education of the newly founded Turkish Republic published a Turkish history written by Rıza Nur, a member of the last Ottoman parliament in Istanbul.[75] In 1920, Rıza Nur joined the nationalist movement in Ankara and became a member of the cabinet, as well as a member of the delegation to Lausanne, where the nationalists succeeded in revising the post-World War I treaty imposed on the Ottoman Empire. Later, Rıza Nur became an opposition figure and was forced into exile. He was able to return to Turkey only after the death of Mustafa Kemal.[76] In what was probably the first official history publication of the new Republic, Rıza Nur gives the 1622 incident an emphasis that differs from Mehmed Murad's. Although he presents Osman as a reformer who could have forestalled the empire's decay, Rıza Nur does not depict the soldiers as a foreign element. Instead, he claims that the religious scholars provoked the soldiers to rebellion by suggesting that Mustafa be brought to the throne and that the soldiers kill Osman.[77]

Neither Mehmed Murad, who had also attacked the religious scholars,

---

Müstetâb," in Yaşar Yücel, ed., *Osmanlı Devlet Teşkilatına Dair Kaynaklar: Kitâb-ı Müstetâb, Kitabu Mesâlihi'l-Müslimîn ve Menâfi'i'l-Mü'minîn, Hırzü'l-Mülûk* (Ankara, 1988); the first editions of two treatises in this collection: Yaşar Yücel, ed., *Osmanlı Devlet Düzenin Ait Metinler I: Kitâb-ı Mustetâb* (Ankara, 1974); *Osmanlı Devlet Düzenin Ait Metinler II: Kitâbu Mesâlihi'l-Müslimîn ve Menâfi'i'l-Mü'minîn, Tıpkıbasımı* (Ankara, 1980); *Osmanlı Devlet Düzenin Ait Metinler III: Kitâbu Mesâlihi'l- Müslimîn ve Menâfi'i'l-Mü'minîn, Metnin Türk Harflerine Çevirisi ve Değerlendirmesi* (Ankara, 1981), pp. 2-4 (in old Turkish letters, pp. 6-8). I thank Derin Terzioğlu and Nicole van Os of Koç University for drawing my attention to this point.
75. Rıza Nur, *Türk Tarihi*, 12 vols. (Istanbul, 1924-26).
76. Feroz Ahmad, "Rıdâ Nûr," *EI²*, VIII: 511.
77. Rıza Nur, *Türk Tarihi*, III: 236-42.

although to a lesser degree, nor Rıza Nur can be identified as a radical secularist. On the contrary, with regard to issues of religion, both were in the conservative camp at their respective times. They believed in and emphasized the role of religion and religious institutions in society. Thus, their attack against the religious scholars has to be understood within the context of their political struggle. As members of a new intellectual elite, however, they had to distinguish themselves from and fight against the political influence of the ulema, whose role they were trying to assume. This new elite, whether liberal or conservative, identified with progress and blamed the old intellectual elite, the scholars of religion and law, for obstructing progress.

During the late 1940s and the early 1950s, the new portrayal of the 1622 incident entered one of the most commonly used Turkish reference works, the *Explained Chronology of Ottoman History* by İsmail Hami Danişmend.[78] According to Danişmend, Osman's plans included replacing the degenerated, decaying, and cosmopolitan central military organization with a national one recruited from the Turks of Anatolia, Syria, and Egypt. Moving the capital from Istanbul to Anatolia would substitute a national environment for a cosmopolitan one and break down the political and financial power of the religious scholars.[79] As is clear from these examples, Osman was re-evaluated according to the nationalist and secularist ideology of the new intellectual elite of modern Turkey.

A history of Ottoman Turkish reform that starts with Mahmud II in the early nineteenth century, or even with Selim III in the late eighteenth century, has to deal with the uncomfortable claim that Ottoman reform resulted entirely from the impact of the West. Danişmend alludes, however, to the fact that Osman's position as a reformer is the proof of the national and local basis of the Ottoman Turkish renovation movement.[80] In other words, Ottoman Turkish reform did not stem from an inferiority complex vis-à-vis the West or from a wish to imitate western institutions. In Danişmend's book, Mehmed Murad's concept of a nation based on religious and local ties is replaced by an ethnic nationalism. At the same time, Mehmed Murad's remark, "[L]et us no more be unaware of the identity and character of our own existence," is made explicit. In both authors' works, the soldiers, who the seventeenth-century chronicles have making justifiable demands of a sultan surrounded by misguided advisers, now become rebels, responsible for Ottoman decay, even though the twentieth-century historians base their studies on those very same seventeenth-century chronicles.

Although I elsewhere cite quite a number of more recent Turkish sources,[81] I will limit the present discussion to a single significant interpretation of Osman and the 1622 incident. Yaşar Yücel, the president of the Turkish Historical Society in the aftermath of the 1980 military *coup d'état*, published in 1983 a literary source for the reign of Osman.[82] In Yücel's introduction, "Osman II is the first sultan who

---

78. İsmail Hami Danişmend, *İzahlı Osmanlı Tarihi Kronolojisi*, 4 vols. (Istanbul, 1947-55).
79. Ibid., III: 290-92.
80. Ibid., III: 291.
81. See my "Searching for Osman," mentioned in n. 8.
82. See n. 6 above.

tried to solve the problems faced after Kanunî's time. At the end of the sixteenth century, the Ottoman Empire reached a turning point. The need for many radical changes began to be seen. This went on until the succession of Osman II to the throne."[83]

All recent interpreters of the reign of Osman and the 1622 incident share the characteristics of elitism and statism. The well-educated Osman recognizes all the problems and knows all the answers. The state is the place where the reform movement begins and from which it is imposed upon society. Similarly, the guiding principles of modern Turkish politics are reform led by an enlightened leader, change from the top down, and state interference in political development through military *coups d'état*.

It is not only Turkish scholars who subscribe to elitist and statist views. Stanford Shaw, the author of an Ottoman history that has been widely used as a textbook and reference work, claims, on the basis of information from an eighteenth-century French novel,[84] that the sultan was "[t]rained in Latin, Greek, and Italian by his Greek mother, as well as Ottoman Turkish, Arabic, and Persian."[85] Shaw cautions that "[w]hether Osman II was a conscious reformer or whether conditions and problems simply led him to actions that can be called reforms is uncertain."[86] Still, he is convinced that Osman wanted to "Turkify" both the palace and the military organization. "[Osman] seems to have thought of moving the Ottoman government from the *devşirme* center of Istanbul to some place in Anatolia where Turkish traditions and values would prevail, perhaps to Bursa or Ankara, thus presaging the reforms of Mustafa Kemal Atatürk by some three centuries."[87] In this case, the interpretation of Danişmend is echoed for an audience that appreciates Third World leaders who guide their countries through development in accordance with modernization theory.

In 1993, finally, an *Ottoman Encyclopaedia* was compiled by a committee

---

83. Yücel, ed., *Zafer-nâme*, pp. xxix-xxx.
84. Madeleine-Angélique de Gomez, *Histoire d'Osman, premier du nom, XIXe empereur des Turcs, et de l'impératrice Aphendina Ashada*, 2 vols. (Paris, 1734), trans. by John Williams as *The Life of Osman the Great*, 2 vols. (London, 1735). Mme. de Gomez (1684-1770) was born into a family of comedians in Paris, married a well-to-do Spanish man, and spent her life writing numerous novels: *Dictionnaire des littératures de la langue française*, II (Paris, 1984): 959. Her works are cited as examples of sentimental and heroic novels: Henri Coulet, *Le Roman jusqu'à la Révolution*, vol. I: *Histoire du roman en France* (Paris, 1967), p. 182; Robert Niklaus, *A Literary History of France: The Eighteenth Century, 1715-1789* (London and New York, 1970), p. 356. A very extensive treatment of her novels, which include others that are inspired by the Ottoman and Safavid empires, is available in Joseph de Laporte (1713-79), *Histoire littéraire des femmes françoises*, 5 vols. (Paris, 1769), III: 466-644. I thank Professor Lionel Gossman of the Department of Romance Languages and Literatures, Princeton University, who referred me to these titles.
85. Stanford J. Shaw, *History of the Ottoman Empire and Modern Turkey*, vol. I: *Empire of the Gazis: The Rise and Decline of the Ottoman Empire, 1280-1808* (Cambridge, 1976), p. 191.
86. Ibid., I: 192.
87. Ibid.

composed largely of "Turkish Muslim intelligentsia."[88] Its presentation of the 1622 incident is closer to Kâtip Çelebi's account than to the modern interpretation just discussed.[89] The conclusion reads, "Thus Sultan Osman II, who took his place in history as a young and inexperienced ruler trying to open a new path, was killed on 20 May 1622."[90] The phrase "who tried to open a new path," reflecting the modern interpretation, thus is counterbalanced with "young and inexperienced." The soldiers are reproached for engaging in rebellion although their demands are justified. The value of Osman's projects is recognized but with emphasis on the fact that he was unrealistic and inexperienced.

The encyclopaedia's account does not simply reflect a middle ground between the two alternatives. Rather, it is related to the Muslim critique of Turkish political development, in which reforms were imposed on society from above. Just as there were different interpretations of the 1622 incident in the seventeenth century, in the twentieth and early twenty-first centuries, some also disagree with the hegemonic interpretation of the time.

REEVALUATION

The radical difference between the seventeenth-century interpretation of the 1622 incident, which more or less justifies the soldiers' actions, and the twentieth-century portrait, which depicts the soldiers as rebels or tools of conservative forces, should be clear by now. The question is whether we can claim that the new interpretation is an absolute re-creation. Certainly it has serious factual flaws. Osman did not for one moment think of Turkification, and the soldiers he was going to recruit would include Arabs and Kurds, as well as Turks.[91] Moreover, he probably did not decide to abolish the policy of recruiting Christian boys altogether.[92] In short, the modern interpretation cannot be substantiated and is plainly the product of an epoch in which nationalism is one of the strongest

---

88. *Osmanlı Ansiklopedisi: Tarih--Medeniyet--Kültür*, 7 vols. (Istanbul, 1993). I use "Turkish Muslim intelligentsia" to refer to those intellectuals who are seen as "Islamist" by some members of the secular Turkish intelligentsia.
89. Ibid., IV: 19, 22-25.
90. "*Böylece Osmanlı tarihinde çığır açmaya çalışan genç ve tecrübesiz bir padişah olarak tarihe geçen II. Osman, 20 Mayıs 1622 tarihinde öldürüldü.*"
91. Sir Thomas Roe, *The Negotiations of Sir Thomas Roe in His Embassy to the Ottoman Porte* (London, 1740), pp. 43-44.
92. See the document published by Ahmed Refik, "Devşirme Usulü, Acemi Oğlanlar," *Edebiyat Fakültesi Mecmuası*, 15 (1927): 1-14, at pp. 4-5. Moreover, there was a large *çıkma*, or advancement of the *devşirme*s from service in the palace to the military regiments, in the last few months of Osman's reign, suggesting that a radical change in the system of recruitment was not seriously considered, at least in the short term; see Kâtip Çelebi, *Fezleke*, II: 8; and the contemporary appointments register (*rü'ûs defteri*), Başbakanlık Osmanlı Arşivi, Kamil Kepeci 257, pp. 65-71, 74-75, 79-80.

ideologies.

Therefore, one would be justified in claiming that the new interpretation of the 1622 incident has much more to do with the political stage today than the historical situation then, as I have tried to show throughout this discussion. Recognition of the unfounded socio-political use of the past in the new portrayal does not warrant discarding it entirely, however: the gist of the portrait that presents Osman in a positive light and the soldiers in a negative one was present in the seventeenth century, in interpretations such as Peçevi's and the anonymous Jewish author's. Similarly, a recent interpretation of the 1622 incident, the one by the Turkish Muslim intellectuals, still carries important traces of the earlier portrait. It is not a question of one or the other. Just as the recent interpretation reflects the political agendas of the interpreters, the contemporary ones display the stakes of the chroniclers in the system of that time. The portrayal that became hegemonic in the seventeenth century did so only because the army and its supporters won the day in May 1622. All of the narratives hold clues to the serious conflict of interests within the political elite of the empire and to the efforts of the various interests to legitimize their claims in terms of the "ancient law" (*kanun-ı kadim*). The seventeenth-century chroniclers' point that Osman deviated from the path of Ottoman tradition provides us with the essence of the main controversy.

The concept of innovation was a negative idea on the eve of modernity. The arguments in J.G.A. Pocock's *Ancient Constitution* hold for the Ottoman political stage, as well.[93] All of the so-called reform tracts of the late sixteenth and early seventeenth centuries suggest cutting down the number of soldiers in the central army or cutting down the expenses of the treasury. These suggestions are not identified as renovations, however, but explicitly called a return to the "ancient law." One tract presented to Osman, for instance, states, "What is contrary to the 'law' (*kanun*) is that whereas the number of soldiers in the infantry corps (*yeniçeri kulları*) used to be 12,000 in old times, today just the number of the retirees (*korucu ve tekâ'üd*) has grown to more than 7,000."[94] The soldiers and their sympathetic chroniclers use the same justification: "On the same day the soldiers petitioned the sultan [Mustafa] for the execution of those who left the path of the ancient law (*kanun-ı kadim*) and invented new laws."[95] Yet to be written is a history of the 1622 incident that addresses this controversy over the definition of the ancient constitution. Although both parties involved in the controversy were actually engaged in some kind of renovation, both legitimized themselves as upholders of the very same past. The next historian of the 1622 incident now must map the various

---

93. J.G.A. Pocock, *The Ancient Constitution and the Feudal Law: A Study of English Historical Thought in the Seventeenth Century--A Reissue with a Retrospect* (Cambridge, 1987; 1st ed. 1957).
94. Anonymous, *Kitâb-ı Müstetâb*, ed. Yücel, p. 9 (in old Turkish letters, p. 17).
95. Kâtip Çelebi, *Fezleke*, II: 19; compare Naima (d. 1716), *Tarih-i Naima*, 6 vols. (Istanbul, 1281-83 A.H.), II: 224-25. Kâtip Çelebi's source is Hüseyin Tugi, H.O. 74, fols. 19b–20a; compare Bibliothèque nationale, MS Turc. 227, fol. 28b; MS Suppl. Turc. 871, fol. 27b; and Solakzade, *Solakzade Tarihi*, p. 717; see also n. 19 above.

interest groups around this controversy, identify their members, and then re-examine the incident, not as a dichotomy of reformer vs. conservative, but as a conflict over the direction of change.

University of Wisconsin-Milwaukee

Palmira Brummett

The River Crossing:
Breaking Points (Metaphorical and "Real")
in Ottoman Mutiny*

> Before us the thick dark current runs. It talks up to us in a murmur become ceaseless and myriad, the yellow surface dimpled monstrously into fading swirls traveling along the surface for an instant, silent, impermanent and profoundly significant, as though just beneath the surface something huge and alive waked for a moment of lazy alertness out of and into light slumber again.
> William Faulkner, *As I Lay Dying* (New York, 1985; originally published New York, 1930), p. 141.

> The river itself is not a hundred yards across, and Pa and Vernon and Vardamon and Dewey Dell are the only things in sight not of that single monotony of desolation leaning with that terrific quality a little from right to left, as though we had reached the place where the motion of the wasted world accelerates just before the final precipice. Yet they appear dwarfed. It is as though the space between us were time: an irrevocable quality. It is as though time, no longer running straight before us in a diminishing line, now runs parallel between us like a looping string, the distance being the doubling accretion of the thread and not the interval between. The mules stand, their fore quarters already sloped a little, their rumps high. They too are breathing now with a deep groaning sound; looking back once, their gaze sweeps across us with in their eyes a wild, sad, profound, and despairing quality as though they had already seen in the thick water the shape of the disaster which they could not speak and we could not see. Ibid., pp. 146-47.

INTRODUCTION

William Faulkner, in *As I Lay Dying*, has written perhaps the most moving passages in American literature on what it means to cross a river. We feel not only

---

* This article was previously published with the same title in *Rebellion, Repression, Reinvention: Mutiny in Comparative Perspective*, ed. Jane Hathaway (New York: Praeger Press, 2001), pp. 215-231.

the fear and determination of the men but the terror of the mules as they prepare to descend into the flood, obeying commands, fulfilling a "promise," taking Addie Bundren to be buried at "New Hope." In Faulkner's story, crossing the river becomes a crucible for testing the very nature of man and for illustrating the differences among men. His novel is a metaphor, not only for the river crossing itself but for the acts of mutiny that the demand to cross engenders. Each of his characters responds to the terrible task in different ways: one refuses to risk his mule; others go around; one approaches the river with a fury of determination, another with a detached acceptance of death, another with the stoic consciousness of duty. Faulkner provides a poetic comparative frame for assessing the episode of the river crossing in history; in his characters and the full range of their emotions, the elements of Ottoman mutiny are invoked and magnified.

Faulkner, however, does not have a monopoly on imagery of the river crossing; indeed, the notion of surviving the flood, of crossing over to the other side, constitutes a centuries-old metaphor for life, for redemption, and for the inevitable trials imposed by duty or by nature. The river in world literature leads to adventure or oblivion; one crosses it into paradise (the Jordan) or hell (the Styx). The idea of crossing the water is also critical in narrations of mutiny. Commonly, the term "mutiny" is associated with shipboard revolt. Most apparently, the isolation of the sea crossing and its hardships provide both the environment and the opportunity for seagoing mutiny. But the "crossing" is not only a factor in mutinies at sea. On land, the river crossing becomes a quintessential symbol of men's breaking points. The river is the boundary beyond which men cannot or will not go. Crossing the river breaks men in both body and spirit. Rivers, of course, act as natural boundaries between territories. But, more than that, they represent the point at which armies must regroup and reconsider their positions and their allegiances. They represent a surrendering of men, horses, and equipment--not an involuntary surrendering but a voluntary, calculated surrendering. Of course, there are many such points of decision in the course of a military campaign. But the river is often a particularly formidable barrier (especially in eras and societies in which few could swim). Crossing the river, at best, demands ignominious ablutions; at worst, it signifies vulnerability, cold, illness, injury, and death.

The struggle of battle and the struggle of life itself are often characterized in water and flood imagery. Kings, gurus, and military commanders, in these metaphors become those who can enable men to cross the water. The great spiritual leader of the Jains is called *tirthankara*, ("ford-maker"). The Buddha is depicted as a miraculous river-crosser who can transport his followers across the swollen Ganges.[1] According to Rashīd al-Dīn, Kublai Khan, undaunted, crossed the sea-like

---

1. When the Buddha decided to break his fast, he ate and then decided to cross the river. But the Ganges was overflowing. Some of his followers began to look for boats or to weave rafts, but the Buddha, "as instantaneously as a strong man would stretch forth his arm, or draw it back again when he had stretched it forth, vanished from this side of the river, and stood on the further bank with the company of the brethren." The Buddha then noted: "They who cross the ocean drear, making a solid path across the pools, whilst the vain world ties its basket

River Keng to pursue his conquests, although he had to use a talisman of birch-bark to accomplish the task.[2] The inept commander or the bad king is he who fails to meet the challenge of the flood. As noted in the great Indian epic the *Mahabharata*: "The king who ignores his principal ministers and makes vile ones his favorites meets with disaster, and, suffering, he never finds a safe place to ford the stream."[3] In the *Arthasastra*, the brilliant third-century manual of advice for kings, Kautiliya mentions both floods and rebellions as "calamities" that befall armies. He discusses how to guard troops from such calamities. Kautiliya also recommends river worship to prevent floods.[4] If, then, rivers provide the occasion for military calamities, then military leaders must control the waters, conceive plans for fording them successfully, and guard against the flood's producing the calamity of rebellion. Indeed, in the face of a threatening enemy, even those who are not warriors may serve this guardian function, according to the *Mahabharata*, which notes that if a nonwarrior emerges to protect the people threatened by a "barbarian army," then that person should be rewarded:

> If someone would serve as a further shore, when there is no further shore in sight; if someone would serve as a boat, when there is no boat at hand, he deserves respect in every way, whether he is a Shudra or something else. When people who have no protector, or those oppressed by barbarians, get protection... they ought to pay that man respect with joy, as if he were their own kinsman.[5]

This paper analyzes the river crossing in the context of Ottoman military campaigns and suggests the ways in which river crossings hold the potential to generate mutiny. It examines the modes and strategies of river crossing, the differences between crossings made while advancing and those made while retreating, the different responses of leaders and men to the crossing event, and the

---

rafts, these are the wise, these are the saved indeed." From the Mahaparinibbanasutta, in *Buddhist Suttas*, trans. from the Pali by T.W. Rhys Davids (New York, 1969, reprint of the 1881 Oxford ed.), pp. 21-22; see also pp. 178-84 for more river-crossing imagery, this time criticizing the brahmins.
2. John Boyle, ed. and trans., *The Successors of Genghis Khan, Translated from the Persian of Rashid al-Din* (New York, 1971), p. 248.
3. *The Mahabharata*, trans. from the Sanskrit by James L. Fitzgerald (Chicago, forthcoming), Book 12, 94:1.
4. Kautiliya, *The Kautiliya Arthasastra*, Part 2, trans. R.P. Kangle, 2nd ed. (Bombay, 1972), pp. 262-63, 392, 409, 413, 435, 460. He also argues that the king who fights with only a small army "perishes, like one plunging into the ocean without a boat." Perhaps the epithets of Genghis Khan (Oceanic Ruler) and Sultan Süleyman the Magnificent (Lord of the Two Lands and Two Seas) were meant to symbolize not only the extent of their rule but their ability to control the waters.
5. *Mahabharata*, Book 12, 79:37.

rhetorics by which the narrative sources present these crossings. These rhetorics will then be compared to those of Faulkner and, by way of a postscript, to those of the Mughal ruler Babur in his memoirs.

STRATEGIES

In the sixteenth century, the Ottomans were already masters in the art of crossing rivers. They built pontoon bridges, made bridges of boats, and constructed more enduring bridges of lumber and stone.[6] When preparing campaigns, the Ottomans demonstrated their awareness of the critical nature of river crossings by attempting to plan and provide for the logistics of river crossings in advance. There is ample evidence, for example, in the chronicle of Mustafa Naima (1665-1716) of bridge-building in the Ottoman wars (1593-1603) in Hungary. Naima recounts how the Ottoman commanders called for the transport of bridge-building personnel and material and for the strategic locating of boats early on in the preparations for campaigns.[7] This was often (but not always) fairly easily accomplished at points that the Ottomans already held along the Danube. But as the Ottoman armies moved farther from this major water course and from their own points of supply, bridge-building became difficult or impossible. What was lacking in river crossings was not, then, expertise but rather supplies, labor, and time. The logistics of transport and the vagaries of weather meant that the Ottoman forces often had to cross rivers without the benefit of bridges.[8] Indeed, when one looks at the campaigns against the Hapsburgs, one is tempted to say that it was not superior forces or a lack of valor that kept the Ottomans from taking Vienna but a combination of water and mud.

Of course, even where bridges were available, they did not always smooth the passing of the river. When Ottoman forces were in retreat, bridges constituted murderous bottlenecks that were counted upon for salvation but that often resulted

---

6. At Pruth in 1711, the Ottomans built three pontoon bridges overnight to protect the opposite shore; hundreds of Janissaries (*serdengeçti*s) and Tatars swam across. They also crossed with barges to face the Russian advance guard trying to prevent the crossing. Thanks to Virginia Aksan for this account.
7. In this essay, I cite two versions of the work of the chronicler Naima: (1) an Ottoman edition: Mustafa Naima, *Tarih-i Naima*, vol. I (Istanbul, 1281-83 A.H./1864-66 C.E.) and (2) the English version: Mustafa Naima, *Annals of the Turkish Empire from 1591-1659 of the Christian Era*, trans. Charles Fraser, vol. I (London, 1832). Notes indicate the pagination from the Ottoman text, followed by a slash, and then the pagination from the translation. Fraser's translation is flawed and sometimes incomplete but more accessible than the rather scarce Ottoman editions. There are sufficient differences between the Ottoman edition and the translation that I would suggest that the manuscripts from which they are taken are different.
8. For a thorough study of the logistics of Ottoman campaigns in Hungary, especially the logistics of provisioning, see Caroline Finkel, *The Administration of Warfare: The Ottoman Military Campaigns in Hungary, 1593-1606* (Vienna, 1988).

in panic, chaos, and the abandoning of artillery and heavy equipment when melées occurred while large armies were trying to cross narrow bridges. Even when forces were not retreating, bringing an army across a single bridge was a time-consuming affair. Naima relates that in 1594 the *agha* (senior officer) of the Janissaries ordered a bridge of boats built across the Danube; the construction took four days. It then took one entire day for the army, ordinance, and baggage train to cross the bridge.[9] This gives some idea of why fleeing armies, having lost all order of march, suffered such disasters when they encountered bridges. Even with bridges in place, river crossings were a timeless dilemma, as illustrated by Rashīd al-Dīn's account of the Mongol army's crossing the Yangtze in 1260 as it returned from victories in Annam (in present-day Vietnam). Rashīd al-Dīn relates that one of Kublai's commanders, named Uriyangqdai, built a bridge of boats over the Yangtze. Then an immense army of the Sung arrived, and the Mongol army struggled to get across the bridge. In the ensuing chaos, many "fell into the water or perished."[10]

When no bridges were available, the Ottomans on an orderly march used boats, fords, and rafts and swam their horses across.[11] They also used wagons and ropes, just like the Bundrens in Faulkner's novel. But when no boats were available, or when rivers and streams were swollen to flood levels, then transporting an army across a river became a nightmarish endeavor. The commanders' demands that men cross such flooded rivers provoked anger, frustration, despair, and mutiny. I have described one such episode, as the Ottomans were engaged in the eastern campaigns of 1578-80, in a previous article.[12] On that occasion, faced with the prospect of drowning, the soldiers mutinied, threatened their commanders, and attempted to seize the campaign treasury. Each difficult river crossing thus became a test of the commanders' ability to exercise authority over their men. If the troops had endured long periods of deprivation prior to the crossing or, as we shall see later, if they had already endured flood conditions and river crossings in which they had witnessed their fellows drowning, they became demoralized and were more likely both to break ranks and to engage in other sorts of rebellious behavior.

RESPONSES

As I Lay Dying presents the dilemma of the individual faced with a river crossing. In Ottoman historical accounts, we seldom get such personal visions.

---

9. Naima, p. 142/73.
10. Boyle, *Successors of Genghis Khan*, p. 227.
11. Comte de Marsigli, *L'État militaire de l'Empire Ottoman* (La Haye, 1732), II: 49-50. Marsigli, who was intimately familiar with the Ottoman military, illustrates what he calls the Ottomans' "barbarous mode" of crossing rivers while on campaign. The mode, however, sounds and looks well-ordered.
12. Palmira Brummett, "Subordination and Its Discontents: Ottoman Campaign, 1578-1580," in Caesar Farah, ed., *Decision-Making and Change in the Ottoman Empire* (Kirksville, MO, 1993), pp. 101-14.

When faced with the crossing, men may follow orders; disobey orders; act courageously or display cowardice; act out of duty, honor, or fear. They cross because they are ordered to do so, because their fellows cross, or because they see themselves as having no alternative. Some instances of river crossing are clearly more potentially conducive to mutiny than others: those that do not accomplish their objectives; those that lead to subsequent (disastrous) losses; those that result in many men lost to drowning; and those that seem to be ill-conceived, ill-executed, or even ill-starred.

Men respond to this challenge in different ways: they may try to go around, wait for boats, try to escape the crossing, or plunge ahead regardless of the risk. In most cases, we simply do not know how men felt when they were faced with a river crossing. The rhetorics of our narrative sources are often constructed after the fact by non-participants who focus on certain behaviors (especially of leaders) in retrospect, when the outcome of the crossing is already known. We have very little direct evidence of individual thoughts or actions during the actual river-crossing episode. That being the case, our accounts of Ottoman mutiny must be viewed, in part, as admonitory tales that suggest the bad things that can happen when the right military decisions are not made. They are used to advise rulers and to allocate blame to officers. Nonetheless, I think that these river-crossing narratives can illustrate the high degree of duress to which Ottoman troops were exposed. In addition to overwork, no pay, lack of provisions, and long campaigns, the Ottoman troops were subjected to the crises of river crossings that tested the mettle of the commanders and the loyalty (and strength) of the men. Rhetorically, these accounts also demonstrate the panic engendered by being trapped between a river and a charging foe. They show the paradox of military ideals confronted with the realities of river crossings that presented no particular opportunity for valor or reward and, at the same time, great opportunity for injury and loss.

NARRATIVES OF OTTOMAN RIVER CROSSING

Naima's chronicle of the Ottoman-Habsburg Wars presents a series of episodes in which the Ottomans are stymied in their efforts by rivers. Naima, of course, is quick to assign blame when river crossings led to disaster. But the overall picture that he presents of these campaigns suggests (1) that the Ottomans took great pains to provide for river crossings and to protect the bridges that were in place and (2) that multiple rivers (particularly away from the Danube itself) and flooding constituted especially difficult obstacles in the progress of campaigns in the Balkans.

Two episodes, one in 1593 and the other in 1595, neatly illustrate how water imagery figures prominently in tropes of leadership and warfare. The first concerns the expedition of Hasan Pasha of Bosnia into Croatia. At Siska, Hasan threw two bridges over the Kupa River and sent one of his warriors across to reconnoiter. He returned to report that the Austrian force was "covered with steel" (*ahen-pus*) and advancing in great numbers like the waves of the sea.[13] Hasan Pasha, who had been playing chess, accused his subordinate of cowardice for letting the size of the enemy army cow him. Mounting his horse, he led his troops across the bridge into battle. The Ottoman army, however, could not contend with this foe and was driven back to the bridges, where Hasan Pasha fell into the river and lost his life (*gark u nabud oldu*). Eight thousand Ottoman troops were "drowned and martyred." Naima cites Hasan for his bravery, but his account suggests that the commander was rash. Nonetheless, the news of the slaughter inspired the "ocean-like zeal" (*derya-i gayret*) of the sultan back in Istanbul to pursue the war effort with great vigor.[14]

In the second episode, in 1595, Sinan Pasha, the grand vizier, has launched a campaign into Wallachia. He leaves a newly-constructed bridge under guard on the Danube at Yergögü. Plagued by Michael, the *voyvoda* (governor) of Wallachia, the Ottoman army retreats, only to find the bridge virtually unattended. Naima tells us that the garrison was in the habit of abandoning its post to go out and despoil the countryside. After a few nights encamped at Yergögü, the Ottoman army is confronted with the imminent arrival of Michael and his army. Sinan crosses the bridge by night, leaving his soldiers to do what they can. In effect, the commander saves himself and leaves his troops to follow as they may.[15] Meanwhile, the enemy arrives, seizes the abandoned gear of the Ottomans, and sets up its cannon on a high point in order to bombard the bridge and the fleeing Ottomans. The scene is reminiscent of Faulkner's river crossing but on a much grander scale:

The bridge was cut in two by cannon fire, and the soldiers and heavy equipment upon it were cast into the Danube. Some on the bridge, crying to God for aid, fell into the flowing river, and their wails and moans caused the earth to tremble. At this point, the merciless infidels put to the sword the Muslims who were on the far side of the river and unable to cross. They did not spare a single soul. 1,000 souls were obliterated,

---

13. Naima, pp. 80-81/14-15. In this metaphor the glinting of armor is compared to the glinting of the waves at sea, but there are many literary images that compare armies and battlefields to the "raging waves of the sea." For two examples, see Virginia Aksan, *An Ottoman Statesman in War and Peace: Ahmed Resmî Efendi, 1700-1783* (Leiden, 1995), p. 150 (citing Vasif); and *The Mahabharata*, trans. J.A.B. van Bruitenen (Chicago, 1978), Book 5, 50:26, which describes the prospect of challenging the warrior Bhimasena thus: "Only fools would attempt to cross that shoreless, plumbless, impassable ocean called Bhimasena, an ocean stormy with arrows."
14. Naima, p. 81/15; Ibrahim Peçevi, *Peçevi Tarihi*, Turkish ed. prepared by Bekir Baykal (Ankara, 1982), II: 118-19. Peçevi's account of this event omits the dramatic confrontation of commander and subordinate.
15. Naima, p. 133/65. Peçevi, II: 161, does not specifically blame Sinan Pasha for leaving the troops in disarray, but he does say that Sinan got his just deserts from God for bearing a grudge against Ferhad Pasha, the grand vizier most recently deposed: "...*kazdığı derin kuyuya kendisi düştü, büyük Allah'tan cezasını buldu*" (He himself fell into the deep well that he had dug and found his punishment from almighty God).

their blood flowing in streams. Among the *akıncıs* (raiders), not one of those who found himself on the opposite shore escaped. They were cut to pieces. Most of the cannons and munitions fell into the hands of the enemy.... Never has there been such a rout, nor calamity and destruction of this magnitude.[16]

Naima, of course, uses a bit of hyperbole when he suggests that this was the worst disaster ever recorded. But Sinan here, according to Kautiliya's model, proved himself a bad commander, exposing his troops to crisis and leaving them at the mercy of the enemy and the river. Sinan was (temporarily) deposed in disgrace, and Naima tells us that the Ottoman notables and Muslim populace "went mad" (*ciğerleri biryan oldu*; literally, "their livers were broiled") when they heard the news of this ignominious defeat.[17]

There is no mention in Naima of mutiny in the ranks in the immediate aftermath of the Yergöğü disaster, although there are several accounts of mutinous behavior in the aftermath of Hasan Pasha's defeat in 1593. In 1596 Mehmed III (1595-1603) himself marched out with the Ottoman army. Naima relates that the army was impeded by marshy ground and a flooded stream but nonetheless marched valiantly on to engage the enemy.[18] He speaks disapprovingly of the sultan, however, who remained behind, too timid to cross and confront the enemy directly. This again, as so often happens in Naima's account, suggests that certain elements of the Ottoman leadership are lacking in valor. If the sultan is timid, how can he expect his commanders to inspire the troops? Inspiration and valor (along with rivers, mud, and bad luck) are key elements in Naima's accounts of war.

One particular river-crossing episode, retold in rather apocalyptic fashion by Naima, suggests both that the Ottoman commanders are not proper "ford-makers" and that heaven itself may be opposed to the Ottoman advance. In 1598, without benefit of a bridge, the Ottoman troops under Satırcı Mehmed Pasha face a very difficult crossing of the Mureşul River. They experience "a thousand hardships" crossing rivers and marshes until they finally arrive at Varad in Transylvania.[19] Mehmed decides to besiege Varad but soon realizes that it will not be easily taken. Then the rains begin. "By God's command, it rained without letting up for over forty days." That number, one suspects, is not coincidental.[20] The Ottoman troops watch the waters rise just as the Bundren family watch the river rise as their mother lies dying. In both cases, this watching is the prelude to disaster. At Varad the river overflowed, and the entire camp became a quagmire. Soldiers could not pass from

---

16. Naima, pp. 133-34/65.
17. Ibid., p. 135/66.
18. Ibid., pp. 154-55/83-85. This river was fordable in places.
19. Ibid., p. 191/118.
20. Ibid., p. 193/120-21. Peçevi's version, II: 202, does not use the figure forty for the days of rain; he says "more than a month". Like Naima, he recounts the misery of the troops and the food profiteering that goes on as the army withdraws and searches for provisions.

one tent to another, the wind tore out the tent poles, and the animals were belly-deep in the mud. The army was completely demoralized. Then terrible news arrived: 80,000 enemy troops were besieging Buda, Michael had taken Nicopolis, and the infidel was seizing territory right and left. But Mehmed Pasha's troops were faced with "rivers like seas," making it difficult to send aid to the beleaguered Ottoman forces.[21] Ismail Pasha of Temeşvar was instructed to build bridges to aid Mehmed Pasha's withdrawal, but he did not build them. So the army had to cross (under great duress) twelve rivers, with the men chilled from the cold, many animals drowned, and their provisions soaked, causing disease among the men. The chronicler conjures a harrowing vision of men abandoned by the roadside: cold, starving, and pinioned in the mud. Naima relates admiringly that three of the brave pashas, in order to inspire the troops, put their own necks to the yokes used to haul artillery across the rivers.[22] This vignette stands in direct contrast to the representation of Mehmed Pasha, whose valor is not questioned but whose errors in judgment are blamed for the army's predicament.

Exhausted, disheartened, and starving, the army moves to Solnok, expecting supply boats with provisions to have arrived along the river Tisza. At this point the long march, many river crossings, and hunger cause the army to explode into mutiny. The men become enraged, and the Janissaries rush the *serdar*'s (commander's) tent and pull it down around his ears. That particular action occurs in various accounts of mutinous Janissary behavior. But in this case, the Janissaries go further. They bludgeon the *serdar*, loot his provisions, and seize the treasury: "Each one had taken up a piece of wood, and with countless blows, they split the renowned commander's head."[23] These acts of violence seem to assuage their anger, and the commander is not killed, but his spirit is broken, and he is later executed for his failures. The troops continue their retreat and finally obtain food from provision boats on the Tisza near Segedin. But in order to ward off further mutinous behavior, the Ottoman officers borrow money from the "rich men and merchants of Belgrade" in order to pay the Janissaries before they disperse into winter quarters.[24] So ends the disastrous campaign of Satırcı Mehmed Pasha, whose ill-considered siege of Varad left him as a sort of pathetic Noah with no tip of land to find among the swollen streams of Transylvania. Here, the river tests the limits of men's obedience-- not a single episode of confrontation with a river but a monotonous repetition of river crossing after river crossing, each flood exacting its toll.

RYCAUT

One of the most pointed and dramatic accounts of an Ottoman river crossing is told by the intrepid Paul Rycaut, secretary to the English ambassador at the court of

---

21. Naima, p. 194/122.
22. Ibid., pp. 195-96/123.
23. Ibid., p. 196/124.
24. Ibid., p. 197/124.

Mehmed IV (1648-1687).[25] Rycaut visits the Ottoman camp to observe its order and recounts the misadventures of its recent campaigns. The story is worth quoting at length both for its details and its suggestion of the rhetorics of war (emphasis added):

> The Vizir made many and various attempts to pass the River Raab, to make some conquests in the parts of Croatia and Styria, but by reason of the forts the Christians had made along the banks of the River, in every adventure lost considerable numbers of men; at which loss of men and time, and the ill success near Lewa, the Vizir being greatly moved, made another adventure on the twenty seventh of July 1664, advancing with the gross of his army as far as Kerment, a place between the rivers Raab and Terne, endeavouring there to make his passage with better success; but by the valour of the Hungarians and the affiliance of the General Montecucoli were repulsed with extraordinary slaughter.
>
> On the first of August following, the Turk made another considerable attempt and passed over in one place 6,000 Janissaries and Albanians, and in another where the River was fordable, and not above ten paces broad, the whole body of the Turkish Horse crowded over in vast numbers, which caused the Christians to join their Forces into one Army, and retreat farther into the Country, and put themselves into a posture of giving battle to the Enemy.
>
> As soon as the Turkish army had thus waded over the water, the night following fell so much rain, and such a deluge came powering down from the mountains that the River which was fordable the day before did now overflow its own banks and [was] not passable without Floats and Bridges. As soon as the Army was thus passed the River, the great Vizir dispatched immediately Messengers to the Grand Signior [sultan] to acquaint him of his progress and passage; which news he knew would come very grateful; because in all Letters from the Grand Signior he was urged by threats and positive commands to proceed forward in his march, *and not to suffer the impediment of a narrow ditch to be an interruption to the whole Ottoman force, which was never before restrained [even] by the Ocean.* The Grand Signior having received this intelligence, *as if the whole Victory and Triumph over the World consisted in the passage of the Raab, was transported with such an extraordinary joy and assurance of victory that all Hungary and Germany were already swallowed in his thoughts,* and when by a second message he received intelligence that a forlorn hope of the Enemy, consisting of a thousand men, was cut off, the Ottoman court was transported with the joy and assurance of Victory, that

---

25. Paul Rycaut, *The Present State of the Ottoman Empire* (New York, 1971, reprint of 1668 London ed.), Part 3, pp. 206-07. I thank Virginia Aksan for drawing this account to my attention.

to anticipate the good news, the Grand Signior commanded that a solemn Festival should be celebrated for the space of 7 days and 7 nights...[but the festival had to be cancelled after three days when the Ottomans received word, to their humiliation, that the grand vizier had been routed].

For they being now got over the River, and the Christians drawn up in Battalia, a most furious fight began, which from nine a clock in the morning, until four in the afternoon continued with variable Fortune; at length the Turks assailed by the extraordinary valour of the Christians, which were now of equal numbers to them, began to give back and put themselves into a shameful flight, leaving dead upon the place about 5000 men, and the glory of the day to the Christians: the Turks *who always flye disorderly* knowing not the art of the handsome retreat, crowded in heaps to pass the River, the Horse trampling over the Foot, and the Foot throwing themselves headlong into the water, without consideration of the depth, or choice of places fordable after the great rains; those sinking, catching hold of others that could swim, sunk down and perished together; others both of men and horse through the rapidness of the stream were carried down the River and swallowed up in the deeper places: the water was dyed with blood and *the whole face of the River was covered with Men, Horse, Garments, all swimming promiscuously together; no difference was here between the valiant and the cowardly, the foolish and the wise, councel and chance, all being involved in the same violence and calamity.*

Perhaps Faulkner read Rycaut's account of the Ottoman disaster before he penned *As I Lay Dying*. This last passage in particular sounds much the same as Faulkner's description of the Bundren brothers' being flung into the raging current. For the Ottoman sultan, as for the Bundrens, the whole world, at least for some seemingly endless moments, was compressed into the confining space between the banks of one flooded river. Both confrontations with the river caused mutinies, but the outcomes of Rycaut's and Faulkner's stories were not the same. The Bundrens lost no rich spoils, although they lost much of what little they had, and there were no enemies shooting at them from the banks. For the Ottoman troops, there came peace, at least for a time, after this bloody defeat, and the soldiers got to go home. The Bundrens, too, returned home, but for them there was no peace.

Rycaut, who makes much of his Christian sympathies, notes how the whole Ottoman nation was shamed by this catastrophe: Muslims, who days before had boasted of victory, were now too ashamed to look Christians in the eye. The sources for Rycaut's account must have included eyewitness accounts from the Ottoman camp, intelligence reports from the capital, and circulating rumors. Although it has the trappings of literary convention, Rycaut's account also bears the marks of reality, the same very believable unbridled panic and helter-skelter tossing together of man and horse, coward and hero, that we find in images of real floods and that we associate with the realities (not the ideals) of war. The rhetoric of valor and cowardice and the sultan's taunting of his general also ring true. Over and over again, we see in these campaigns the men at the front pressed by the demands of the unenlightened capital, forced into decisions they might otherwise not make.[26]

Rycaut's account of this debacle also resonates with Faulkner's narrative when it recounts the after-effects of the river crossing:

> The minds of the Soldiery after this defeat were very much discomposed, tending more to sedition than to obedience, everyone took license to speak loudly and openly his opinion, that the War was commenced upon unjust and unlawful grounds; that the Comets lately seen to fall were prodigies foretelling the ill success of the War; that the total eclipse of the moon, which portends always misfortunes to the Turks, should have caused more caution in the Commanders of engaging the Army, until the malignancy of that influence had been overpassed; and calling to mind the solemn Oath with which the Sultan Suleyman confirmed his Capitulations with the Emperor, particularly vowing never to pass the Raab or places where the Turks received their defeat, without a solid or reasonable ground of War; all concluded that this Invasion was a violation of the Vow, and an injury to the sacred memory of that fortunate Sultan, and that all enterprises and attempts of this War would be fatal and destructive to the Muslims or Believers, and the end dishonorable to the Empire.

So the soldiers become mutinous after the catastrophe of the river crossing, and they call up signs to demonstrate the legitimacy of their rebelliousness. The commanders are blamed, and the "fortunate" sultan Süleyman is conjured up to illustrate the faults of the current leaders. A vow has been broken, and the heavens have shown their displeasure with the undertaking. Again, the story of Noah comes to mind. Why did the leaders not properly interpret and act upon these signs? Of course, there are always plenty of excuses not to fight, even without signs and portents. But the Ottoman soldiers, like the characters in Faulkner's novel, look to the heavens to find an explanation for that which is otherwise too terrible to explain.

---

26. This was clearly demonstrated in the following century when, in 1770, the grand vizier, fearful of "the scattering of the army and the anger of the padishah [sultan] at the possible defeat," crossed the Danube against his better judgment and exposed his army to defeat at Kartal and a disastrous recrossing under fire, during which a third of the army was drowned. In this episode, there was no bridge and only a few boats. See Aksan, *Ahmed Resmî Efendi*, pp. 150-53.

CONCLUSION

When they face the swollen river and its burden of deadly logs, each of the participants in Faulkner's novel responds in his or her own way. The younger brother and sister are sent to cross at the broken bridge, where the danger is less formidable. One is preoccupied with her own terrible secret; the other fantasizes to ward off the blow of his mother's death. The self-absorbed father, too, claiming age and infirmity, takes for himself this easier crossing. One brother, Cash, approaches the task in workmanlike fashion, trying to discover the best tactics for driving the wagon loaded with his mother's coffin across the river. A second brother, Darl, loses himself in the details, meditating on the river as a live and evil thing. The third brother, Jewel, flings himself into the river on his horse, daring the others to delay, and attempting to exorcise his own demons in the drama and danger of the undertaking. But the river seizes the wagon, spilling its contents, drowning the mules, and almost drowning Cash. As they drag themselves, wagon, and coffin from the flood, each character assesses the reasons for the failure. Anse, the father, blames his own personal misfortune. Jewel blames the lack of fortitude of his fellows, while Cash looks at logistics: the coffin was not set "square" in the wagon. But many of their neighbors blame the family patriarch for his foolhardy decisions; for his own cowardice, and for his placing his children, his mules, and his wife's remains at risk. They are like the Ottoman chroniclers who blame the military commanders (fathers) who are not proper "ford-makers" or who blame divine providence. As the family wends its weary way toward New Hope, observers look at the disaster of the river crossing as a sign: God is punishing Anse for his arrogance; the family is cursed; Addie Bundren was never meant to be buried at New Hope. Faulkner's grim family procession passes a sign reading "New Hope 3 miles," pointing to the road that has become impassable due to the flood. It looks, thinks Darl, "like a motionless hand lifted above the profound desolation of the ocean."[27]

In *As I Lay Dying*, the Bundren siblings, with one exception, all mutiny against the authority of their father, the hardness of their task, and the intolerable nature of their lives. While they are finally successful in crossing the river and bringing the nine-day-old and stinking carcass of their mother to New Hope for burial, they cannot escape their punishing existence; they are all victims forever trapped by fate in the swirling flood of their lives. Only the pragmatic and stoic Cash sees some small relief in the simple pleasure of a newly acquired phonograph. Only the selfish and cowardly father, Anse, he who declined the trial of the flood, gets what he wants by sacrificing each of his children in turn. In the Ottoman armies, the fathers also sacrifice their children to the river. Some men mutiny; some stoically follow orders; and others merely talk of rebellion, of the inadequacy of their leaders, and of the cruelty of fate. They seem to suffer the same fate as the Bundrens, and if they survive, they remain stuck in the floodwaters of war, deprivation, and the

---

27. Faulkner, *As I Lay Dying*, p. 108.

internecine squabbles of their commanders. Whether they believe in fate, divine providence, or their own survival skills we do not know. But they bear out the warning of an old Egyptian proverb: "Walk a mile rather than cross a canal."

POSTSCRIPT: COMPARISON WITH BABUR

The memoirs of the founder of the Mughal dynasty are famous for their apparently candid and direct commentary about the life and thoughts of a ruler. As Babur (ruled 1526-30) unfolds the details of his campaigns into India, he mentions at least twenty-four river crossings and many episodes of rebellious behavior. Interestingly enough, however, in all his crossings of rivers, the two coincide only once. Of the twenty-four crossing events, only seven take place during battle (only five recount Babur's own battles).

Babur's narrative suggests that his forces used many of the same crossing modes as the Ottomans: barges; boats; fords; dragging supplies over by ropes; and swimming horses, camels, and donkeys across. Sometimes parts of the army swim their horses over, and the rest search for a ford farther downstream or upstream. In many accounts, Babur states flatly that a river is crossed and comments no further. In others, he mentions the difficulties involved when rivers are swollen or when sudden rains come. In particular, he speaks of the difficulty of swimming armored horses and men across, noting how the warriors have to "strip down" their horses.[28] When Babur is leading larger forces, it may take more than a day to cross a river, often on narrow fords like those faced by the Bundrens in Faulkner's novel. On the one occasion when Babur has a bridge constructed (most of his accounts involve rafts and boats) to cross the Ganges near Chanderi, it takes a week to build; the troops then pass over the bridge, and the supply camels cross at a ford downstream.[29]

Unlike the Ottoman accounts, when Babur narrates difficult river crossings during engagements, it is usually to comment on the heroic feats of himself or others. Hence he tells us, in the eulogy for Sultan Husayn Mirza, that Sultan Husayn once swam his horse across the Gurgan River and defeated a band of Uzbeks.[30] He recounts with glee the story of his henchman, Qul Bayezid, who strips down his horse and swims it across the broad Indus all alone to put the enemy to flight. "What bravery," Babur writes, and he grants Qul Bayezid a promotion.[31] On another occasion when his troops are faced with crossing a flooded stream, Babur notes that he had to make his horse swim across the "rushing water," thus showing

---

28. Zahiruddin Muhammad Babur, *The Baburnama: Memoirs of Babur, Prince and Emperor*, trans. Wheeler M. Thackston (New York, 1996), pp. 126, 192, 278.
29. Ibid., pp. 194-95, 275, 278, 284, 400-01 (bridge).
30. Ibid., p. 206.
31. Ibid., p. 192.

himself to be a proper commander and inspiring his "scared" men.[32] When Babur does narrate a battle in which troops are pinned against a river and forced to cross under fire, the enemy Uzbeks are routed and drowned in the swollen Kishm River.[33] One instance in the monarch's account, however, suggests a more universal association of river crossings with danger. Babur has asked Khusrawshah when his younger brother will cross the Oxus and show himself at Babur's camp. Khusrawshah replies, "If he finds a crossing, he will come speedily, but when the water rises, the crossings change; as the saying goes, `The water carried off the crossing.'"[34]

In this memoir one episode echoes some of the hardship and mutinous feelings narrated in the Ottoman campaign accounts. It occurs after Babur has taken Agra (1525-26). Food and fodder are scarce, many of the men have sickened, and the beys, or commanders of the tribal cavalry, lose heart; they are unwilling to stay in Hindustan and begin to leave.[35] Babur says, "I expected that if I went into fire or water and emerged [a ford-maker] they would come in with me and emerge along with me and be at my side wherever I went--not that they would speak out in opposition to my purpose."[36] He calls a council and gives an inspirational speech (common enough in this type of narrative), and most of the beys decide to stay with him. Khwaja Khan, however, remains adamant and abandons the cause. Babur permits him to go (he cannot really stop him) and graciously awards him some territory. Then Khwaja Khan adds insult to injury by penning the following verse:

If I cross the Indus in safety, may my face turn black if I ever desire to see Hindustan again.[37]

The difference between Babur's narrative and those of the Ottoman chroniclers lies perhaps in the nature of Babur's battles, the size of his army, the differences of time and place, and the nature of Babur's rhetoric. He is speaking of himself and not of a commander whom he wants to criticize. In India Babur seldom found himself in the predicament that the Ottomans in Hungary frequently faced: that of retreating in haste and having to cross a river in the course of the retreat. The nature of Babur's military was also different: his forces were generally much smaller and organized on a less formal basis.

When Babur speaks of rebellion, he speaks of two kinds of mutiny. One is the mutiny of the conquered kings ("heel-snappers") who submit under duress and then refuse to cooperate once Babur's army has left the immediate vicinity. The second

---

32. Ibid., p. 278.
33. Ibid., pp. 229-30, in May/June 1506.
34. Ibid., p. 165.
35. Ibid., p. 354.
36. Ibid.
37. Ibid., p. 355.

type of mutiny that Babur recounts comes in the form of "going home" or "failing to show up." Babur's tribal cavalry forces are, in general, still treating him as a first among equals. As such, his ability to force his troops to remain in the field seems quite limited. On various occasions, Babur speaks grudgingly of this bey or that who has decided to remain at home or who has rebelled against him by refusing to participate. Not so for the Ottoman campaigns or the Ottoman narratives. The Ottoman soldiers were more highly organized and had fewer options; they could desert, but they could not simply go home. The Ottoman chroniclers of the sixteenth and seventeenth centuries, unlike Babur, were quite content to dwell on the details of defeat: mutinies, inadequate commanders, enemy victories. They are all part of the litany of how the Ottoman military has gone wrong.

Conversely, Babur, although he waxes poetic on gardens, food, and the loyalty that he feels he deserves but does not always get from his subordinates, tends to be rather matter-of-fact about hardships in the course of battle. When he crosses a river, often he simply says it was crossed. When his sister is captured in an enemy siege, he seems to mention it only as an afterthought. In fact, Babur's memoir in some ways is strangely reminiscent of more modern literature. It is eloquent on the author's feelings, woes, or pleasures and short on some of the specifics of war, although Babur is quite fond of the heroic vignette. Perhaps he took to heart the images of kingship in the Indian classics; by his own account, he was a leader who successfully forded rivers and whose troops, apparently, were never left to founder and be sucked under by the raging waters.

University of Tennessee

The Ottoman Balkans in the 18th and 19th centuries

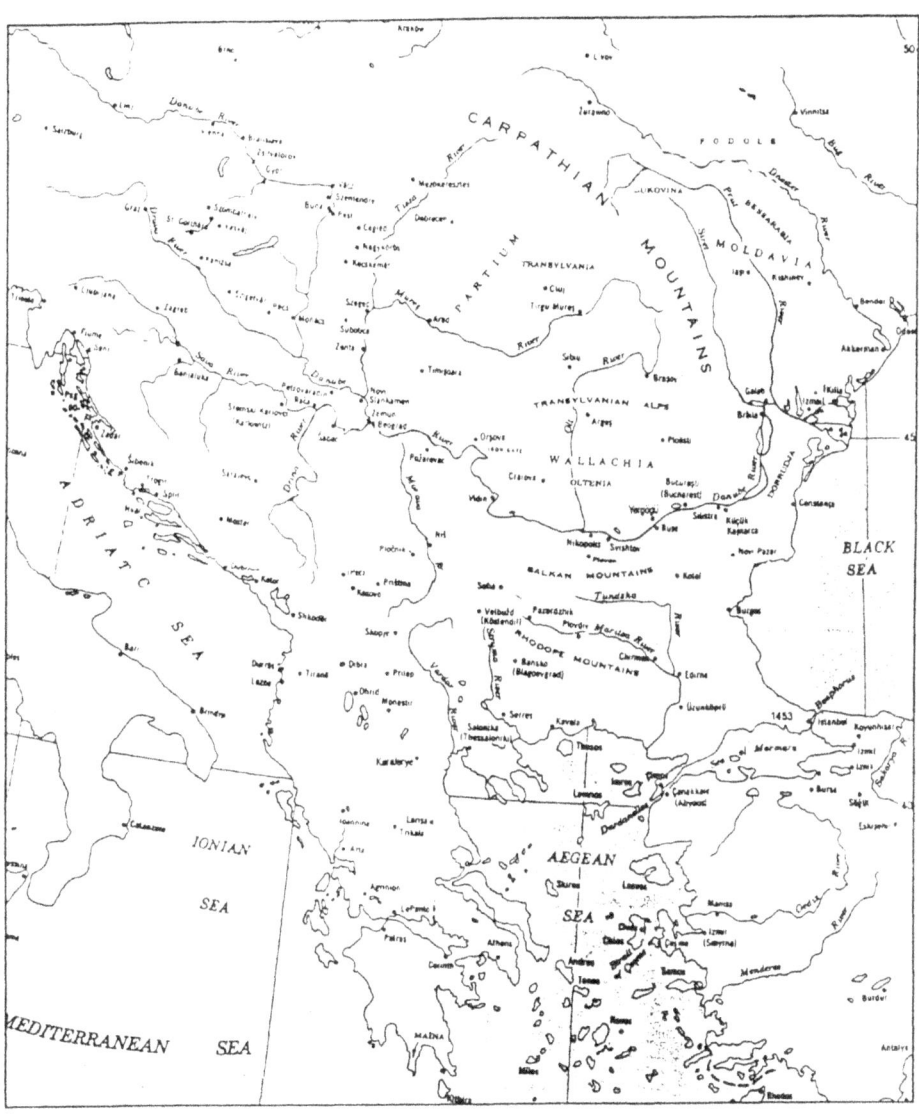

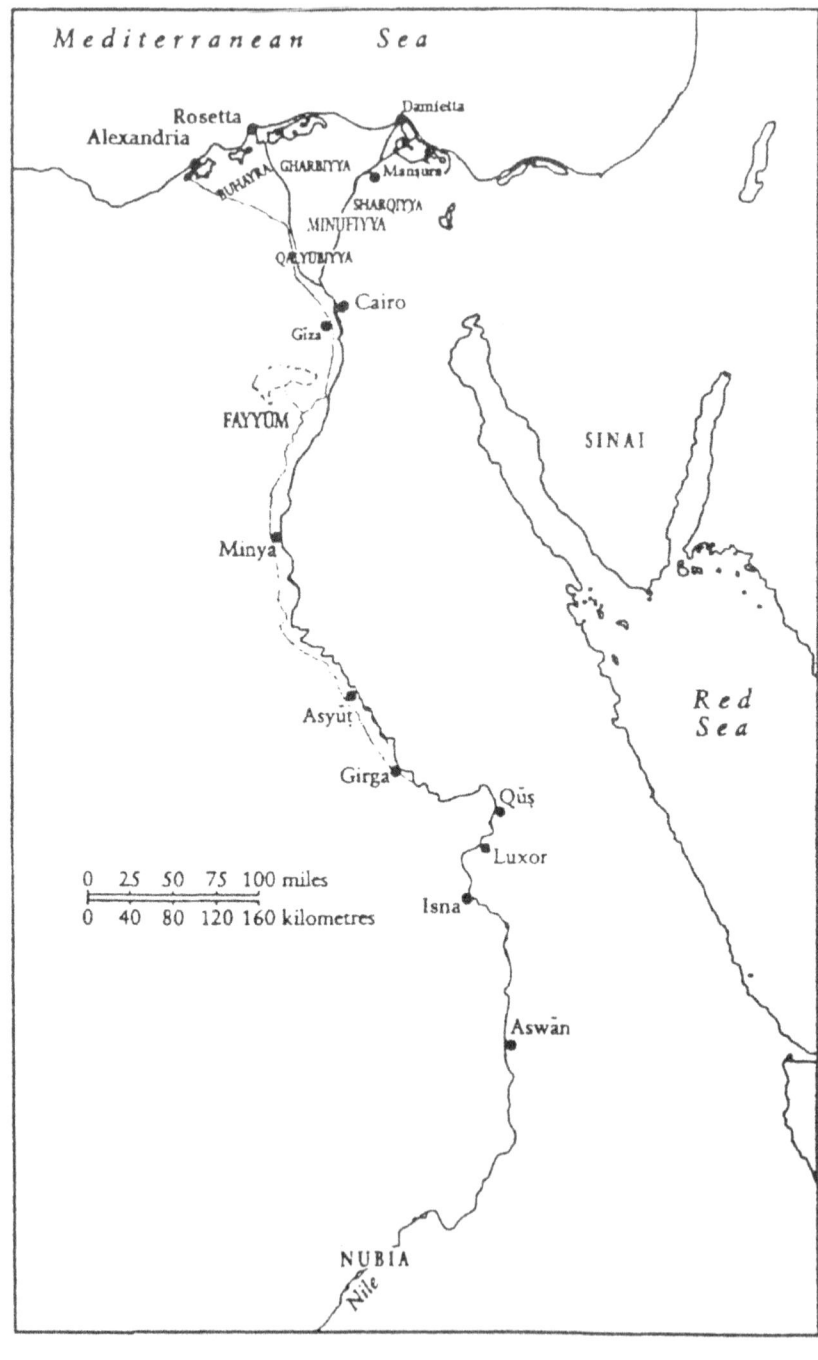

Egypt in the 19th century

Virginia H. Aksan

MANNING A BLACK SEA GARRISON IN THE EIGHTEENTH CENTURY: OCHAKOV AND CONCEPTS OF MUTINY AND REBELLION IN THE OTTOMAN CONTEXT

For most of the eighteenth century, Ochakov (Özü) was one of the largest of the Ottoman fortresses on the Belgrade-Azov defensive line along the Danube and the northern shore of the Black Sea. That line became the do-or-die border for the empire in the late eighteenth century, contested territory between the Ottomans and the Romanov emperors of Russia. Located on and dominating a thirty-mile-long estuary at the mouth of the Dnieper River, Ochakov was the key to control over the coast between it and the Dnieper, and the scene of some of the bloodiest confrontations between the Russians and the Ottomans in 1737 and again in 1788. Ochakov was surrendered finally to the Russian forces under Marshal Grigorii Potemkin and ceded to the Russians with the treaty of Jassy in 1792, when they gained the land between the Dnieper and Bug Rivers. Ochakov was permanently attached to Russia with the cession of Bessarabia in the Treaty of Bucharest, 1812.

In times of peace, the Janissary garrison at Ochakov probably numbered between 6,000 and 8,000 men.[1] During the famous sieges of the period, the garrison stood at more than 20,000 men--Janissaries and other auxiliary forces--reflecting its importance to the Ottoman line of defense. That partly explains why the Ottomans chose to prolong debilitating wars in the latter half of the eighteenth century and were obdurate in negotiations about Ochakov's possible surrender. In 1737 and again in 1771, in the course of peace conferences to attempt mediation and the end of hostilities between the Russians and the Ottomans, the status of Ochakov was one of the more contentious issues.

This paper proposes to consider why the ways in which the Ottomans manned the Ochakov fortress were, *ipso facto*, a recipe for insubordination, rebellion, and mutiny. It will focus on archival and chronicle evidence from the 1768-74 Ottoman-Russian war following a brief review of the more famous confrontations before and after. This discussion will lead to some concluding speculative arguments about the

---

1. Istanbul, Başbakanlık Osmanlı Arşivi (B.O.A.), Bab-ı Defter Baş Muhasebe Kalemi Defter Kataloğu (D.BŞM) 4274, p. 12, a listing of the Janissary salaries for various of the Ottoman fortresses, gives four years of figures for Ochakov: in 1773, there were 8,267 Janissaries; in 1774, 7,123; in 1775, 7,915; and in 1776, 7,875. The figures are only a gauge, as the Janissary rolls were notoriously inaccurate; and other kinds of local garrison forces are not represented.

relationship between late Ottoman recruitment practices and mutinies.

DEFINITION

Those of us who study the Ottoman Empire have not yet reached a consensus about what constitutes rebellion and/or mutiny in this non-western military context, although Palmira Brummett has recently moved us admirably in that direction.[2] Rebellion was endemic in the last two centuries of the empire's existence, but we still are asking what form revolts took, who joined them, and what they meant. Numerous Ottoman Turkish words--*isyan* (rebellion, riot, mutiny); *eşkıya/eşkıyalık* (bandits, banditry; also rebels/rebellion); *fitne/fitna* (rebellion, sedition, disorder)-- are used in the documents. It would be possible to argue some nuances about the legitimacy of rebellion, as in the case of *fitne*, which to many Muslims constituted the legitimate right to overthrow an unjust government, but the terms were for the most part interchangeable in the period under discussion. The central government considered an *isyan* the most serious form of revolt, requiring a forceful response. A "mutiny" presupposed discipline, an environment in which the men who stood up for their rights understood the consequences of their actions. In the eighteenth-century Ottoman context, discipline was swift but not always predictably applied. Mutinies often ended in negotiation or desertion, rather than discipline, because the locales allowed for flight.

"Mutiny" could be defined as an expression by confined soldiers of perceived legitimate grievances concerning late pay, unjust officers, or revoked privileges. Elsewhere, I have offered an example of that form of "mutiny" in an Ottoman garrison.[3] Here, I would like to broaden the typology of "mutiny" in a non-western setting to encompass four approaches. Regarding the definition of any particular mutiny by a military formation in a battlefield context as well as the subsequent evocation of that mutiny in narratives, those approaches would consider locale, or topography; impetus, or motive; explicit and implicit agendas; and short or long-term memory.

By locale and topography, I mean any confined, restricted, or isolated environment, a definition I would stretch to include mountains, seas, and/or steppes. Ochakov, for example, was surrounded by much unsettled as well as deserted territory and easier to approach by sea than by land. Supplying it was very difficult, maintaining a garrison a hazardous proposition. Disease, desertion and ill-trained, undisciplined soldiery were problems common to all armies who fought there.

---

2. Palmira Brummett, "Classifying Ottoman Mutiny: The Act and Vision of Rebellion," *Turkish Studies Association Bulletin* 22:1 (1998): 91-107. She concludes by calling for more studies of battlefront mutinies, as opposed to the Istanbul versions of the sixteenth and early seventeenth centuries that are her examples (pp. 106-07).
3. See my "Mutiny and the Eighteenth Century Ottoman Army," *Turkish Studies Association Bulletin* 22:1 (1998): 116-25.

The impetus for resisting military commands was most often desperation, coercion, or the basic urge to self-preservation, all pressure points *in extremis*. Explicit agendas might include hunger, missing pay, or regimental or fraternal "rights," such as the right of plunder or camaraderie. Implicit agendas might be the recognition and preservation of status or traditions, or the perception that societal contracts had been broken or that the make-up of ruling circles was based on class, ethnicity, or religion. In Ochakov, Cossacks, Tatars, Christians, and Muslims, but more specifically Albanians, Bosnians, Kurds, and others populated a military landscape commanded by the Ottoman Istanbul elite. The very nature of the strategies of conscription and utilization of non-Janissary recruits in this context incubated mutinous behavior.

The evocations of revolts in eyewitness reports and later chronicles impart an iconographic importance to resistance. In the imperial setting, such narratives may well have provided an oblique critique of Ottoman policies. As Brummett notes, "Mutiny was the yardstick by which the justice of the regime and the loyalty of its subjects were measured."[4]

THE SIEGE OF 1737

Before discussing the events of 1769, I would like to describe the two largest sieges of Ochakov in order to convey the scale and human cost of defending this fortress. The siege by General Münnich and his Russian troops began on 10 July 1737. "...Münnich and his army of 60,000 men, encumbered by an enormous baggage train, had taken over three months to reach Ochakov. By the time they got there the heat was appalling, and for over eight miles around there was not a stick of wood, a scrap of forage or a drop of water."[5] They found Ochakov well defended and well stocked, with over 20,000 men and sufficient artillery and supplies for a sustained siege. Turkish sources, however, claim that the Ottoman commander Yahya Paşa appealed to the grand vezirial camp on the Danube for men as well as supplies, having only 6,000 in the fortress. Grand Vezir Silahdar Mehmed Paşa ignored the appeal, but 4,000 troops were sent by Bender field commander (*serasker*) Muhsinzade Abdullah Paşa, who later became grand vezir in place of the incompetent Silahdar Mehmed.[6] In either case, the Ottomans were outnumbered by at least three to one.

The garrison repelled the first storm of the fortress by the Russian troops,

---

4. Brummett, "Classifying Ottoman Mutiny," p. 107.
5. Lavender Cassels, *The Struggle for the Ottoman Empire, 1717-1740* (London, 1966), p. 132.
6. Cevat Erbakan, *1736-1739 Osmanlı-Rus ve Avusturya Savaşları* (Istanbul, 1938), pp. 27-30. Muhsinzade Abdullah had a distinguished career as a soldier and statesman and was the father of Muhsinzade Mehmed Paşa, the most experienced of the generals of the 1768-74 War, grand vezir on the Danube from 1771-74.

although Yahya Paşa failed to follow up the advantage gained. The Russians were without their large artillery, had to cross a large trench around the fortress, and lacked proper equipment for scaling the walls. Nevertheless, on the second day of the siege a Russian mortar blew up the fortress powder magazine, killing an estimated 6,000 defenders. The fortress capitulated, and in the ensuing slaughter, in spite of the white flag, all but 3,000 of the garrison died. "[Within] twenty-four hours the stench of decaying corpses was such that the Russians had to withdraw fifteen miles from the fortress."[7] Russian casualties were estimated at 4,000, but disease and hunger took an additional toll, making the Russian losses more than equal to those of the Ottomans.[8]

In October, which is usually late in the campaign season, the Ottomans attempted to retake Ochakov, besieging it with an estimated 20,000 soldiers and an additional 20,000 Tatars.[9] Huge losses, torrential rains, and desertions on all sides forced the Ottomans to abandon the siege in early November.[10] By the time of the Belgrade treaty in 1739, however, the Russians had been forced to withdraw from Bessarabia and the Crimea because of the impossibility of maintaining healthy and well-supplied garrisons in the area. At Ochakov alone, some 60,000 Russians were lost before it was leveled and abandoned in 1738.[11]

THE SIEGE OF 1788

Ochakov remained the key to naval control of the northern Black Sea coast and the mouth of the Danube. In 1788, the Russian and Ottoman fleets played a larger role in the defense of the fortress than they had in 1737. Since Kilburun, the sister fortress across the estuary from Ochakov, had been surrendered to the Russians in 1774, the first Ottoman objective after declaring war in 1787 was its recapture. An assault by 6,000 Ottomans on that fortress, however, was repulsed by General Suvorov. His name has been forever linked with audacity and genius, in part, at

---

7. Cassels, *Struggle*, p. 132.
8. Edward S. Creasy, *History of the Ottoman Empire* (London, 1878), still a generally impartial, lively, and passionate account, pp. 365-68. Creasy and Cassels blame the Cossacks for the slaughter of the Ottoman side. General Münnich had a reputation for severity and brutality.
9. The numbers are probably overestimated: Karl A. Roider, *The Reluctant Ally: Austria's Policy in the Austro-Turkish War, 1737-1739* (Baton Rouge, LA, 1972), pp. 123-24.
10. Louis Feliz Keralio, *Histoire de la guerre des russes et des impériaux contre les Turcs en 1736, 1737, 1738 & 1739 & de la paix de Belgrade qui la termina* (Paris, 1780), I: 144-52.
11. Cassels, *Struggle*, p. 152. At the Belgrade siege the same year, an estimated eighty to one hundred Austrian troops died each day of plague, malaria, and dysentery (p. 153).
Excavations are underway at Ochakov although the modern town is built upon the site, making it difficult to proceed. Caroline Finkel and Victor Ostapchuk are members of the group studying the Ottoman fortress rebuilt after 1739, using both on-site and archival evidence to do so (personal communications with both).

least, because of his defense of Kilburun and the taking of Ismail on the Danube in 1790, but he was wounded before the final assault on Ochakov.[12]

Between the middle of June and December, when the fortress surrendered, Potemkin cautiously moved 50,000 troops to surround the fortress from the land. The Ottoman garrison was estimated at 20,000. The Russians invested the fortress by August, but the Ottomans were able to continue to supply it by sea, running a Russian blockade with 1,500 troops as late as the middle of October. Potemkin ordered the final assault on 16 December, after a month of heavy shelling from the fleet in the harbor:

> Valour, maddened to ferocity, was shown on both sides.... The Turks of Oczakof, had before the siege, surprised a Russian village in the vicinity, and mercilessly slaughtered all the inhabitants. Potemkin and Suwarrow caused the Russian regiments that were there to assault the town, to be first led through this village as it lay in ashes, and with its streets still red with the blood of their fellow countrymen....[The] Russians advanced on the 16th of December.... Whole ranks were swept away by the fire of the besieged; but the supporting columns still came forward unflinchingly through musketry and grape; 4,000 Russians fell; but the survivors bore down all resistance, and forced their way into the city, where for three days they reveled in murder and pillage. No mercy was shown to age or sex; and out of a population of 40,000 human beings, only a few hundreds (chiefly women and children) escaped....[13]

The war of 1768-74 on the same terrain had been tame by comparison. Largely because the operations of the main Russian army were concentrated in Moldavia and along the Danube, Ochakov was not similarly besieged except for one occasion in August of 1771, when the Turkish garrison repulsed the attempt to capture the fortress. Evidence of the ways the Ottomans saw to manning the fortress during this war, however, are instructive.

In August 1769, Ochakov commander Canikli Süleyman Paşa reported a mutiny among the *yamak*s (Janissary recruits) under his jurisdiction. An enemy raiding party, made up of Cossacks, had crossed into Ottoman territory, where they were joined by many of Süleyman Paşa's own garrison, who revolted, plundered and burned a number of the nearby Ottoman fortresses, and killed many of the local residents before crossing back over the Bug River into enemy territory. Süleyman himself had gone after the mutineers, then deserters, with loyal troops, following them for some distance, but he was forced to return to Ochakov for fear of an attack on the fortress by the enemy. He requested reinforcements led by an experienced

---

12. Creasy, *History of the Ottoman Empire*, p. 428.
13. Ibid., p. 432, says 16 December; Isabel de Madariaga, *Russia in the Age of Catherine the Great* (London, 1981), pp. 404-05, has the date as 17 December.

commander, arguing that the 5,000 soldiers remaining were insufficient to defend the fortress. His request was seconded by both the *kadı* (judge) of the fortress and his fellow officers. In the end, he was sent an additional 5,000 troops, some of them Janissaries but more than half of them *levend*s (state-funded militias) under the command of Karasu *mutasarrıfı* Abdullah Paşa and *Binbaşı* Osman Ağa, a *levend bölükbaşı* (present-day equivalents might be major and captain, respectively).[14]

One of the most interesting aspects of the account by Sadullah Enverî, summarized above, is the paragraph just before it, which argues that Muslim soldiers were accustomed to raids (*çete tarikiyle*) into infidel territory as part of their official duties.[15] The implicit message is that they had been prevented from undertaking such raids, forcing a mutiny and flight of large numbers, irresistibly drawn to natural inclinations that were traditionally sanctioned as an honorable aspect of their service.

There are two categories of soldiers mentioned in the account: *yamak* and *levend*. Mobilization in 1768-69 involved a combination of systems. Included were the salaried corps--the Janissaries and their recruits, the *yamaks*--and the state-funded militias--the *levend*s, who signed on for a limited period, usually six months, and were paid in cash, either at the place of mobilization or upon arrival at the battlefront. Because the commanders and suppliers of those militias were drawn from the countryside power-brokers, by the late eighteenth century tax farmers or tax collectors had become the vital link to successful campaigning for the Ottomans. John Lynn has called this style of recruitment "aggragrate contracting," a mixture of a core permanent force and soldier bands who could be quickly organized and just as quickly disbanded.[16]

The Janissary corps, which had not been on campaign for more than twenty-five years, had to be completely rebuilt in 1768. The Istanbul contingent probably numbered no more than 20,000; most of the recruitment to increase the size of the corps occurred on the road in the spring of 1769. A record of the Ochakov Janissary garrison from that period conveys the problem: of the 8,216 listed in the register, 3,227 were listed as "new" *yamaks*, an additional 989 as "old" *yamaks*, probably meaning present at the last roll call, in total some 4,216 untrained troops.[17] Without

---

14. Sadullah Enverî, *Tarih*, Istanbul University Library, MS T. 5994 (1780), fols. 48b-49. One documentary account corroborates these events, an official appeal to the Bender field commander, Dağıstanlı Ali Paşa, to send more troops to Özü, as the garrison had already engaged 10,000 of the enemy (B.O.A. Mühimme Defteri 168, p. 1). The events sound very much like the situation in 1737.
15. Enverî, *Tarih*, fol. 48b.
16. John A. Lynn, "The Evolution of Army Style in the Modern West, 800-2000," *International History Review* 18 (1996): 514.
17. B.O.A., Cevdet Askeriye (CA) 30706, dated 1771 but referring to the previous two years. "Old" may well refer to age. Rumiantsev, victorious field marshal of the Russian army, commented after the renowned victory at Kagul (Kartal) in the summer of 1770, "... the ancient janissaries and sipahis, who seemed so by their appearance and age,...perished here completely." P.A. Rumiantsev, *Sbornik documentov* (*Collected Documents*) (Moscow, 1953), I: 345, translation by Maryna Kravets.

a doubt, the newly enrolled caused most of the trouble at the beginning of the war. The number of registered Janissaries at Ochakov rarely topped 8,000 throughout the war.[18]

Each year of the campaign, the army had to be rebuilt. Meanwhile, the grand vezir stayed on the frontier, generally at his headquarters in Babadağı, south of the Danube in present-day Romania. In January 1771, a fleet of ten ships left Istanbul with men and supplies, for the specific task of refortifying Ochakov. Four of the ships carried an estimated 600 Janissary *serdengeçti*s, in this war a term synonymous with *yamak*. When the ships stopped at ports *en route* to gather more supplies (Varna and Köstence, for example), many of the new recruits fled, forcing guards to round them up and put them back on the ships bound for Ochakov.[19] One can only speculate how many actually arrived there.

The other main source of cannon fodder for the Danube in 1768 was the *levend* system. Men from all over the empire, both infantry and cavalry, were organized into detachments of fifty or one hundred men each (*bayrak*), commanded by the chief officer of the *sancak*, called the *mutasarrıf*. This system of recruitment, pay, and provisioning was completely cash based. Generally, the provincial *mutasarrıf* took responsibility for feeding his men; the money for (substantial) sign-on bonuses and six months' pay came from the sultan's purse or, on account, from the pocket of the commander himself, who was required to report to the front with his own entourage of over 200 troops, plus 1,000 to 2,000 *levend*s. A special tax, the *imdad-i seferiye*, was assigned to the commander appointed to bring the troops to the front.[20]

Two records of substantial numbers of *levend*-style troops called up specifically to guard Ochakov have been found. The first, dated September 1768, represents a call to arms for a winter contingent of 10,000 troops to guard the fortress and, presumably, to be present for the campaign that would get underway the following May. Each of the ten *mutasarrıf*s was exhorted to arrive with 200 of his household guard, as well as 500; 1,000; or 2,000 infantrymen (*piyade*), to make a total of 12,200 men.[21] The most interesting aspect of this particular record is the

---

18. One register lists 7,311 Janissaries at Ochakov in 1770-71 (B.O.A., Maliyeden Müdevver (MM) 17405, p. 108); the same register records 9,709 Janissaries in 1771-72 (MM 17405, p. 121); for later years, see above, n. 1. There seems to be little difference between war and peacetime mobilization, suggesting fictional registers. I have discussed the problem of fictional Janissary rolls elsewhere: "Whatever Happened to the Janissaries?" *War in History* 5 (1998): 23-36.
19. *Serdengeçti*s were soldiers who volunteered for difficult, sometimes suicidal, duty and were given bonuses accordingly. The eighteenth-century versions were generally new recruits, which is why I equate the term with *yamak*. Enverî, *Tarih*, fols. 180b-181. Both Enverî and another contemporary source say 10,700 men were to be sent from Istanbul and Anatolia; see Şemdanizade, *Şemdanizade Fındıklılı Süleyman Efendi Tarihi Müri't-Tevârih*, ed. M. Münir Aktepe (Istanbul, 1980), IIB: 61. Şemdanizade puts the number of ships carrying the 600 men from Istanbul at 6 *firkate*.
20. Described in Aksan, "Whatever Happened to the Janissaries?"
21. B.O.A., CA 16288; also Mustafa Cezar, *Osmanlı Tarihinde Levendler* (Istanbul, 1965),

geographic source of the recruits: Albania, Macedonia, Bosnia, and northern Greece (among the *sancaks* listed: Prizren, Üsküp, Delvine, Avlonya, Elbasan). The second record is from June 1773, listing a total of 12,500 troops largely from the same area, whose commanders are being compensated for passage to the Danube in order to guard the frontier fortresses.[22] Getting men to the frontier was no easier for the provincial commanders than for their Janissary equivalents. In 1775, the *mutasarrıf* of Köstendil, Mehmed Paşa, was requested to return the balance of the advance he had been given, for while waiting for transportation to Ochakov from the port of Burgos on the Black Sea, 600 of the 1,000 infantrymen he was supposed to mobilize had fled.[23]

Mobilizing a largely untutored and undisciplined force, especially after a hiatus of a quarter of a century, obviously contributed to the massive failures of the 1768-74 war. Mutinies, such as those of Süleyman Paşa's garrison at Ochakov, were more commonplace than exceptional. *Yamak*s were probably drawn from the same sources of manpower as *levend*s even though their records were separately maintained. This army, once mobilized, dissolved rapidly when soldiers deserted and formed autonomous bands and raiding parties. Severe discipline and the exercise of command were serendipitous on the battlefront. Frequent cash rewards for valor, a significant incentive, were very often more than double the six-month salaries of the *levend* recruits.[24]

Even with an army unsuitable for the defense of a garrison line, there were heroic stands and able commanders. No sustained siege occurred at Ochakov in the 1768-74 war, but the garrison did repulse Russian attackers in the summer of 1771, one of the very few occasions when Ottoman arms were successful in this particular war. The soldiers were supported by the Ottoman fleet in the harbor as in 1788,[25] a contemporary recounted.

> The Russians surrounded the fortress from one sea to the other. A number of courageous ones (*dilaver*) left the fortress and engaged the enemy for five hours. As the Russians fled, they were fired upon from both the fortress and the fleet in the harbor, and many of the infidels were destroyed....Three days later they came back, but as before many were disgraced. When the news of this bravery was learned, 3,000 *altın* was sent by the grand vezir, 350 *kise* by the *devlet* (sultan).[26]

---

pp. 438-39.
22. B.O.A., CA 12906. This followed a two-year truce; war was resumed early in 1773.
23. Ibid., CA 9247. These are samples of hundreds of documents that make difficult and confusing reading.
24. The miserly monthly salary for *levend* recruits remained 2.5 *kuruş* for over a century. Refer to Aksan, "Whatever Happened to the Janissaries?"
25. Enverî, *Tarih*, fol. 219.
26. Şemdanizade, *Şemdanizade Tarihi*, IIB: 74.

Although Bender had fallen in 1770 after a lengthy siege, the Russians made no further advance after the unsuccessful attempt on Ochakov. They had instead invested most of the Danubian fortresses by the end of 1770. The Ottomans, however, would not admit defeat until the spring of 1774, when Russian field marshal Rumiantsev surrounded the Ottomans at Şumla (Shumla), deep in Ottoman territory south of the Danube. Grand Vezir Muhsinzade Mehmed reputedly had fewer than 10,000 troops with him by that time.[27] Under the terms of the treaty of Küçük Kaynarca, the Russians acquired Kilburun, considerably facilitating their final capture of Ochakov in 1788, as described above.

The fourth approach to the definition and subsequent evocation of mutiny concerns memory, both long and short-term. Şemdanizade framed his story of the defense of Ochakov in 1771 with an interview of Abaza Mehmed Paşa, the renowned field commander, that Şemdanizade had conducted just prior to Abaza Mehmed's execution for insubordination the same year. Ordered to go to the defense of the Crimea by sea, Abaza had refused to land and sailed to Sinop on the northern Anatolian coast instead. Explained the now-disgraced soldier: "I had no money. I requested twenty *kise* from the grand vezir. 'Lend me the money, [I said], so that I can procure soldiers, in the customary fashion of a commander.' He didn't give it to me. So I came [here], thinking that if I were to disembark [there], I would be enslaved and scorned by the army, damaging the imperial honor." Şemdanizade chided proponents of Abaza Mehmed's speedy demise for executing such an honorable man, whose martyrdom was celebrated in infidel church services.[28]

A critique of the government was implicit in the narrator's championing of a loyal Ottoman mountain man. (Abaza referred to a soldier of Abkhazian origin, a distinguished/notorious line of able servants turned state rebels throughout the centuries.) The interview with Abaza Mehmed is followed by the Ochakov account and several others of the bravery of individual soldiers in the face of the infidel onslaught. Demonization of the Abkhazian (and/or Albanian and other mountainman) soldiers' excesses in official documents contradicted both the realities of the battlefront and the persistence of the *topos* as a popular model of bravery.[29] The occasional clear-eyed commentator, in this case a judge, revealed the essential dilemma in the recruiting system that prevailed by the end of the 1768-74 war. Mobilization strategies and incentives brought the Ottomans only temporary raiding parties, of dubious loyalty and quick to flight.

---

27. See my *An Ottoman Statesman in War and Peace: Ahmed Resmî Efendi (1700-1783)* (Leiden, 1995) for a fuller description of the war; Creasy, *History of the Ottoman Empire*, pp. 403-10.
28. Şemdanizade, *Şemdanizade Tarihi*, IIB: 73-74.
29. See my "Mutiny and the Eighteenth Century Ottoman Army" for a further example.

CONCLUSION

Late Ottoman military recruitment was a combination of voluntary and coercive systems, some permanent and some contractual. Its mobilization systems thus resemble those utilized by other early modern empires. So, too, do the persisting ethos of the individual warrior and the admiration for the man with the horse and cold steel. There are, however, a number of unique aspects to the Ottoman context.

Integral to the Ottoman pursuit of war was the maintenance of a wide band of frontier-style borders, defended by clientage relationships, which included the Danubian Principalities and the Crimea. The eighteenth-century evolution from a hegemonic to a territorial empire meant the delineation of fixed borders and the move to a garrison defense line along the Danube. This, in turn, required a different style of warfare, with more disciplined and continuous garrisons. In a territory of scarce men and supplies, troops had to be brought in from greater and greater distances, in two senses of the word. Geographically, Kurds and Abkhazians were sent to the Danubian shores, while Albanians were sent to the Caucasus. Culturally, newly recruited mountain men were introduced to high Ottoman palace-style elitism. The net result was increased nomadization and loss of control on the peripheries of Ottoman territory, as well as continuous tension between the grand vezirial command (and household politics) and undisciplined provincial prowess on the battlefield.

McMaster University

Antonis Anastasopoulos

LIGHTING THE FLAME OF DISORDER: *AYAN* INFIGHTING AND STATE INTERVENTION IN OTTOMAN KARAFERYE, 1758-59[*]

The aim of this paper is to discuss the state intervention during 1758-59 to restore order in the town of Karaferye (Veroia in Greek), center of a *kaza* in the *sancak* of Salonika. That discussion, in turn, illuminates the role of the *ayan* in the Ottoman provinces and shows that the actions of even minor *ayan*s could upset not only local life but also the state authorities. Eventually an analysis of comparable cases from other areas could establish a pattern, demonstrating both how the state dealt with disruptions of order in the provinces and how its efficacy can be evaluated.

Our information about the incident in Karaferye comes primarily from one of the *sicil* volumes of the town's Islamic court, in which were registered incoming orders and locally issued documents. Reports of the Venetian consul in Salonika provide supplementary accounts, although the *sicil*s of that city contain no information about the affair despite the significant involvement of the *sancak* authorities.[1] In this case, the *kadı* of Salonika must not have been among the addressees of state documents because Karaferye lay beyond his immediate jurisdiction. The sources that set the limits of our knowledge about the incident cover the period from November 1758 to June 1759, with a gap between mid-February and late March 1759. Neither the state documents nor the consular reports supply a detailed account of the events but focus on the state's reaction to the problem.

The Venetian consul noted in a report dated 27 October 1758, that a civil war between two ağas of Veroia had been raging for several weeks.[2] State documents also refer to a conflict (*kavga, cidal, mücadele, muhasama*) among the *ayan* of

---

[*] A different version of this paper forms part of the author's Ph.D. dissertation, "Imperial Institutions and Local Communities: Ottoman Karaferye, 1758-1774." Research was made possible through grants from the A.G. Leventis Foundation, the A.S. Onassis Foundation, the British Academy, Peterhouse, the Skilliter Centre for Ottoman Studies, the Martin Hinds Travel Fund, and the Worts Travelling Scholars Fund.
1. There is only a passing remark about the need to appoint a *mütesellim* (deputy governor) because the new paşa of Salonika was still in Karaferye: Selanik Sicilleri, vol. 94, pp. 78-79 (10 June 1759). The year of all *sicil* entries and documents cited is 1759 unless otherwise stated.
2. K. Mertzios, "Sympleroma eis ta `Mnemeia Makedonikes Historias,'" *Eis Mnemen K.I. Amantou* (Athens, 1960), p. 59. The consul also mentions similar conflicts in Yenice-i Vardar (Yannitsa) among Janissaries and in Siroz (Serres).

Karaferye and identify the two most important figures in this clash as Kara Ahmed and "his enemy" (*aduv*) Molla Mustafa. Even though the formulaic expressions used in the sources do not allow for a detailed analysis of the impact of the conflict on the town and the surrounding area, it becomes obvious that everyday life was gravely disturbed (*katl-i nüfus ve gasb-i emval ve ihtilal-i nizam*).³ The people of the *kaza* submitted petitions to the state, and the authorities intervened to defend their suffering subjects (*fukara-yi ahali ve reayaya türlü türlü cevr ü eziyet ve isal ü hasaret eylediklerine binaen*) and restore order (*tahsil-i nizam*).⁴ The *ayan* leaders, who were promptly denounced as tyrants, rebels, and brigands (*mütegallib eden[ler]*, *eşkıya*, *şekavetpişe[ler]*), found themselves the subjects of government orders to be discussed below.⁵ It must be said, however, that they apparently had never intended to attract the attention of the state, let alone to rebel against it. Instead, the factional leaders had wished to carry out their operations "discreetly" and legally, and not to be outlawed.

Essentially, the problem appears to have been administrative and fiscal abuses in the context of a struggle for local power.⁶ One office around which the problem revolved was the *voyvodalık*, an indication of its increased importance in local life in the eighteenth century. The voyvoda of Karaferye was the tax farmer of the *mukataa* of the region, as well as the *de facto* governor. Karaferye was an imperial *hass*, or private holding, that was farmed out as *malikâne*, a life-tenure hereditary tax farm. The *malikâne*-holder subsequently sublet the *mukataa* on a yearly basis to a holder called voyvoda. The voyvoda, therefore, was not a government agent; he

---

3. The terms *fitne* and *fesad*, meaning "sedition" and "disorder," are also used to describe the situation.
4. The same sequence of actions may be observed in numerous other cases. A petition against Kara Ahmed is discussed a little later, while Başbakanlık Osmanlı Arşivi (B.O.A.), Rumeli Ahkam Defterleri (hereafter RAD) defter 14/no. 861 and RAD 14/869, also discussed later, refer to the dismissal of Molla Mustafa following complaints of the Karaferye population. For the important place of justice and the protection of the empire's subjects from oppressive officials in state ideology, see Cornell Fleischer, "Royal Authority, Dynastic Cyclism, and 'Ibn Khaldunism' in Sixteenth-Century Ottoman Letters," *Journal of Asian and African Studies* 18 (1983): 198-220, esp. 201-202; Halil İnalcık, "Adâletnâmeler," *Belgeler* 2 (1965): 49; Norman Itzkowitz, "Men and Ideas in the Eighteenth-Century Ottoman Empire," in Thomas Naff and Roger Owen, eds., *Studies in Eighteenth-Century Islamic History* (Edwardsville and Carbondale, IL, 1977), p. 25. See also Bistra Cvetkova, "Recherches sur le système d'affermage (*iltizam*) dans l'Empire Ottoman au cours du XVIe-XVIIIe s. par rapport aux contrées Bulgares," *Rocznik Orientalistyczny* 27 (1964): 130-31, for the dismissal of a *muhtesib* in Siroz in 1728 after complaints of the local people against him. Koca Mehmed Ragıb Paşa, grand vezir at the time of the incident, was particularly harsh toward oppressive officials and *ayan*.
5. Terms and excerpts come from Karaferye Sicilleri (hereafter KS) defter 81/microfilm exposure 3/page 368/entry 2, KS 81/16/2 (1758), KS 81/20/230/3.
6. One accusation against several individuals, including Molla Mustafa and his accomplices Ramiz Efendi and Arnavud Hasan Ağa, as well as against Kara Ahmed's brother, Elhac Mehmed Ağa, was the illegal transformation of *vakıf* villages of the *kaza* of Karaferye into *çiftlik*s: RAD 14/939, RAD 15/1164 (1760).

was an individual who held administrative power through his involvement in the tax-farming system. The fact that he was included among the addressees of state decrees suggests that the state acknowledged his contribution to provincial administration. So, too, does the urgency with which replacement voyvodas were appointed after the dismissal of the proper ones in the case under examination. The affairs of the *kaza*, in particular those involving collections in money or kind for the state, apparently could not wait.[7]

The first of the two principal figures, Kara Ahmed, was the subject of the state documents issued between November 1758 and February 1759, but from April onwards Molla Mustafa became the target. While there are two separate sets of decrees and the two "rebels" were dealt with independently, they were related to each other, and their unlawful actions formed part of the same incident, as did those of other persons. Among the others was Ahmed's brother Mustafa, who is cited as his collaborator. Another brother, Elhac Mehmed Ağa, appears not to have been involved in this particular case, despite cooperating with Ahmed in several other ventures over a number of years. Molla Mustafa's most prominent associate was Ramiz Mehmed Efendi, a former professor in the imperial *medreses* of Edirne and an important landholder of Karaferye. All five were counted among the regional *ayan*. Kara Ahmed's name, in particular, appears quite often in the Karaferye *sicils* of the third quarter of the eighteenth century. Molla Mustafa was from Sarıgöl (Ptolemais) but was obviously interested in developments in and the resources of a richer district.

The state authorities moved in two directions to restore order. One was to punish those involved in the power struggle and the oppression of the local population; the other was to render the local administration operational again. The state ordered that Kara Ahmed and Molla Mustafa be sent to the fortress of Kavala in eastern Macedonia, while Ramiz would be detained in Mağusa (Famagusta), Cyprus. Ahmed's brother Mustafa had already fled to Alasonya (Elassona) when the first available order was issued, and the authorities appear not to have given any concrete instructions about him. Other minor figures were also to be banished. The implementation of the penalties was initially entrusted to Mehmed Paşa, governor of Salonika, who sent a special agent to Karaferye. Later, responsibility was transferred to his counterpart in Köstendil, Abdi. After both failed to apprehend any of the "rebels," the state compromised by keeping the fugitives outside the *kaza* borders, or at least in hiding. Responsibility thus was transferred once again, this time from the state agents to the local community, which was forced to undertake collective responsibility for preventing those involved in the affair from ever re-entering the *kaza*, or pay a heavy fine. The second task, the restoration of administrative order, was connected primarily with the appointment of a voyvoda.

---

7. For more information about the voyvoda of Karaferye, see Antonis Anastasopoulos, "Imperial Institutions and Local Communities: Ottoman Karaferye, 1758-1774," unpublished Ph.D. dissertation, Cambridge University, 1999, pp. 38-43. See also Halil İnalcık, "Centralization and Decentralization in Ottoman Administration," in Naff and Owen, eds., *Studies in Eighteenth-Century Islamic History*, pp. 35-36.

As indicated, in the first phase of the affair the state dealt with Kara Ahmed. According to a *ferman* issued in early November 1758, Kara Ahmed and his men had already fled in "cowardly" fashion to Karaferye, while his brother Mustafa had sought refuge with the voyvoda of Alasonya. It was pointed out that the punishment of Ahmed, who here is called *şaki*, was an imperative religious duty and that he should be arrested and sent to Kavala. The state, however, took only one practical measure toward his arrest. It ordered the people of Karaferye to submit a document ratified by the *kadı*, according to which they would be collectively fined if they permitted Ahmed to return to the *kaza* without arresting him and turning him over to the paşa of Salonika. The *ayan* and officers of Karaferye specifically were warned that not only would they be made to pay the fine, but they would also suffer other unspecified penalties should they fail to arrest Kara Ahmed upon his return. As for Ahmed's rival, Molla Mustafa, he remained as acting voyvoda, for someone needed to take care of the affairs of the *kaza*, and Mustafa had held the same post previously, as well. Nevertheless, he was to dismiss all except "five or six" of his Albanian troops.[8]

Unfortunately, the sources do not reveal who held the *voyvodalık* before Molla Mustafa took over as acting voyvoda. Kara Ahmed is cited only as an oppressive *ayan* "whose ambitions lit the flame of disorder and strife" (*ayanlık iddiasıyla...cevr ve eziyet, ikad-i naire-i fitne ve şıkak eden*), not as a dismissed voyvoda, yet he may well have been one. In fact, we know that Ahmed had held the *voyvodalık* at a certain point and, along with his brother Elhac Mehmed, had held as well the *mukataa* of the *cizye* (the poll tax on *zimmi*s, or non-Muslims). This information comes from an *arzuhal*, or petition, of the people of Karaferye (*ahali ve reaya fukarası*) that bears no date but, from internal textual indications, may be dated November 1758. In the petition, the people complained that the two brothers had collected illegal amounts of money with the endorsement of the "corrupt" (*mürtekib*) *kadı* of Karaferye. Their abuses included collecting almost three times the usual amount of local taxation, imposing illegal fees, and collecting the *cizye* at a single rate instead of at three graded rates. As a consequence, the population was fleeing the *kaza*. The people alleged that two earlier *arzuhal*s had brought no result, apparently because the two brothers had connections with figures in Istanbul, such as Derviş Efendi, an official formerly in charge of the sipahi corps payroll (*sabıka sipah kâtibi*) and in-law of a former grand vezir.[9] The Porte ordered in its reply to the *arzuhal* that the two brothers be arrested and tried, but we do not have any information as to the actual outcome of the petition.

Because the petition is undated, it is not possible to say that it was directly connected with the events of 1758-59. The fact that the *ferman* of November 1758

---

8. KS 81/16/2 (1758). Mustafa undersigned a document dated 23 February 1759 as "voyvoda" (KS 81/21/232/3). This is an indication that he had managed to become voyvoda of Karaferye by that date. What is strange from a palaeographic point of view is that it seems as if one *mim* is used for both "Molla" and "Mustafa."

9. B.O.A., Cevdet Tasnifi-Adliye 629. Derviş is accused of having been bribed by the two brothers in order to secure the Karaferye tax farms for them.

does not refer to Elhac Mehmed indicates that it is not. We may well assume, though, that Ahmed had somehow managed either to cling to or to regain the *voyvodalık* and that by late 1758 similar complaints had been submitted against him once more. When he was dismissed and outlawed, a replacement was found in Mustafa, whose enmity with Ahmed and Mehmed was of long standing. As early as 1755-56, Molla Mustafa, while still an *ayan* of Sarıgöl, had denounced the two brothers as patrons of the brigands who had attacked several itinerant merchants, and he had demanded their punishment in accordance with the *şeriat*.[10]

In any case, on 7 January 1759, a *hüccet* was issued in response to the *ferman* of November 1758.[11] This is the first of three similar documents entered in the Karaferye *sicil*. Ninety-three persons, representing twenty-three *mahalle*s of Karaferye, undertook on behalf of the whole town the obligation to pay 10,000 *kuruş* to the *beytülmal* (public treasury) if they tolerated the return of Ahmed to Karaferye. There were four representatives from each *mahalle* and only five from the Muslim *mahalle* of Kemal Bey. In all, the Muslim representatives included sixteen ağas, thirteen *ulema* (including five *imam*s), seven *bes*es (a generic term for "elder"), two *berber*s (one was also a çelebi), two çelebis, two scribes (*yazıcı*), three sipahis, and one person who held no title but was a "-*zade*" *seyyid*. The Christians bore no titles at all, so it is very difficult to say anything about them, except that there were only three priests. The *hüccet* was signed by six *şühudul-hal*, or "professional witnesses," who were efendis, ağas, and çelebis.[12] None of them appeared in the next *hüccet* either as a *mahalle* representative or as a witness, and it is not clear why they were set apart from the rest of the community.[13]

In the *hüccet*, whose phrasing followed the *ferman* word for word, Muslims and Christians were listed in separate *mahalles*. We cannot tell whether the separation reflected real circumstance or was made solely for administrative purposes, but it suggests segregation on religious lines. It should be added that not only is the number of *mahalle* representatives different in the other two *hüccet*s; the number of listed *mahalles* also differs. For instance, the next *hüccet*, drawn up five months later, included twenty-eight *mahalles* instead of twenty-three. The discrepancy may be simply a scribal error, or it may reflect our inability to understand the principles according to which these documents were composed.

Ramiz Mehmed Efendi's turn came some time after that of Ahmed and his brother. He was on Molla Mustafa's side although his exact role in the case is not explained. He was, however, the only one dealt with by the authorities of the *eyalet* of Rumeli, according to a *buyruldu* of 1 February 1759. Unless there are gaps in the sources, the special treatment reserved for Ramiz may be attributed to his important

---

10. I. Vasdravelles, *Historika Archeia Makedonias, B'Archeion Veroias-Naouses, 1598-1886* (Thessaloniki, 1954), pp. 161-163 (document 184-1756).
11. KS 81/17/224.
12. See Claude Cahen, "À propos des Shuhūd," *Studia Islamica* 31 (1970): 71-79, for the *şühudul-hal* in classical Islam.
13. Actually, one of them must be the same in both *hüccet*s, only that he is efendi in one and ağa in the other.

ulema status. In fact, the authorization of the *şeyhülislâm* was given for his detention in Mağusa. Whatever the case, when the *vali*'s agent arrived in Karaferye, Ramiz was no longer there. In wording reminiscent of the *ferman* regarding Kara Ahmed, the arrest of Ramiz was incumbent upon the people of Karaferye, who were to be held collectively responsible for the payment of 10,000 *kuruş* to the state and liable to "the most severe punishment" if they tolerated his return.[14]

Separate treatment was reserved for each party involved in the affair. A *ferman* issued two weeks later (16 February) and addressed to the paşa of Salonika focused on Kara Ahmed and his brother without implicating Ramiz Mehmed or anyone else. As would happen in the future, too, the Porte extended the meaning of the *hüccet* to place responsibility for the arrest of Ahmed on the entire population of the *kaza*, not just on the urban population, and to cover any disturbance of public peace as well as Ahmed's return. Furthermore, the state warned that it would collect twice the amount pledged in the *hüccet* if its wishes were not honored.

Two months after the *buyruldu* against Ramiz Mehmed, Molla Mustafa became the target of state action. A gap in the sources does not permit a full understanding of the circumstances, but we do know that Mustafa was by then voyvoda of Karaferye. His document of appointment (*zabt temessüğü*) by the *malikâne*-holders of the *mukataa* of Karaferye, copied in the *sicil* of Karaferye, covered the period from March 1759 to February 1760. The name of the holder of the *voyvodalık* was left blank, which was not unusual for such documents.[15] Later *fermans* referred to this *temessük* as an open-named *temessük* (*ismi acık iltizam temessüğü*) that had been granted to him. Like Ahmed and Mehmed earlier, Mustafa also undertook the collection of the *cizye* from the *zimmis* of Karaferye. He subleased that *mukataa* from its holder for the *sancak* of Salonika.[16]

According to a *buyruldu* of 14 April 1759, Karaferye residents had complained to the Porte that Molla Mustafa was roaming free with a significant force of 400 Albanians and oppressing the *reaya*, undeterred by the orders about the banishment or imprisonment of those who had been involved in the *ayan* clash. The central authorities branded Mustafa a tyrant and a brigand and ordered that he be contained in Karaferye and even killed if he resisted. The authorities of Salonika were to cooperate with Abdi Paşa of Köstendil, who was charged with restoring order in Karaferye;[17] several men and the *kethüda* of the paşa of Salonika were sent to assist

---

14. KS 81/18/225. The *hüccet* that must have been issued as a result of the *buyruldu* has not survived in the *sicil*.
15. KS 81/21/232/1. Amnon Cohen, *Palestine in the Eighteenth Century: Patterns of Government and Administration* (Jerusalem, 1973), p. 204, n. 4, notes: "The tax was to be levied on the land, which fact explains why the name of the relevant *vali* [the *vali* was the main lessee in the *eyalet* of Sidon] was often missing or else inserted only later in red ink." However, it is still not clear why the name should be left blank when the lessee was known. Perhaps such a practice facilitated transfer of the document from one person to another.
16. KS 81/9/380/1.
17. Abdi Paşa eventually reached the offices of *vali* of Anatolia, Rumeli, and Bosnia, and died in 1204 A.H. (1789-90) as *vali* of Silistre. It is interesting that in 1762, he was posted to Belgrade, where he successfully restored order; as a result, he received the title of vezir:

Abdi. The *buyruldu* confirmed that Ramiz Efendi was still at large but falsely suggested that Kara Ahmed and his brother Mehmed (not Mustafa) had been banished as a punishment for their behavior. A *kapıcıbaşı*, Osman Ağa, was appointed as state agent, and he acted as the eyes and ears of the palace through his reports to Istanbul.[18] In addition, his *mübaşir* and the *kadı* of Karaferye were to compile an inventory of the assets of Molla Mustafa, which had been confiscated by the state.[19]

The *buyruldu* suggested that Molla Mustafa was still in Karaferye when it was issued and that the *kethüda* of the paşa of Salonika was to arrive there first. It instructed the people and authorities of Karaferye to resist and avert Mustafa's flight, but when Abdi himself reached the town, Mustafa was no longer there. According to the Venetian consul in Salonika, this resulted in tension between the authorities of Salonika and Abdi, who imprisoned the *kethüda* for notifying Mustafa of his imminent arrival. The *kethüda* was freed three weeks later, after the Porte intervened at the request of the governor of Salonika. The consul also noted that Abdi had imprisoned the *kadı* of Karaferye for collaborating with Mustafa and had had the *serdar* of the town decapitated for the same reason.[20] Nothing was mentioned about these developments in the *sicils*. On the contrary, the Ottoman sources indicate that Şükrü Mustafa Efendi, *kadı* in November 1758, still held the post in March 1760.[21] The consul also connected Abdi's mission in Karaferye with cleansing the area of the Albanians who spread anarchy, but that issue did not come up in state documents until some time later.

As stated earlier, the authorities expected the population of Karaferye to contain Molla Mustafa and his irregulars in the town. That was apparently not easy. After regular troops failed to track down Mustafa, possibly because they were outsiders in a *kaza* with mountainous areas and excellent hideouts, a *buyruldu* dated 21 April ordered the recruitment against him of all the local Muslims who were able to bear arms. This constituted a case of *nefir-i âm*, or general call-up (even though it is not called this in the *sicil* entry), a step taken in emergencies. The document was addressed not only to the *serdar* and the *ehl-i İslâm*, but also to the inhabitants of the villages and of the *çiftlik*s, most of whom were Christians. It is tempting to assume that such non-Muslims, possibly in armed groups, were expected to play a part in the campaign. What seems more likely is that they were only being warned against

---

Mehmet Süreyya, *Sicill-i Osmanî*, III (Istanbul, 1311/1893-94): 411-12.
18. KS 81/3/368/2.
19. KS 81/4/370/1. The inventory has not survived. All we know is that Mustafa had a large house and pieces of land (*çiftlikler*) in Karaferye, as well as movable goods that were to be sold in Salonika (KS 81/9/380/1).
20. Mertzios, "Sympleroma eis ta 'Mnemeia Makedonikes Historias,'" pp. 61, 63. According to the *sicil* entries, Mustafa Ağa of the second *cemaat* (division) of the Janissaries was appointed *serdar* in early February 1759 (KS 81/23/235/1). The next appointment was that of Pehlivanzade Haseki Hüseyin Ağa in late June, after the previous *serdar* had been "removed" (*ref olunub*). Seyyid İbrahim Ağa was also appointed *serdar* in the meantime.
21. KS 81/24/870/2 (1758), RAD 15/907 (1760). It is still possible that the *kadı* was detained for a short while and then released and restored to his duties.

offering provisions or other support to Mustafa. The *buyruldu* pointed out that it was permissible to kill Muslim "rebels" when they had been disobedient to the state and ravaged the *kaza*. Threats of severe punishment for any negligence in carrying out the orders were placed at the end of the *buyruldu*, as usual. It is interesting that Molla Mustafa was not cited as a former voyvoda or even as an *ayan*, as Kara Ahmed was earlier; he was described simply as an inhabitant of Karaferye (*kasaba sükkânından*).[22]

Apart from arresting Mustafa, the other pressing issue was to restore the operation of local administration and especially to appoint a new voyvoda. Final orders were expected from Istanbul, but Abdi appointed an acting voyvoda on 22 April. The *kadı* ratified the appointment, which was justified on the same grounds as that of Molla Mustafa a few months earlier: the flight of the former voyvoda had left the affairs of the *kaza* in disarray, and someone needed to supervise them.[23] The appointee was Seyyid Ibrahim Ağa, a *çavuş* of the Janissaries of the Porte, who had been appointed to the retinue of Abdi and promoted to *serdar* of Karaferye in late March.[24] His particular task was to ensure that order was maintained after the departure of Abdi Paşa and that those banished would not return. If the Venetian consul's report is accurate, Abdi had executed Ibrahim's predecessor.

There was a small complication in the appointment of a proper voyvoda. According to a *buyruldu* issued on 18 May, the post was allocated to an influential *ayan* of Salonika, Abdurrahman Ağa, pending ratification by the Porte.[25] Abdurrahman must have been Abdi Paşa's selection, as the Venetian consul in Salonika wrote in a report dated 22 May.[26] Other sources suggest, however, that the *malikâne*-holders in Istanbul had subleased the *mukataa* of Karaferye to Elhac Osman, a *gedikli*, or office-holder, of the Porte, for one year. A petition Osman submitted in May claimed that Mustafa had already collected a large amount of the *mukataa* revenues and that these now should be recovered with the assistance of the

---

22. KS 81/3/368/1. See Halil İnalcık, "Military and Fiscal Transformation in the Ottoman Empire, 1600-1700," *Archivum Ottomanicum* 6 (1980): 304-311, on *nefir-i âm*.
23. KS 81/4/369/1. The dates of issuing and of registration of the *buyruldu* coincide, which means that Abdi must have issued it in Karaferye.
24. KS 81/4/369/2, KS 81/4/369/3. His appointment is announced by a *ferman* and a letter of the ağa of the Janissaries at the Porte. Abdi Paşa is cited in both documents, which means that his appointment took place not later than 20 March.
25. KS 81/5/372/1. Abdurrahman was *baruthane nazırı* and *gümrük emini* of Salonika, as well as *mütesellim* of various paşas, and held the title of imperial *kapıcı başı*: V. Günay, "H. 1159 (M. 1746) Tarihli Karaferye Kazası Şeriye Sicili (Transkripsiyon ve Değerlendirme)," unpublished thesis, Izmir, 1993, p. 232, document 60; N. Svoronos, *Le Commerce de Salonique au XVIIIe siècle* (Paris, 1956), pp. 17-18 and 18, n. 4. Svoronos notes that the customs officer (*gümrük emini*) was the most important among the tax farmers of Salonika, while in the *eyalet* of Sidon, too, those who farmed the customs revenues of the port towns were also appointed governors and represented the *vali*'s authority (Cohen, *Palestine in the Eighteenth Century*, p. 125).
26. "Abdi returns to Köstendil....[H]e appointed customs officer Abdurrahman as his deputy and voyvoda in Karaferye" (Mertzios, "Sympleroma eis ta ʽMnemeia Makedonikes Historias,'" p. 64).

local court and given to Osman, whose appointment had started in March. The Porte accepted Osman's request and ordered an investigation of the accounts of Molla Mustafa. Mustafa's dismissal was a result of complaints from the local population, the petition indicated.[27]

Osman's name was not mentioned again. On the contrary, the appointment of Abdurrahman was made official in a *ferman* dated 2 June.[28] He enjoyed Abdi's support and that of the local population, according to the formulas used in official documents (*cümle ahali-i vilâyetin istidasiyla...esseyyid Abdurrahman Ağa... voyvoda nasb ve tayin*). Apparently, it was believed that the *mukataa* no longer belonged to the *malikâne*-holders but formed part of Mustafa's confiscated property, for it was eventually discovered that the latter had prepaid its full value without having had time to start collecting from the local population. Consequently, the state was entitled to intervene and order the *malikâne*-holders to appoint whomever it chose as voyvoda. To avoid further complications, it was specified that no individual complaint would be accepted unless supported by a *mahzar* (decree), an *ilâm* (written judgment) of the *kadı*, and a letter from the voyvoda. The "open-named" *temessük* that was still in Mustafa's possession was declared void, and the *malikâne*-holders issued a new one specifically bearing Abdurrahman's name and clarifying that he would collect the *mukataa* revenues fairly on behalf of the public treasury.[29] He was obviously also allowed to collect a fee for his services, but there is no mention of such an allowance in the *fermans*. Abdurrahman probably appointed an agent (*vekil*) instead of moving to Karaferye himself.

The only evidence of Abdurrahman's *vekil* is a *tevzi defteri* (distribution register) compiled on 24 May, which includes payments to the officials involved in the incident. The name of the *vekil* was Ibrahim Efendi. Ibrahim Ağa, the *çavuşbaşı*, was also included in the *defter*, and despite having been a *voyvoda vekili* himself, he should not be confused with his efendi namesake. The total payment amounted to 4,236,000 *akçes* (35,300 *kuruş* at a rate of 120 *akçes* per *kuruş*). Abdi Paşa was allocated 42.5% of the total, Osman Ağa 28.3%, the *kethüda* of the paşa of Salonika 4.25%, Ibrahim Ağa and the voyvoda 2.8% each (as a collection fee for the latter), and Ibrahim Efendi 0.3%. The remaining amount represents expenses for provisions and fees for the court of law and the retinues of the officials.[30] The sum of 4,236,000 *akçes* was a very substantial amount; the expenses entered in the regular *tevzi defteri* of 1764 amounted to only 2,262,650 *akçes*. The *hazariye* tax, to provision dervish lodges for which the governor of Salonika was responsible, in the same *defter* came to 226,975 *akçes* (at least one-third of that amount must have been administrative fees), while Abdi Paşa received 1,800,000 *akçes* for his part in the campaign against Mustafa.[31]

---

27. RAD 14/861, RAD 14/869; Cevdet Tasnifi-Maliye 9014.
28. KS 81/11/383/1. A second *ferman* about the same matter was issued on 3 June (KS 81/9/379).
29. KS 81/12/385/2.
30. KS 81/7/375/1.
31. KS 85/6/427-9 (1765).

Abdi Paşa was appointed governor of the *sancak*s of Salonika and Kavala on 2 June 1759, apparently as a reward for his services in Karaferye, for which he was praised. He was expected to restore full order in Karaferye before departing for Salonika. The special relationship between Abdi and Abdurrahman is confirmed by the fact that the former appointed the latter as his *mütesellim* on 10 June.[32] Minor appointments took place in Karaferye at around the same time (from 18 May to 25 June), marking the return to normality. They included those of a *subaşı*, a *muhtesib*, and a *bölükbaşı* with two hundred men.[33]

Normality was supposedly guaranteed by two more *hüccet*s. The first was drawn up on 19 May and signed by 184 Muslims and 156 Christians of the town, distributed in twelve Muslim and sixteen Christian *mahalle*s.[34] This time, representation was not uniform but ranged from five to twenty-four persons per *mahalle*, perhaps on the basis of *mahalle* sizes. Christians, listed solely by given name, must have represented the *mahalle* leadership. (No priests are indicated while seven *imam*s are cited in the Muslim *mahalle*s.) Muslim titles appear as they do in the first *hüccet*, beginning with that of Rüşdi Ali Efendi, the "recognized" *ayan* of the *kaza*.

The *hüccet* of 19 May is similar to the one about Kara Ahmed. It covered Molla Mustafa, noting that he fled six days before the arrival of Abdi, as well as Ramiz Mehmed and Kara Ahmed. According to the text, the signatories undertook the obligation to pay 50,000 *kuruş* to the public treasury if any of the three *ayan*s returned and was not immediately arrested. It is not known whether the extraordinarily high sum was based on an estimate of the actual financial resources of the *kaza* or set arbitrarily to terrorize the population. Signed by the urban population, the document applied to the whole *kaza* (*cümle ahali-i kazayı canib-i mîrîye ellibin guruş nezre ket eylediklerinde...*). This may be a testimony to the domination of the urban center over the rural areas although on other occasions the villages were independently represented. It should also be noted that Ahmed's penalty was clearly stated to be detention in the fortress of Kavala and not exile, as suggested in the *buyruldu* of 14 April.

According to the *ferman* confirming receipt of the *hüccet*, the inhabitants of Karaferye would have to pay much more than they had pledged if they tolerated the return of either of the two *eşkıya*, Ahmed and Mustafa, or of Ramiz. Furthermore, the *ferman* maintained, the population of the *kaza* had undertaken the pledge voluntarily (*bilcümle ahali-i kaza taahhüd...huzur-i ser'de bittav v'ür-rıza verdikleri hüccet*).[35] The Venetian consul, however, denied that claim categorically in his report of 22 May, attributing the imposition of the 50,000-*kuruş* pledge to Abdi.

Following a *buyruldu* of the *divan* of Salonika, another *hüccet* was issued on 24 June. In it, the people of Karaferye undertook to pay 5,000 *kuruş* to the public

---

32. KS 81/12/386/1, KS 81/12/386/2. The date of the appointment of Abdi is given as 3 June in the document appointing Abdurrahman as his *mütesellim* (see n. 1).
33. KS 81/5/372/2, KS 81/12/386/3, KS 81/14/390/2.
34. KS 81/6/373-74.
35. KS 81/9/380/2.

treasury if twenty-seven listed minor accomplices of Molla Mustafa were allowed to return to the *kaza* without being arrested.[36] The accomplices' names seem to have been indicated by imperial *ferman*.[37] Fifteen were Janissaries;[38] Mustafa Ağa, the brother of Kara Ahmed, was also among them as were a nephew of Molla Mustafa and his two sons and two brothers from Sarıgöl. The *hüccet* contained the names of 160 inhabitants (including nine *imam*s) from only the Muslim *mahalle*s of the town, obviously because the offenders resided there. The representation pattern was different again. For instance, the *mahalle* of Cami-i Atîk was represented by twenty-four persons in the earlier *hüccet* but by fifteen in this one; first ten, now sixteen, persons represented Su Kapısı.

At this point, the problem in Karaferye can be connected with the issue of the Albanian presence in the region. Incidentally, the Venetian consul in Salonika referred to Molla Mustafa as "leader of the Albanians" in one of his reports.[39] Two *ferman*s issued in late May-early June 1759 treated the 50,000-*kuruş* pledge as obliging the *kaza* to be cleansed of all the Albanian brigands (*eşkıya*) who were active there and pointed out that the killing of Muslim brigands was canonically permissible in response to resistance and battle. In addition, the authorities and populations of the neighboring *kaza*s (Yenice-i Vardar, Vodina, Ağustos) were ordered to expel Albanians and to assist the people of Karaferye, for, it was claimed, order could not be established until Albanians were altogether expelled from the region. The officers and *ayan* of the *kaza*s received particular warnings against allowing the return of Albanians. The authorities apparently deemed the issue so important that one of the *buyruldu*s was addressed not only to the officials and the *ayan* of Karaferye but also to the Christian *kocabaşı*s and even to the village population.[40] Including the Christian majority of the *kaza* among the addressees of state decrees was extremely rare, but it happened twice--this time explicitly--in the course of this particular case.

---

36. KS 81/14/389/1, KS 81/15/391.
37. KS 81/11/383/2, KS 81/11/384/3. These are undated lists of names under the headings *derbeyan-i Yeniçeri eşkıyası* and *vürür ferman-i âlide mukayyed eşkıyanın defteridir*. Even though the lists may have been copied from a *ferman* confirming the *hüccet*, it seems more likely that the Porte was notified of the names and consequently demanded the drawing up of a *hüccet*.
38. It is specified in the *buyruldu* that not only the inhabitants of the *mahalle*s but the *serdar* and the elders of the Janissaries should be bound by the undertaking.
39. According to a *sicil* entry of 1770, however, Mustafa was "Türk" (KS 91/3/850). This entry has been published by Vasdravelles, *Historika Archeia Makedonias*, pp. 184-85 (document 202).
40. KS 81/10/381, KS 81/10/382. The first entry has been published by Vasdravelles, *Historika Archeia Makedonias*, pp. 168-170 (document 189). *Buyruldu*s of the *divan* of Salonika inform the Karaferye *kaza* population of the orders for the extermination of the Albanian *eşkıya* and hold the *bölükbaşı* of Karaferye responsible for carrying out the cleansing (KS 81/12/385/1, KS 81/14/389/2). The Venetian consul in Salonika refers to *ferman*s about the expulsion of the Albanians as early as mid-April 1759 (Mertzios, "Sympleroma eis ta 'Mnemeia Makedonikes Historias,'" p. 61). Copies of such *ferman*s have not survived in the *sicil* of Karaferye.

After 1759, as well, the Ottoman authorities dealt with the Albanians of southern Rumeli and the Peloponnese on several occasions. For instance, during a well-known campaign in 1779,[41] a *ferman* specified that the central authorities would not tolerate any more Albanian *ayan* in Rumeli since their *ayanlık* ambitions already had brought chaos and anarchy to several towns.[42] In the case of the *sancak* of Salonika, *fermans* and *buyruldus* of late 1764 and 1765 called for the extermination of Albanian brigands who had raided the whole of southwestern Macedonia and Thessaly, and the same documents criticized the lack of respect for the orders sent to Abdi Paşa concerning the expulsion of the Albanians.[43] Abdi himself had been appointed *serasker* in the campaign against the Albanians in 1759, but complaints of the *reaya* had led to his removal and eventual transfer from Salonika to İnebahtı (Lepanto, Naupactos) in mid-February 1760.[44]

The *fermans* dealt with others besides the Albanians. One of the two demanded that three inhabitants of Karaferye be exiled "to distant places," charging that *kaymakam nakib-i sabık* Seyyid Mehmed, Hasan *sipahi*, and *imambaşı* Elhac Ibrahim had participated in the troubles in some capacity. More important, another Albanian, Hasan Ağa, his sons, and his men were to be kept out of the *kaza* of Karaferye. Hasan, who was the *de facto* ruler of the nearby town of Katerin and also the biggest landholder in the *kaza* of Karaferye, was denounced as an associate of Mustafa. According to the document, Mustafa borrowed money from Hasan, transferred the debt to the population of the *kaza* by forcing them to sign notes of acceptance, then terrorized them for its repayment. It is not clear, however, what was to happen to the lands and the *mukataa* held by Hasan in the *kaza* of Karaferye. His control over the *mukataa* of Çitroz, in the southern part of that *kaza*, had been renewed just a few months earlier, until the end of February 1760.[45]

Government activity concerning the incident *per se* ceased after the promulgation of the decrees against the Albanians and the *hüccets*, at least according to the Karaferye *sicil*. Nevertheless, repercussions of the case persisted some time after an appearance of normality returned to the life of the town.[46] In December

---

41. On the extermination of the Albanian beys, see the contemporary reports of J.V. Arasy in M. Lascaris, *Salonique à la fin du XVIIIe siècle d'après les rapports consulaires français* (Athens, 1939), pp. 37-40. See also Svoronos, *Le Commerce de Salonique*, pp. 29-31.
42. Vera Mutafčieva, "L'institution de l'*ayanlık* pendant les dernières décennies du XVIIIe siècle," *Études Balkaniques* 2-3 (1965): 237.
43. KS 85/11/425/2 (1764), KS 85/9/301/2, KS 85/15/770/1 (1765).
44. Mertzios, "Sympleroma eis ta 'Mnemeia Makedonikes Historias,'" pp. 65-68. According to the French consul in Salonika, Abdi made two campaigns against Albanians in Thessaly and took office in Salonika only on 16 December 1759, after he had had them dispersed. During his absence, Salonika was governed first by his *kethüda*, and then by an interim paşa: Svoronos, *Le Commerce de Salonique*, pp. 22-23 (document no. 18), 373 (document no. 161).
45. KS 81/5/372/3. The Venetian consul in Salonika reports on 19 June that Abdi Paşa is planning to pursue a certain Arnavud Paşa (sic) who is protecting Molla Mustafa. Arnavud Pasha might be a mistake for Arnavud Hasan (Mertzios, "Sympleroma eis ta 'Mnemeia Makedonikes Historias,'" p. 65).
46. Apparently, state performance in the case was not convincing enough to avert further

1759, the guilds of Karaferye claimed that a Christian family of the town, the Kritopoulos, had in their possession 15,000 *kuruş* that Molla Mustafa had given to a certain Küçük Kritopoulos in order to bribe officials in Istanbul into pardoning the molla. Allegedly, after Kritopoulos found out about the *ferman* against Mustafa, he returned to Karaferye and died without delivering the money. The guilds had a claim of 3,000 *kuruş* against Mustafa and demanded that it be paid from the Kritopoulos money. The clever claim attracted the attention of the state, which was determined to keep the remaining 12,000 *kuruş* as part of Mustafa's confiscated property. Consequently, the Porte referred the case to the *divan* of Rumeli and to the *kadı* of Karaferye and appointed an imperial *kapıcıbaşı* to collect the money.[47]

The investigation that followed led to the collapse of the entire case, as revealed in a *ferman* issued in early February 1760. The people of Karaferye denounced the guilds' claim as calumny resulting from private grievances, and an examination of the inventory of Molla Mustafa's assets provides no evidence to support it, either.[48] The case does demonstrate that local competitions were still going strong in the aftermath of the *ayan* conflict: the guilds versus the *bazirgân* (merchant) Kritopoulos and the townspeople (*Karaferye ahalisi*) versus the guilds. It is noteworthy, too, that the cooperation between Mustafa and a Christian did not sound unlikely to the authorities, even if the claim proved not to be true. Apparently, a merchant with business and contacts in Istanbul was particularly useful as mediator with the central authorities. What is not known is whether Mustafa had a patron in Istanbul or not.

Mustafa's immediate fate is also not known. Some years later, in 1764, the *zimmi*s of Kilindir village complained that a certain Mustafa from Sarıgöl had forcibly and illegally collected a fictitious seven-year-old debt of 600 *kuruş*.[49] According to a *defter* of 1765, Mustafa owned only a small share of land in the village of Makroğuz, but he was in a position to lead troops for the Ottoman army in 1770.[50]

As for Hasan Ağa of Katerin, he submitted a petition to Istanbul in early December 1759 against rival *ayan*. The petition and the reply of the Porte did not include any reference to the decree against him. On the contrary, Hasan stressed his role as guarantor of order against brigands and other outlaws, as if he were never banished from Karaferye for terrorizing the population.[51]

---

oppression of the population: in early September 1759, the Christian community complained again of the attempt of the *cizyedar*, Hasan Ağa, to collect the *cizye* twice (RAD 15/135).
47. KS 81/23/868/1, KS 81/23/868/2, RAD 15/473. These documents are also useful in that they state that Mustafa has not been arrested yet in December 1759 and that the mission of Abdi concerning the restoration of order in Karaferye has been terminated. The Kritopoulos family is best known as Charitopoulos, but this appears to be due to a misreading of Ottoman documents. KS 81/23/868/1 has been published by Vasdravelles, *Historika Archeia Makedonias*, pp. 170-171 (document 190), though with several mistakes.
48. KS 82/1/613, RAD 15/667 (1760).
49. RAD 21/497 (1764).
50. KS 85/17/774 (1765), KS 91/3/850 (1770).
51. RAD 15/470.

More interesting information is available about Kara Ahmed. In spring 1760, the people of Karaferye petitioned the Porte via reports of the *kadıs* of Karaferye and Yenice-i Vardar, requesting that he be pardoned. According to their petition, Ahmed had repented for his past behavior and undertook not to employ Albanians again. It was claimed that Ahmed's enemy (*hasım*), Ramiz, was dead.[52] It seems that the only effect of the pledges imposed upon the people of Karaferye had been to precipitate their reconciliation with Ahmed so that Ahmed could return to the *kaza*, and the population could be spared the danger of paying a heavy fine. The Porte, however, was reluctant to accept the request until confirmatory sealed and signed *mahzars* had been submitted directly by the Karaferye population.

Before closing, it is useful to discuss an important detail about the registration of the decrees in the *sicil*: several of the *buyruldus* concerning the case were issued and recorded in the Karaferye *sicil* on the same day. Abdi Paşa or his subordinates must have issued those orders on the spot. The *ferman*s were recorded in the *sicil*s with a delay of at least eight days. The *ferman* of November 1758 dealing with Kara Ahmed was recorded two months after it had been issued, and another *ferman* was recorded with a delay of one month, but most were recorded within twenty days. Although it still is surprising that important and urgent orders required such a long time to be registered, their immediate recipients, such as Abdi, seemed to receive them much faster. For instance, the *ferman* concerning the claim of the guilds against Mustafa was issued in the first ten days of December and probably sent to the *vali* of Rumeli, who issued his *buyruldu* on 19 December; then both orders were forwarded to Karaferye and registered in the *sicil* on 27 December.[53]

CONCLUDING REMARKS

The incident discussed in this paper was one of several in the struggle for supremacy among *ayan* in the Balkans, a major theme in eighteenth-century Ottoman history. Vera Mutafčieva cites several more examples of such clashes, the earliest being set at Razgrad in 1747.[54] Bruce McGowan also mentions competition for domination among the *ayan* of Siroz and of Vidin in the 1760s.[55] Control of the

---

52. RAD 15/907 (1760). A later document contradicts the claim that Ramiz was dead (RAD 24/231 [1768]). As already noted, Ahmed's "enemy" was Molla Mustafa, according to the *ferman* of November 1758.
53. Five out of seven *ferman*s issued on 2-3 June 1759 were recorded in the Karaferye *sicil* on 14 June and the remaining two on 18 June. Were they received as a batch, or was their simultaneous copying in the register a coincidence?
54. Mutafčieva, "L'institution de l'*ayanlık*," pp. 236ff.
55. Bruce McGowan, "The Age of the Ayans, 1699-1812," in Halil İnalcık, ed., with Donald Quatert, *An Economic and Social History of the Ottoman Empire, 1300-1914* (Cambridge, 1994), p. 665. See Cohen, *Palestine in the Eighteenth Century, passim.*, for the case of Zahir al-Umar in Palestine. The scale is certainly different, but there are some analogies with the case of Karaferye in terms of both notables' ambitions and state reaction to them.

local financial and productive resources was a major motive for such competitions, and both Kara Ahmed and Molla Mustafa were accused of overtaxation and financial abuses.

State control was never at serious risk in Karaferye. The issue was, rather, checking oppressive officials and notables and restoring administrative order. The oppression and collapse of order necessitated the intervention of the state, giving it an excellent opportunity to perform its role as guarantor of justice and thus reinforce its bond with its subjects. The state responded to the requests from the people for action by dispatching decrees, agents, and troops, but it proved unable in the short term to arrest any of the wrongdoers. In the long term, it was unable to avert similar phenomena or even the return of the "rebels" of 1758-59 to the *kaza*.[56] We therefore have grounds for asserting that the Karaferye incident refutes, on the one hand, any suggestion that the central government had totally lost control over the Ottoman provinces but demonstrates, on the other hand, how flawed its control was. The state did not seek to remedy the roots of the problem, which were located in the prevailing administrative, fiscal, and social structures. Rather, it adopted a symptomatic analysis of the events and acted as if replacing and banishing a few corrupt individuals could end misgovernment and oppression. In fact, because the priority of the state was to restore the uninterrupted collection and flow of tax revenues, once a new voyvoda had been appointed, the issue was considered practically settled.

If we review the steps taken, the process of restoring order in Karaferye seems to have begun with reports and petitions that rendered Istanbul aware of the situation. Subsequently, the Porte issued decrees outlawing those who had oppressed the population and had participated in the *ayan* clash, and it dispatched paşas, troops, and agents against them. This leg of the government's policy did not result in the arrest of the subjects of the decrees but only forced them to hide or to flee Karaferye. The second leg concerned administrative appointments, especially that of the voyvoda, who would supervise the smooth running of local and state affairs. As the aim of state policy changed from arresting Ahmed, Ramiz, and Mustafa to keeping them out of the *kaza*, so the responsibility for carrying out the decrees was shifted from the state to the local society by applying the familiar principle of communal responsibility.[57] The community thus became bound by legal documents, as in several other cases, and the flow of state decrees about the incident was terminated.

As noted above, the Ottoman government focused on individuals rather than

---

56. In 1782, Hacimehmedağazade Osman Bey, his two sons, one Osman Ağa, and twenty of their followers raided the house of the *serdar* of Karaferye and murdered him. The *mütesellim* of Salonika, an agent of the central authorities, and the *naib* of Karaferye were ordered to restore peace and order: Vasdravelles, *Historika Archeia Makedonias*, pp. 224-225 (document 235-1782).

57. See KS 72/fol. 46r (1748), published by Vasdravelles, *Historika Archeia Makedonias*, pp. 156-157 (document 179), with several mistakes. According to this entry, the population of Karaferye undertook collective responsibility for the security of the roads and mountain passes of the *kaza*.

on institutions, but it did proceed to one generalization. That was connecting the Karaferye problem with the presence of Albanians in southwestern Macedonia. These Albanians were considered responsible for several instances of oppression and disorder in the region, and if Molla Mustafa alone were followed by 400, one can see why the state was worried about them. Once the authorities decided to use force against them, the local population had to be enlisted either to make the Albanians return to their homeland or to exterminate them. In the long run, however, the state failed again, and Albanians remained a factor in the life of the region.

Less than a year after calm had supposedly returned to Karaferye, the first attempts to negotiate the status of people such as Kara Ahmed started. Despite the Porte's reluctance, the sources suggest that Ahmed eventually managed to return to the *kaza* and regain his power and influence.[58] The claim of the guilds regarding Kritopoulos indicates that an oppressive official could reasonably expect to negotiate his place within the Ottoman system as long as he had the proper connections and patrons.

It should not be overlooked that although the abuses of the *ayan* undoubtedly were a heavy burden, the population also had to bear the very substantial cost of the state emissaries sent to alleviate the suffering of the *reaya*. Furthermore, the shift in responsibility for the arrest of those wanted from the state to the community and the subsequent imposition of the pecuniary pledges both signified that the population was in danger of paying an even larger amount of money before the case was closed. Because the menace of the fine, as opposed to the monotonous abstract threats of strict punishment, was the only concrete measure that could really contribute to the implementation of state policy, it is legitimate to ask what the local community or its leadership expected to achieve by applying to the Porte. In other words, how did they perceive their position within the Ottoman polity? To answer such questions, however, we would need to establish first what the terms "community" and *ahali* stood for in the Ottoman context, an extremely difficult task for the modern scholar.

University of Crete

---

58. For instance, Ahmed was expected to lead 300 foot soldiers to the war front in 1772 (B.O.A., Mühimme Defteri 171, nos. 207, 329, 403, 459; see Y. Nagata, *Muhsin-zâde Mehmed Paşa ve Ayânlık Müessesesi* (Tokyo, 1976), p. 105).

Robert Zens

PASVANOĞLU OSMAN PAŞA
AND THE PAŞALIK OF BELGRADE, 1791-1807*

The Serbian uprising of 1804 and the events surrounding it have been the subjects of a variety of studies, but the major figure behind them, Pasvanoğlu Osman Paşa, has been neglected by most scholars. Pasvanoğlu's revolt against the Ottoman central government began the Serbian uprising. In fact, one can state safely that Pasvanoğlu prepared the groundwork for it in the same way that Tepedelenli Ali Paşa laid the foundation for the Greek revolution of 1820. Pasvanoğlu's actions against the sultan and state-appointed officials were a turning point in Ottoman history in the sense that the local administrators, or *ayan*s, achieved the full control over the community and its economic resources that allowed them to defy the authority of the central government. Pasvanoğlu achieved such firm control over the *paşalık* of Belgrade that he forced the state to arm the *reaya*--the very group that the state was supposed to rule, protect, and tax--and use them against its own representatives. In the great paradox of the situation, the state used non-Muslim subjects against its fellow Muslims, enabling the non-Muslims to seek control over their own security and economic well-being and making the Ottoman administration redundant.

Pasvanoğlu's rise to power was facilitated by issues that affected everyone in the Balkans in the last decade of the eighteenth century. Foremost was a struggle for control of the land. The *ayan*s continually sought to wrest control of the land from the state, that is, to transform *miri* (state) lands into *mülk* (private property) in order to gain the right to cultivate it according to the needs of the market economy. Pasvanoğlu, who resided in Vidin near the Habsburg border, could draw great wealth from the sale of agricultural goods to his Habsburg neighbors if he could establish control over and extend his landholdings. Pasvanoğlu's acquisition of land, however, diminished the security and economic stability of the *reaya*, especially those in the *paşalık* of Belgrade.

Closely tied to the struggle for land ownership was the issue of centralization. During the reign of Sultan Selim III (1789-1807), a policy of centralization was introduced to re-impose state control over economic means.[1] Because the land was the chief economic asset, its potential master (the state, *ayan*, or other landowner)

---

* A prior version of this paper was delivered at the 2001 Middle East Studies Association conference.
1. For a detailed account of Sultan Selim's reign and reforms, see Stanford J. Shaw, *Between Old and New: The Ottoman Empire under Sultan Selim III, 1789-1807* (Cambridge, MA: Harvard University Press, 1971).

could achieve control of the community. Among the sultan's centralizing measures was the establishment of a modern military unit, the *Nizam-i Cedid*, which was to become the state's standing army, allowing the sultan to free himself from the growing power of the *ayans*. The reaction to Selim's reform efforts was generally negative, but especially so in the Balkans, where the increasingly powerful and wealthy *ayan*s, such as Pasvanoğlu, had the most to lose. Pasvanoğlu made Vidin, the center of his *ayanlık*, the hub of discontent with the sultan and his reforms. His cause attracted thousands, such as the Janissaries, who were adversely affected by the reforms, as well as impoverished individuals who simply wanted to join the *eşkıya* (brigands) to partake of the booty.

Pasvanoğlu was not merely the catalyst that set the Serbian uprising in motion, but he also was the individual who, directly or indirectly, established the socio-military infrastructure for the entire rebellion. That rebellion was rooted in the social and economic conditions of the eighteenth and nineteenth centuries; it was not, as Serbian nationalist writers have claimed, the culmination of the Serbian national resistance that began after the defeat at Kosovo in 1389. From its social origins, it next became political, and, ultimately, nationalistic.

Pasvanoğlu Osman Paşa's rise to power is key to understanding better the state of the *paşalık* of Belgrade in the last decade of the eighteenth and the first decade of the nineteenth century. Osman was born in 1758 in the important Danube fortress city of Vidin. His father Ömer, originally from Tuzla in Bosnia, was awarded a large number of villages in the *sancak* of Vidin.[2] The wealth and land that Ömer accumulated were said to have surpassed those of the richest *ağa*s of the region.[3] After Ömer fell from grace, for unknown reasons, and was expelled from Vidin, he served as *ağa* of the thirty-first division of the Janissary corps at a border fortress in Belgrade.[4] By distinguishing himself in battle, he was able to return to prominence in the *sancak* of Vidin, where he was rewarded with two villages and made an *ayan*.

As Ömer grew prosperous, powerful, and independent, his status put him at odds with the central authorities and especially with the *muhafız* (fortress commander) of Vidin. He was accused of inciting the local population against the "authorities and the rules of the *şeriat* in these dire times for the state," and of

---

2. One source states that Ömer possessed more than 200 villages in the *sancak* of Vidin, probably a great exaggeration. Shteryu Atanasov, *Selskite V'staniya v B'lgaria k'm Kraya na XVIII vek i nachaloto na XIX vek i S'zdavaneto na B'lgarskata Zemska Voiska* (*Rural Revolts in Bulgaria at the End of the Eighteenth and the Beginning of the Nineteenth Century, and the Creation of the Bulgarian Rural Army*) (Sofia: D'rshavno Voenno Izdatelstvo, 1952), p. 47.
3. Grégoire Yakichitch (Grgur Jakšić), "Documents et Mémoires: Notes sur Passvanoglou, 1758-1807," *La Revue slave* 5:1 (1906): 266.
4. *Arzuhal* from the legal representative of Ömer Pasvanoğlu to the commander of the *vilayet* of Vidin, 23 October 1764, in D. Ihchiev, *Turski D'rzhavni Dokumenti za Osman Pazvanoglu Vidinski* (*Turkish State Documents on Osman Pazvanoglu from Vidin*) (Sofia: D'rzhavna Pechatnitsa, 1909), p. 10. The documents in Ihchiev's book are from the *sicil defterleri* of the Sofia and Vidin *kadı* archives, which are now located in the national library in Sofia. This fall from grace most likely was related to the raids Pasvanoğlu conducted in Serbia and Wallachia. See Yakichitch, "Documents et Mémoires," p. 267.

engaging in "unlawful activities by a forceful acquisition of the properties and livestock of the innocent *reaya*."[5] The sultan sentenced him and his son Osman to death, together with some other "rebels," and in the same *ferman*, ordered the central government's representatives in Vidin "not to let any rebels enter the *hududs* [borders] of Vidin," repelling their attempts by any means. The Janissaries were transferred from Vidin to other border fortresses for fear they would join or help the rebels, as many eventually did.[6] Ömer was publicly executed in late spring 1788; his property was confiscated by the state and sold at auction.[7]

Osman escaped to Serbia, then moved to Albania, where he served under a renowned brigand and later organized his own *haydut/eşkıya* (bandit/brigand) band.[8] During the war with Austria, Osman and his band displayed such extraordinary bravery and skill while fighting the Austrians in Wallachia that the sultan allowed him to return to Vidin and gave back part of his family property.[9] Osman was also given the right to collect the head tax on non-Muslims (*cizye*) from the gypsies in the province of Vidin.[10]

Recovering a portion of his father's territory was not sufficient for the ambitious Osman, who desired to avenge his father's death. A steady source of income from his job as a tax collector allowed him to consolidate and expand his domain with help from the *eşkıya* who had been under his command since his days in Albania and from the dissatisfied Janissaries and brigand bands dispersed in Rumeli after the Peace of Sistova in 1791.[11] His personal militia soon numbered one thousand, including the Janissaries, the *yamaks* (irregulars) who had fled the *paşalık* of Belgrade immediately following the peace, and those forcibly evicted by Ebu Bekir Paşa, the *muhafız* of Belgrade, in 1792. These "refugees" from Belgrade would be responsible for Osman's tremendous impact on the entire *paşalık* and for the Serbian uprising in 1804.

---

5. *Ferman* of Abdülhamid I to the commander of Vidin, 9 December 1787, in Ihchiev, *Turski D'rzhavni Dokumenti*, pp. 11-12.
6. Ibid.
7. *Hüccet* issued by the court of Vidin, 6 June 1788, and *ferman* from Abdülhamid I to the şeriat court of Vidin, 6 July 1788, in ibid., pp. 13-14. Memiş Paşa of Adakale viewed Ömer and Osman as brave men, invaluable in the Ottoman war against Austria, and pleaded in vain for their pardon. See Dušan Pantelić, *Beogradski Pašaluk: Pred Prvi Srpski Ustanak, 1794-1804* (*Belgrade Pashalik: Prior to the First Serbian Uprising*) (Belgrade: Srpska Akademija Nauka, 1949), p. 7.
8. Yakichitch, "Documents et Mémoires," p. 269.
9 Maria Teofilova, *Bunt't na Pazvanoglu i Negovoto Znachenie za B'lgarskoto Osvoboditelno Dvizhenie v XIX vek* (*Pazvanoğlu's Rebellion and Its Meaning for the Bulgarian Liberation Movement in the Nineteenth Century*) (Sofia: Hemus, 1932), p. 33.
10. *Buyrultu* from the chief commander of Vidin to the authorities of the Vidin *vilayet*, 7 August 1792, in Ihchiev, *Turski D'rzhavni Dokumenti*, pp. 15-16.
11. For a detailed study of the role of the *eşkıya* in the Balkans and their importance in the activities of Pasvanoğlu, see Yücel Özkaya, *Osmanlı İmparatorluğunda Dağlı İsyanları, 1791-1808* (Ankara: Ankara Üniversitesi Dil ve Tarih-Coğrafya Fakültesi Yayınları, 1983).

Almost immediately after re-establishing himself in the *sancak* of Vidin in 1791, Pasvanoğlu began raiding Wallachia to the north and Serbia to the west. These raids brought in a great deal of wealth and encouraged other discontented individuals to join the marauding band, emboldening Pasvanoğlu in his defiance of the central government in Istanbul. The sultan responded with a *ferman* ordering the immediate capture of Osman Pasvanoğlu and his accomplices, Haci Bey Bulgarzade from the fifty-fifth Janissary division and Selimzade Bekir Ağa from the twelfth Janissary division.

Actually, according to the *ferman*, Pasvanoğlu and his friends already had been captured and were awaiting exile to Kars. When they petitioned the sultan for forgiveness, Selim III granted them amnesty as "a fatherly grace" that was supposed to serve as an example for his subjects.[12] Besides requiring the promise that "from now on all rebels will remain quiet and be obedient slaves to governmental orders,"[13] the sultan also issued a *ferman* ordering the authorities in Vidin to chase out the *kircalıs* (brigands) or Deliorman Turks who had any connection to Pasvanoğlu.[14]

Judging from the subsequent series of *fermans*, Pasvanoğlu did not turn into a "respectful and loyal servant." On the contrary, he gained increasing power and strength and continued "to incite the population to rebellion and disobedience against the authorities."[15] Eventually besieging Vidin and launching several attacks on it, he defeated the *muhafız* of Vidin, Alo Paşa, in front of the city gates and entered the city.[16] Sultan Selim, in April 1793 and again in June 1793, sent another *ferman* to the *serasker* (commander-in-chief) of Vidin, ordering him to capture and "immediately put to death" Pasvanoğlu Osman.[17] Nevertheless, almost all of the notables of Vidin, including government officials in the fortress of Vidin--the *ulema, suleha* ("pious ones"), *imams, meşayih* (şeyhs), *hatib* (preacher), *turnacı başı* ("crane-keeper": commander of the sixty-eighth Janissary division), *mütekaidīn* (retirees), *eskiyan* ("elderly"), *çorbaci* ("colonel"), *çavuş* ("sergeant"), *odabaşı* (barracks commander), *ayan, alemdar* (standard-bearer), *et al*.--petitioned the sultan to pardon Pasvanoğlu, pledging his innocence "in all aspects" and his utmost respect for the law and the people.[18] This evidence suggests that Pasvanoğlu's extremely wide base of support left the government helpless in its insistence on execution. The sultan, upon receiving this petition, once more pardoned Osman on the familiar

---

12. *Ferman* of Sultan Selim III to the authorities in Vidin, 26 November 1792, in Ihchiev, *Turski D'rzhavni Dokumenti*, pp. 17-19.
13. Ibid., p. 18.
14. *Ferman* of Sultan Selim III to the authorities in Rumelia, 17 May 1793, ibid., pp. 19-20.
15. *Ferman* from Sultan Selim III to the commander-in-chief of Vidin to capture Osman Pasvanoğlu, 19 April 1793, ibid., p. 21.
16. Teofilova, *Bunt't na Pazvanoglu*, p. 36.
17. *Ferman* from Sultan Selim III to the commander-in-chief of Vidin to capture Osman Pasvanoğlu, 19 April 1793, Ihchiev, *Turski D'rzhavni Dokumenti*, p. 21.
18. *Masbata* from the notables of Vidin to Sultan Selim III, 21 July 1793, ibid., pp. 24-25.

conditions that he would not undertake any unlawful activities or challenge the authority of the state.[19]

Pasvanoğlu was not the only powerful Balkan *ayan* to defy state-appointed officials and maintain an entourage of brigands. What separated him from these other independent-minded individuals was the strategic land he held. The city of Vidin, which was central to many of the trade and communication routes in southeastern Europe, enjoyed easy access to the surrounding areas and to the Habsburg border. The series of wars fought with the Habsburgs and Russians in the eighteenth century left many Janissaries and others who had lost their homes searching for new places to settle and new ways to earn a living. Pasvanoğlu offered them protection and a life of brigandage that was much more appealing than farming or living off a meager state salary.

After his second pardon, Pasvanoğlu spent the next several years acquiring *çiftliks* (landed estates) and recruiting more men to his service.[20] As a result, he emerged as the most powerful *ayan* in Rumeli and the leader of many of the smaller *ayan*s in the region, attempting to manage their activities. He consolidated his rule in Vidin by purchasing land, sometimes forcibly, and the acquisition of these great tracts of private property enabled Pasvanoğlu to become even wealthier through trade with his Austrian neighbors to the north.[21] His activities were aided greatly during the summer of 1794 by the interregnum between Mehmed Paşa's appointment as *muhafız* of Vidin and the departure of his predecessor, which left no government-appointed individual to oppose him. As it turned out, Mehmed Paşa proved to be a mere figurehead who had no power or willingness to stand up to Pasvanoğlu.[22]

Pasvanoğlu gained popular support by knowing what the different groups needed and promising them a better life. Portraying himself as the protector of the masses against government arbitrariness, he opposed any new policies or reforms, which the masses always associated with higher taxes. His conservative spirit also won him the support of many Janissaries, the *ulema*, and leading officials in Istanbul. Although, in theory, Pasvanoğlu recognized the need for military reforms, in practice, he became famous for his reactionary policies and dedication to the "old order." Obviously, he wanted independent rule over his domain, and any policies the government might implement to strengthen central control could end his free rein.

---

19. *Ferman* from Sultan Selim III to the *şeriat* court of Vidin, 11 December 1793, ibid., p. 29.
20. *Hüccets* from 12 August 1793, 9 September 1793, 20 October 1793, 18 January 1794, 16 June 1794, 8 September 1794, 9 September 1794, 17 September 1794, 24 September 1794 were issued from the court of Vidin regarding the selling of immovable property to Osman Pasvanoğlu. Ibid., pp. 25-35.
21. At his death in 1807, Pasvanoğlu left behind over seven million gold ducats and a great quantity of diamonds, in addition to a vast arsenal of weapons and munitions. See Auguste Boppe, "La Mission de l'ajudant commandant Mériage á Widin (1807-1809)," *Annales de l'École Libre des Sciences Politiques* (1886): 268.
22. Pantelić, *Beogradski Pašaluk*, p. 17.

Pasvanoğlu continued to fortify Vidin and formed a militia of 12,000 loyal and very well trained soldiers from various ethnic and religious backgrounds, including Albanians, Bulgarians, and Bosnians, in addition to Turks.[23] Consequently, the *sancak* of Vidin became an almost autonomous unit, with an extremely efficient administrative and military organization governed in a dictatorial manner by Pasvanoğlu, who paid the troops out of his own pocket from the taxes he levied on the *reaya* in his vast territories.[24] Still, he tried not to overextend himself. Having more soldiers, requiring him to farm more taxes, might have turned the population against him. After all, the chief reason he enjoyed the support of the *reaya* was his promise to relieve their tax burden. He also "collected" additional revenues by continually raiding Wallachia and the Kraina but thus antagonized the *ayan* of Rusçuk; Terseniklioğlu Ismail Ağa believed he alone had the right to such raids in Wallachia and regarded Pasvanoğlu's activities as encroachments on his rightful domain.[25]

By the mid-1790s, Pasvanoğlu had become the leading power in the northern Balkans, controlling much of the area between Belgrade and Edirne. The only individuals in the region with the potential to face up to him were Terseniklioğlu Ismail Ağa and the newly appointed *muhafız* of Belgrade, Haci Mustafa Paşa. Terseniklioğlu was a powerful *ayan* himself, yet loyal to the sultan when it was convenient. He would risk challenging the immense militia of Pasvanoğlu only if his personal interests were threatened. In the winter of 1796, when these two great *ayan*s clashed, Pasvanoğlu completely destroyed many of Terseniklioğlu's villages along the Danube up to Niğbolu (Nikopolis). Haci Mustafa Paşa, a supporter of the sultan's reforms and former *bina emini* (construction supervisor) of Belgrade, was appointed the *muhafız* in July of 1793.[26] It was his job to safeguard the *paşalık* of Belgrade.

In the year prior to Mustafa Paşa's appointment, the sultan had issued a *ferman* expelling the Janissaries and *yamak*s from the *paşalık* because of their disruptive behavior and exploitation of the *reaya*. Ebu Bekir Paşa, Mustafa's predecessor, was required to implement that *ferman* by force, which included the assassination of the leading Janissaries. In addition, all Turks in the *paşalık* were forbidden to reside outside the towns or to extend their hold over the *çiftlik*s; taxes imposed on the *reaya* were fixed and were to be collected by the Serbian *knez*es (chiefs). These reforms created an angry group of Janissaries and *yamak*s who attempted to avenge

---

23. Özkaya, *Osmanlı İmparatorluğunda Dağlı İsyanları*, p. 34.
24. Teofilova, *Bunt't na Pazvanoglu*, p. 39.
25. The region of Kraina, an extremely fertile province of Serbia situated on the Timok River, was an appanage reserved for the daughters of the sultan. Pasvanoğlu ousted the bey of the Kraina, a Greek appointed by the sultan, and installed his own bey. The revenues that were received from this territory were quite considerable.
26. The date of Haci Mustafa Paşa's appointment as the *muhafız* of Belgrade varies. Some accounts place his accession as late as mid-1795.

their disgraceful exit from Belgrade by heading to the leading rebel in the area, Pasvanoğlu.[27]

After the disruptive elements were ousted from the *paşalık*, the area flourished and became rich from swineherding. Annually the *paşalık* made 1,300,000 florins (130,000 pounds sterling) in its trade with Austria alone.[28] Many of the Serbs who had left the region during the last Austro-Ottoman war or the preceding decades were encouraged to return by the improved conditions.[29] This influx, along with a conscientious Ottoman administration, helped the region to prosper. Haci Mustafa Paşa was so protective of the *paşalık* and its inhabitants that he was called *Srpska Maika*, "Serbian mother." So, like any concerned mother, Mustafa Paşa wanted to protect those in his care from the raiding parties sent by Pasvanoğlu.

In an attempt to appease his hostile neighbor to the east, Mustafa Paşa sent gifts to Pasvanoğlu. Pasvanoğlu received a carriage and six horses and gave eighty *kese* (purses of money) to Mustafa Paşa. But instead of leading to peace, this move led to increased conflict. After sending his brigands into the region to pillage and take captives, Pasvanoğlu demanded the payment of seventy-two *kese* as reimbursement for the presents he had made to the *muhafız*.[30] Pasvanoğlu and his brigands formed a coalition with Çelebi Mustafa Ağa, the former *kul kethüdası* (deputy commander of the Janissaries), and four *orta subayları* (battalion commanders) who were located within the *paşalık*. When their coalition force entered the outskirts of Belgrade, Haci Mustafa Paşa had to take shelter in the inner fortress of the citadel along with the city's inhabitants and soldiers.[31]

The Wallachian *kapı kethüdasi* (governor's aide) sent letters to Istanbul stating that Pasvanoğlu's rebellious actions were disrupting communication, trade, and agriculture in all bordering lands and posing an immediate threat to Belgrade.[32] The Porte had soldiers dispatched to Belgrade to aid Haci Mustafa Paşa, but only after Mustafa Paşa led a group of soldiers from the inner fortress with great swiftness and

---

27. Prior to Mustafa Paşa, Pasvanoğlu's friends in Istanbul arranged for the appointment of Şaşit Paşa, who held the position of *muhafız* for only a couple of months, during which time he overturned the reforms enforced by Ebu Bekir. When the Serbian *knez*es threatened to revolt, the state appointed Mustafa Paşa, who was already well-respected in the *paşalık*, to the post.
28. Leopold von Ranke, *The History of Servia, and the Servian Revolution*, trans. Mrs. Alexander Kerr (London: Henry G. Bohn, 1853), p. 70.
29. Also, many Serbs left the Habsburg territories because they felt betrayed by Emperor Leopold's signing of the peace treaty. In the Treaty of Sistova, signed on 4 August 1791, both powers agreed to return to the *status quo* of 9 February 1788. All lands in the *paşalık* of Belgrade were placed under Ottoman control again. Included was the city itself, which had been captured by the Austrian army, with the assistance of the *Freicorps*, containing about 18,000 Serbs. For a copy of the Treaty of Sistova, see Gabriel Noradounghian, *Recueil d'actes internationaux de l'Empire Ottoman*, vol. II (Paris: Librairie Cotillon, 1900), pp. 6-13.
30. Yakichitch, "Documents et Mémoires," Part 1, p. 276.
31. Ahmet Cevdet Paşa, *Tarih-i Cevdet*, vol. VI (Istanbul: Üçdal Neşriyat, 1966), pp. 293-294.
32. Başbakanlık Osmanlı Arşivi (B.O.A.), Hatt-ı Humayun, 14361.

courage were the opposing forces scattered. The surviving brigands fled back to Vidin, while Çelebi Mustafa Ağa was executed, and the members of the four *ortas* who had aided Pasvanoğlu's men in attacking the city they were meant to defend were exiled to Sinop. They were replaced with four *ortas* from the Morea, Menekşe and Hanya in Crete.[33]

Pasvanoğlu played the role of organizer and financial backer for many of the campaigns and raids into Belgrade and other areas. His involvement is clearly laid out in a letter dated 5 July 1795 from Osman, the *tatar* (courier) of Haci Mustafa Paşa, to the Porte. Osman complained that the Janissaries who had been banished from the *paşalık* of Belgrade were ravaging the area around Pozorofça (Passarowitz). Pasvanoğlu was providing the weapons, ammunition, and other necessary supplies that allowed these *matrudlar* (banished ones) to continue raiding the Belgrade countryside.[34] Rarely did Pasvanoğlu ever lead a raid himself after the mid-1790s.

The failure of Pasvanoğlu's attack on Belgrade did not hinder him for long. Within a couple of months, in early summer 1795, he again assembled a group of brigands to cross into Wallachian territory. Their raids were met by the Wallachian *voyvoda* (governor), and Gürcü Osman Paşa, the Rumeli *vali* (governor-general), was sent from Niğbolu to put an end to Pasvanoğlu's disruptive activities.

As a result of Gürcü Osman Paşa's September march on Vidin, Pasvanoğlu declared allegiance to the sultan and his officials. He swore to obey the orders of the new *muhafiz* of Vidin, Ahmed Paşa of Srebrenica, whom Haci Mustafa Paşa had the honor of installing. He also promised not to attack Belgrade or neighboring areas. In addition, he was forced to pay fines for the crimes committed by his brigands and write a formal apology for their actions.[35] The conditions placed upon Pasvanoğlu were very minor considering that in the past year, the *şeyhülislam* had issued four *fetvas* calling for the capture and annihilation of this rebel who had no respect for any authority or for Islam.[36] Many documents even referred to Pasvanoğlu as a godless traitor (*hain bi-din tagi ve bagi*).[37]

Lenient conditions did not keep Pasvanoğlu in check for long. Renewed raids into the *paşalık* of Belgrade prompted Haci Mustafa Paşa to send his *kâhya bey* (steward), Hüseyin Paşa, to attack Vidin. The objective, according to Mustafa Paşa's orders, was to punish Pasvanoğlu and his ally, Poriçeli Köse Mustafa, who had been expelled from Belgrade by order of the sultan a couple of years earlier. The people of Vidin were to be spared, for they were not the enemy.[38] Well informed of all activities in the Balkans, Pasvanoğlu was prepared for this attack; he

---

33. Ahmet Cevdet, *Tarih-i Cevdet*, vol. VI, p. 294.
34. B.O.A., Hatt-ı Humayun, 12538. See Hazim Sabanović, ed., *Turski Izvori o Srpskoj Revolutsiji, 1804* (*Turkish Sources on the Serbian Revolution of 1804*) (Belgrade: Unedio i preveo Hazim Sabanović, 1956), pp. 33-35.
35. Ahmet Cevdet, *Tarih-i Cevdet*, vol. VI, pp. 295-296.
36. *Fetvas* of the Şeyhülislam to authorities in Rumeli, 1794, Ihchiev, *Turski D'rzhavni Dokumenti*, pp. 35-37.
37. For one example, see B.O.A., Hatt-ı Humayun, 12477.
38. Ibid., 3262.

met Hüseyin's troops in open battle and forced their retreat. In addition, the powerless Ahmed Paşa was arrested, requiring the Porte to negotiate with Pasvanoğlu. The state, for the first time, recognized Pasvanoğlu's authority in Vidin by granting him the title of *nazır* (superintendent) and dismissing all his past indiscretions.[39]

Despite his new-found prestige, Pasvanoğlu resumed his attacks on the *paşalık* of Belgrade and raids into Wallachian territory. As these raids helped spread his reputation as the leading *ayan* in the Balkans, discontented individuals from many backgrounds and religions joined him in Vidin. His personal militia was enhanced, for example, when Janissaries upset by the *Nizam-i Cedid* military reforms of Sultan Selim flocked to Vidin in quest of support for their fight to reestablish their positions of privilege. Similarly, many *reaya* who could not afford the taxes levied to finance the military reforms sought refuge in the brigand bands of Pasvanoğlu or other local *ayan*s.

The impact of Selim's reforms was especially heavy in the *paşalık* of Belgrade, where, prior to 1792, the Janissaries had held a great deal of political and economic power. Over the next three years, the *ferman*s from the sultan placed severe restrictions on the Janissaries. All Turks were forbidden to reside outside the towns and villages or extend their hold over the *çiftlik*s. In addition, taxes on the Serb *reaya* were set at a fixed rate, and these taxes were to be apportioned and collected by the Serbian *knez*es. The Serbs were also given permission to repair churches and monasteries and to ring church bells. These *ferman*s favorable to the Serbs were considered a betrayal by the Janissaries and others who had benefited from the absence of state authority in the region.

Seventeen ninety-six was a rather quiet year in the *paşalık* of Belgrade. There is no mention of incursions into neighboring lands although the mere presence of Pasvanoğlu posed a danger to stability in the region. In the summer of 1797, however, Hakkı Paşa, who had embarked on a long campaign to free the Balkans of brigands, was removed from the post of *vali* of Rumeli, creating a power vacuum too tempting for *ayan*s such as Pasvanoğlu to ignore.[40] In the late spring of 1797, Haci Mustafa Paşa, a very conscientious and hard-working *muhafız* of Belgrade, was promoted to *vali* but did not have the power or ability to take on the role of governor of the entire region. Soon he was forced to combat not only Pasvanoğlu, but also Kara Feyzi in the region of Filibe (Plovdiv). Pasvanoğlu took advantage of this situation and sent Macar Ali on a massive raiding campaign that extended his authority to Niğbolu, Tırnovo, and Sistova, in addition to driving Terseniklioğlu out of Rusçuk and Şumnu (Shumen).[41]

Only after Tepedelenli Ali Paşa replaced Mustafa Paşa as *vali* was Pasvanoğlu brought under control. With the assistance of Terseniklioğlu and Haci Mustafa

---

39. Grgur Jakšić, *L'Europe et la résurrection de la Serbie, 1804-1854* (Paris: Librairie Hachette, 1917), p. 23.
40. For a detailed study of Hakkı Paşa's efforts in the Balkans, see İsmail Hakkı Uzunçarşılı, "Vezir Hakkı Mehmed Paşa, 1747-1811," *Türkiyat Mecmuası* 6 (1936-1939): 177-284.
41. Ahmet Cevdet, *Tarih-i Cevdet*, vol. VI, p. 396.

Paşa, Ali Paşa routed Pasvanoğlu's army near Şumnu. Terseniklioğlu reestablished his position in eastern Bulgaria, forcing Pasvanoğlu to march westward. Pasvanoğlu's group of about 1,700 men under the command of Genç Mustafa and Köse Mustafa captured Poriçe Island and the towns of Pozorofça and Semendire,[42] but in Belgrade, a three-pronged attack against the *eşkıya* resulted in several hundred deaths and the capture of 150 prisoners, along with the invaders' flag and ammunition.[43] Although a good number of Pasvanoğlu's men were able to escape to Vidin to participate in future incursions into Belgrade,[44] the Belgrade *kaymakam* (deputy governor) Osman Paşa, Izvornik *mutasarrıf* (administrator) Hasan Paşa, Böğürdelen *voyvoda* Veli Efendi, and others received honorary gifts (*kürkler ve kaputlar,* or furs and cloaks) from Istanbul.[45]

As Pasvanoğlu continued to engage in raids on other neighboring territories in Selva and Tırnovo, Haci Mustafa Paşa was reappointed *vali* on 24 November 1797 and ordered to capture Pasvanoğlu after these new attacks.[46] Beginning on the same date, a series of *ferman*s initiated the preparations to terminate Pasvanoğlu as a threat, and for the next two months, throughout the Balkans, those preparations structured a major campaign against Pasvanoğlu and his headquarters in Vidin.[47] On 9 December an order was sent to Sofia to gather every available soldier in the region to fight Pasvanoğlu.[48] A month later, all *sipahi*s in Rumeli were called to join Haci Mustafa Paşa's military campaign.[49]

In order to guarantee the complete annihilation of Pasvanoğlu and his brigand bands, all roads and mountain passages in the Balkans were to be guarded, and no traders, members of the *reaya*, or other non-military personnel were to be allowed to go to Vidin.[50] In all past campaigns, a sizeable portion of Pasvanoğlu's militia had been able to escape, regroup, and mount new raids in the near future, for his network of brigands under various loyal chiefs could strike several places in the Balkans simultaneously and avoid major open-field battle.[51] Consequently, the only way to eliminate the threat was to destroy Pasvanoğlu in Vidin and capture all of his chiefs

---

42. B.O.A., Hatt-ı Humayun, 2877 A.
43. Ahmet Cevdet, *Tarih-i Cevdet*, vol. VI, p. 405.
44. B.O.A., Hatt-ı Humayun, 2877 C.
45. Ibid., 12277.
46. *Ferman* from Sultan Selim III to Haci Mustafa Paşa, 24 November 1797, Ihchiev, *Turski D'rzhavni Dokumenti*, p. 51.
47. *Ferman*s from Sultan Selim III, 24 November 1797, ibid., pp. 45-51.
48. *Ferman* from Sultan Selim III to Sofia, 9 December 1797, ibid., pp. 55-56.
49. B.O.A., Cevdet Tasnifi Dahiliye, 2722. This document also requests that the campaign against Pasvanoğlu spare those of his followers who had begged forgiveness from the Porte.
50. *Buyrultu* from the *serasker* of Rumeli to Sofia, 13 January 1798, Ihchiev, *Turski D'rzhavni Dokumenti*, p. 60.
51. Among Pasvanoğlu's lieutenants were Macar Ali, Gavur Imam, Molla Idris, Emincik, Aliş, Rami Bayraktar, Poriçeli, Çanak Veli, Muslu, and Kara Mustafa. See Özkaya, *Osmanlı İmparatorluğunda Dağlı İsyanları*, pp. 47ff.

scattered throughout the countryside.[52] The march towards Vidin began on 5 February 1798, under Kaptan Paşa (Admiral) Küçük Hüseyin and Haci Mustafa Paşa, the *vali* of Rumelia, accompanied by many of the leading *ayan*s, including Gürcü Osman Paşa, Tepedeleni Ali Paşa, Ismail Bey of Siroz, Çirmen *mutasarrıf* Silahdar Hüseyin Paşa, Selva *voyvoda* Hasan Ağa, Tersenriklioğlu Ismail Ağa, Adana *mutasarrıf* Yusuf Paşa, and *ayan*s from Bosna, Tırhala, Şumnu, Hezargrad (Razgrad), Varna, and Pravadı (Pravadia).[53] This force was believed to include up to 80,000 soldiers.[54]

For eight months, the coalition forces besieged Pasvanoğlu in the fortress of Vidin, without any hope of his surrender. Although the besieging forces were great in number and included many powerful *ayan*s, they were quick to abandon the coalition when they realized that victory was not imminent. Within the first month of the siege, orders were already being sent to Sofia to bring deserting soldiers under control. The deserters were wreaking havoc in the Balkan countryside as those who would oppose them were fighting Pasvanoğlu.[55] In addition, the siege of Vidin was not able to prevent supplies and food from crossing the Danube into the city. In the last week of September, Sultan Selim III ordered the demobilization of part of the army, and in mid-October the headquarters of the operations moved back to Sofia.[56]

The failure of the massive campaign against Pasvanoğlu resulted in even greater prestige for the rebel. As he had done three years earlier, Pasvanoğlu once again pledged his allegiance to the sultan, and, in return, the Porte now granted him the titles of vezir, *paşa* with three tails, and *muhafız* of Vidin.[57] This recognition legitimized his hold over the territories, including the strategic Kraina, that he had acquired in the preceding years.[58] Due to the French invasion of Egypt, the sultan

---

52. A *ferman* was issued for the capture of Pasvanoğlu's collaborators Macar Ali, Guvar Imam, Sırıklıoğlu, and Emincik on 30 January 1798. Ihchiev, *Turski D'rzhavni Dokumenti*, pp. 65-66.
53. Ahmet Cevdet, *Tarih-i Cevdet*, vol. VI, p. 413. For a detailed list of those at Vidin and the troops they brought with them, see Özkaya, *Osmanlı İmparatorluğunda Dağlı İsyanları*, pp. 54-55.
54. Yakichitch, "Documents et Mémoires," Part 1, p. 418. One observer estimated Pasvanoğlu's force at 40,000 to 50,000 men. See G.A. Olivier, *Voyage dans L'empire Othoman, l'Égypte, et la Perse...* (Paris: H. Agasse, 1801-1807), pp. 211-218.
55. *Buyrultu* from the Rumeli Beylerbeyi to Sofia, 4 March 1798, Ihchiev, *Turski D'rzhavni Dokumenti*, pp. 76-77.
56. *Ferman* from Sultan Selim III to the *serasker* in Vidin, 27 September 1798, and *buyrultu* from *serasker* to Sofia, 16 October 1798, ibid., pp.119-121.
57. B.O.A., Hatt-ı Humayun, 12505. Ahmet Cevdet Paşa states that Pasvanoğlu received this rank on June 21, 1799. The ranks of vezir and m*uhafız* were taken away on September 20, 1800, because of his support for *eşkıya* raids in Niğbolu, Plevne, and Borkofça, but he regained those titles in August 1802: Ahmet Cevdet, *Tarih-i Cevdet*, vol. VII, pp.123, 201.
58. Although he agreed to pass the administration of the Kraina to the sultan and to send the revenues from this fertile region to Istanbul regularly, Pasvanoğlu was able to keep control of the lands and delegated power to his favorite, Molla Idris Ağa: Jakšić, *L'Europe et la résurrection de la Serbie*, p. 24.

could only hope that Pasvanoğlu would remain loyal to the Porte and refrain from launching raids into neighboring territories.

Unfortunately for the state and, in particular, for the *paşalık* of Belgrade, Pasvanoğlu promptly resumed his lawless activities. Without a large army in the Balkans to fight brigands, Pasvanoğlu and others took advantage of the situation. Many of the Janissaries who had fled to Vidin from Belgrade began to return to their former lands. The Serbian *knez*es complained to Haci Mustafa Paşa about these unwelcome intruders, so once again the *muhafız* of Belgrade had to fight Pasvanoğlu on his own.

In the summer of 1799, Mustafa Paşa was quite successful in his campaigns in the Kraina, but the following March, the *knez* of the fortress town of Šabac, Ranko Lazarević, was attacked and killed by a group of Janissaries. Alexa Nenadović, one of the leading *knez*es in the *paşalık*, announced to Haci Mustafa Paşa: "We *knez*es are devoted to your service and the sultan's and it is our duty to give you service from legs to knees and arms to elbows. But we will no longer endure it if we are to be killed in the sultan's market-place by an oppressor...."[59] Mustafa Paşa soon avenged Ranko's death and "so frightened all the Janissaries that the very name Janissary could not be said aloud in the whole *paşalık*."[60] Those Janissaries who did survive the attack fled across the Sava into Bosnia.

Because Haci Mustafa Paşa had to increase the size of his army and keep it properly armed, he also had to raise taxes. The *reaya,* who had experienced a large tax increase just a couple of years earlier, could not afford this necessary expense. The *knez*es, however, offered the *muhafız* the option of arming the Serbian *reaya*. According to this plan, the *knez*es would recruit from their villages men who would be responsible for their own supplies and equipment and would not receive a salary from the state.

Accepting the *knez*es' plan, Mustafa Paşa ordered that a crier should announce in the marketplace of every town and village: "Hear, men! Whoever is a Serb and has not a long musket, two pistols, and a long knife, let him sell a cow and buy himself arms. This is the command of the noble vezir. Whoever does not obey shall receive fifty strokes of the bastinado and pay a fifty-*kuruş* fine. Hear and heed well, for this is the vezir's command."[61] For the first time in centuries, *reaya* were allowed to bear arms and defend themselves. The monumental step of arming the Serbs, along with Haci Mustafa Paşa's earlier victory in Šabac, made him the main target of the Janissaries remaining in Belgrade and those in Vidin and Bosnia.

In 1800, Pasvanoğlu knew that the sultan would not be able to send any troops to hinder his raids. He had the *yamak*s, who for the most part had resided previously in Belgrade, moved from the Kraina and Vidin back into the *paşalık*, and on their way, they captured Pozorofça, Čupria, and Semendire without much resistance. The

---

59. Mateja Nenadović, *Prota Matija Nenadović* (Belgrade: Srpska Akademija Nauka i Umetnosti, 1978), p. 31, which names Bega Novljanin and Çurtoglija as the murderers of Ranko Lazarević.
60. Ibid., p. 32.
61. Ibid., p. 36.

only response from the Porte was to announce restrictions on travel by Albanians and Bosnians to Pasvanoğlu's territory.[62] As the *yamak*s and other supporters of Pasvanoğlu neared the city of Belgrade, they met the first resistance, but the rather small army of Haci Mustafa Paşa could not hold out for long.

Very shortly after Mustafa Paşa requested assistance from his Serbian supporters, the *knez*es from the western part of the *paşalık* advanced with their newly armed soldiers and pushed the invaders back from the city. Knez Birčanine pursued them to the border of the *paşalık* of Vidin, while Alexa Nenadović stayed in Belgrade with the remaining troops to protect Mustafa Paşa. To prevent immediate reprisals from Pasvanoğlu and other groups in Bosnia, the *reaya* militia was not dismissed from duty for several months.[63]

Ultimately, arming the *reaya* resulted in a massive campaign that threw the *paşalık* of Belgrade into utter chaos. The mufti in Belgrade issued a *fetva* stating that it was against the law to drive the Janissaries and *yamak*s, who were Muslim, from their land and possessions in favor of the Serbian *reaya*.[64] That local response was reinforced when the *Divan* ordered Mustafa Paşa to re-admit the Janissaries, even though they had been exiled by a *ferman* several years earlier and had joined Pasvanoğlu, a rebel in the eyes of the state. As a loyal servant of the Porte, Haci Mustafa Paşa was forced to readmit the Janissaries into the province or place himself in open opposition to the sultan. The Janissaries who returned did not press the *paşa* to restore their property but initially were satisfied with their appointments in the customhouses and the court.[65] When the Janissaries began to acquire property by threatening the *reaya*, however, in mid-1801, another round of fighting broke out in the *paşalık*.

The large number of Janissaries in Belgrade, in consultation with Pasvanoğlu, launched a joint operation against the *paşalık*, focusing in particular on Haci Mustafa Paşa. After a group of Janissaries, *yamak*s, and other brigands was dispatched from Vidin to invade the *paşalık*, Haci Mustafa Paşa sent his son, Derviş Bey, to head them off, but as soon as Derviş Bey neared Niş, the Janissaries in Belgrade began to take control of the city. On 6 September 1801, Derviş Bey realized that he had fallen into Pasvanoğlu's trap and sent an urgent letter to the *vali* of Rumeli. He explained the dire situation in Belgrade, where the *yamak*s had entered the citadel and killed the captain of the garrison, and made it clear that the attackers were united with Pasvanoğlu in the desire to make Belgrade like Vidin.[66]

As Derviş Bey rushed back to Belgrade with his army, Haci Mustafa Paşa notified the *knez*es to reassemble their militias. Both the Serbian militia and Derviş

---

62. B.O.A., Cevdet Tasnifi Dahiliye, 2752.
63. Jakšić, *L'Europe et la résurrection de la Serbie*, p. 26.
64. Ranke, *History of Servia*, p. 71.
65. Ibid.
66. B.O.A., Hatt-ı Humayun, 3946. The *vali* received another report stating that those who had been expelled previously from Belgrade were uniting with Pasvanoğlu and causing problems in Belgrade and throughout the region. Ibid., 12371. Even *The Times* of London reported that "the rebels, on this occasion declared themselves in favour of [Pasvanoğlu]." *The Times* (London), 10 September 1801, p. 2C.

Bey with the *mütesellim* (administrative agent) of Niş, Mustafa Ağa, arrived in Belgrade too late. The Janissaries, commanded by Foçoğlu Mehmed Ağa, Küçük Ali Aganli, and Molla Yusuf, stormed the citadel, imprisoned the *paşa* and executed Haci Mustafa Paşa on 27 December 1801. The city then came under the control of the four Janissary leaders who claimed the title *dayı*, the same title used by the local Janissary leaders in North Africa.

With the news of Haci Mustafa Paşa's death, entire bands of Janissaries and brigands emerged from Albania and Bosnia, and throughout Rumeli. Welcomed warmly by the *dayı*s, many of these newcomers received positions in the administration and such titles as *kabadayı* ("swashbuckler"), *binbaşı* (commander of a thousand), *bölükbaşı* (division commander), and *subaşı* (chief of police). They were thus entitled to replace the *knez*es as the representatives of local authorities in the towns and villages throughout the *paşalık*. As all tax-collecting power now passed into the hands of former brigands and rebels, the arbitrary nature of taxation created great hardship within the region. The Serbs were not the only ones who suffered. The *sipahi*s, who had been loyal to the late *muhafız*, were forced to give up their power and a good deal of their property to Janissaries who had helped the *dayı*s take power. Unlike the *muhafız*, the *dayı*s did not need the assistance of the local *sipahi*s; they had the total support of Pasvanoğlu. Besides sending frequent administrative advice and direct assistance to the *dayı*s, he sent "everywhere [especially Bosnia] emissaries to propagate his principles, and try to make the people dissatisfied with the present Turkish government."[67] In order to end the cooperation between Vidin and the *dayı*s in Belgrade, Ebu Bekir Paşa was dispatched from Bosnia to Niş, but his effort had no success.[68]

Derviş Bey, who had fled to Istanbul after his father's death, obtained from the sultan a *ferman* authorizing him to fight against the *dayı*s. With the backing of the Porte and some assistance from Austria, Derviş Bey began purchasing arms and ammunition.[69] This plot was discovered by the *dayı*s before all preparations were made, and future actions against the *dayı*s were hindered by Pasvanoğlu's control of the route from Niş to Belgrade. This control prevented any supplies from reaching the newly appointed but ineffective *muhafız* of Belgrade, Hasan Paşa.

Ultimately, under the tyrannical *dayı*s, conditions in the province became so unbearable that the Serbs and the Ottomans loyal to the sultan launched a joint uprising in late winter 1804. As the Serbian uprising progressed into a large-scale battle, Pasvanoğlu remained the puppet master behind the scenes in Vidin. He sent the *dayı*s in Belgrade letters of encouragement, supplies, and one thousand men under his trusted lieutenant Koşancalı Halil Ağa (Gushanatz Ali).

Despite Pasvanoğlu's assistance, attacks from the Serbs and an Ottoman force under the *vali* of Bosnia, Ebu Bekir Paşa, convinced the *dayı*s that their situation

---

67. *The Times* (London), 9 November 1801, p. 3B.
68. Ahmet Cevdet, *Tarih-i Cevdet*, vol. VII, pp. 189-190. In addition to Ebu Bekir's action, the sultan ordered that no supplies be sent to Vidin; however, there was no way to enforce this ban.
69. Jakšić, *L'Europe et la résurrection de la Serbie*, p. 29.

was hopeless. They fled down the Danube, only to be caught and executed on the island of Orsava by Recep Ağa. The fortress of Belgrade was left to Koşancalı Halil, and Pasvanoğlu sternly commanded him not to engage in negotiations with the Serbs, the Austrians, or the Porte. Because the city of Belgrade was completely surrounded by the Serbs and their Ottoman supporters, Pasvanoğlu was no longer able to send aid directly to Belgrade, but he was able to block the route to Belgrade from the east, preventing any state aid from reaching those loyal to the sultan.

It was no surprise when Belgrade finally fell to the Serbs and Koşancalı Halil had to flee to Pasvanoğlu. What is rather surprising is that Pasvanoğlu all but disappeared from the fighting that ensued in the *paşalık*. True, he welcomed to Vidin any soldiers fleeing the conflict in Belgrade and assisted those *yamak*s still fighting in the region, but for the most part, he turned his attention to the east and the north.[70] Although in 1805 he sent fur caps and coats (*kalpak ve kürk*) as gifts to the Serb leaders,[71] most likely he was trying only to appease the Serbs and protect his western border while he was engaged with Tersenniklioğlu Ismail Ağa and Alemdar Mustafa Paşa.

At the beginning of the Russian-Ottoman war in 1806, Sultan Selim outraged Pasvanoğlu, who saw himself as the most powerful individual in the Balkans, by appointing Alemdar Mustafa Paşa of Rusçuk *serasker* of the Ottoman forces.[72] Pasvanoğlu, however, did not allow his pride to get in the way of defending the Ottoman state from the invading Russian army. First he sent a detachment of battle-ready Albanians under Molla Idris Ağa toward Negolin to cut all communications between Serbia and Wallachia. The Serbs by 1806 had converted their social uprising into a more far-reaching endeavor and were seeking an unhindered line of communication with the Russians. Only Pasvanoğlu's actions prevented the Russians from making direct contact with the Serbs and allowed the state to bring the Serbian uprising under control soon after the war.

Pasvanoğlu Osman Paşa's fascinating life ended on 27 January 1807. Many of its aspects cannot be addressed in a short paper, but the previously neglected topic of his role in the *paşalık* of Belgrade can be summed up in one word: instigator. Without his actions and support, it is very questionable whether the Serbian uprising would have taken place in 1804. The issuance of Sultan Selim's *ferman*s in the

---

70. With assistance from Vidin, which was not taken by the Serbs until late July 1805, one of Pasvanoğlu's disciples, Ömer Ağa, had usurped power in the fortress town of Užice, the second most populous town in the *paşalık*. See Ranke, *History of Servia*, pp. 89-96.
71. B.O.A., Hatt-ı Humayun, 5490.
72. Pasvanoğlu saw himself as the greatest *ayan* in the Balkans not only because of his enormous wealth and prestige, but also because of the various communications he had with foreign envoys. The Russians sought to establish a consulate in Vidin, while Napoleon sent a mission to Vidin in 1801 to convince Pasvanoğlu to aid France in its struggles. Later, Napoleon's consul general, Mériage, arrived in Vidin just after Pasvanoğlu's death. In addition, the British claimed that Pasvanoğlu had French officers and soldiers fighting under his command. See Ahmet Cevdet, *Tarih-i Cevdet*, vol. VIII, pp. 18-19; Boppe, "La Mission de l'ajudant commandant," pp. 264-268; *The Times* (London), 25 August 1801, p. 2D, and 12 July 1802, p. 2D.

1790s and the administration of the beloved Haci Mustafa Paşa might have maintained prosperity and peace in the *paşalık* for several decades, if not until the Russo-Ottoman war of 1877-1878, for the Serbian movement for independence was confined to a few Serbs in the Hapsburg Empire. Only when Pasvanoğlu's raids made living conditions unbearable for both the Serbs and the Ottomans loyal to the sultan was there any sign of rebellion. What then began as a social uprising gradually grew into a larger conflict that sought to prevent such conditions from ever returning to the *paşalık*.

University of Wisconsin-Madison

Jane Hathaway

OTTOMAN RESPONSES TO ÇERKES MEHMED BEY'S REBELLION IN EGYPT, 1730

The early eighteenth century was a time of defining change in the Ottoman Empire's largest province, Egypt. As the realities that had defined Egypt's political culture in the seventeenth century began to unravel, new sources of authority came to the fore. In particular, this period saw the disintegration of the two factions that had permeated Egyptian society since at least 1640. The Faqari faction (derived from Zülfikar) was eclipsed by a household, the Qazdağlıs, that arose from within its midst. By contrast, the Qasimi faction (derived from Kasim) imploded by dividing against itself. That self-destruction began when Çerkes, or "Circassian," Mehmed Bey, the *mamlūk*, or military slave, of Qasimi chieftain Ibrahim Bey Abu Shanab (died 1718), cultivated a rivalry with Ismail Bey b. Ivaz, the fiery young son of Abu Shanab's comrade-in-arms (*khūshdāsh*)[1] Ivaz Bey (died 1711). This rivalry itself is an intriguing instance of the tension between the clients and the sons of grandees in a society in which sons were not necessarily excluded from military roles, as they had been under the Mamluk sultanate, which ruled Egypt from 1250 until the Ottoman conquest in 1517.[2]

---

1. *Khushdash* typically refers to a *mamluk* of the same master. On this phenomenon, see David Ayalon, *L'esclavage du mamelouk* (Jerusalem, 1951), pp. 30-32, 35. There is still disagreement as to the origin of the term. Gerhard Doerfer, *Türkische und mongolische Elemente im Neupersische*, vol. 3: *Türkische Elemente im Neupersischen* (Wiesbaden, 1967), pp. 184-85, claims that the word derives from *hvāga-daş* (i.e., *hoca-daş*), a fellow-servant or fellow "good person." This interpretation, however, is based on a misapprehension of the connotations of the suffix *daş*, which implies not a "fellow"--one of the same status--but rather one who literally *shares*, or inhabits, the noun to which the suffix is attached: thus, *yoldaş* ("comrade"), for example, is someone who shares a road (*yol*), not a fellow road. Furthermore, this interpretation assumes that the *jīm* in *hvaga* assimilates to *şin*, which does not occur in other uses of this term, as for "teacher" or "merchant". I am grateful to Reuben Amitai-Preiss for drawing my attention to Doerfer's explication. An alternative derivation is *hawsh* (Arabic for "courtyard") + *daş*, on the grounds that *mamluks* of the same patron might have been housed and/or trained in the courtyard of the patron's house or in a similar enclosure. This would seem more satisfying from a phonetic standpoint. To me it seems most likely that the word derives from Turkish *koğuş/kovuş* ("chamber") + *daş*, and refers literally to a barracks-mate. This interpretation is bolstered by the fact that in modern Turkish, *koğuş* is used to mean a dormitory room or jail cell. Phonetically, this etymology is problematic: on the one hand, *ghayn*, as in *koğuş*, typically does assimilate to a *yumuşak* "g" or to a "v" in modern Turkish; on the other, it is less common for a *qaf* to assimilate to *khā'*.
2. On sons of Mamluk sultans and emirs, known as *awlād al-nās* (literally, "children of the people"), see David Ayalon, "Studies on the Structure of the Mamluk Army," Part 2, *Bulletin*

The competition between the two beys dominated Egypt's political life during the 1720s. It was not, however, limited to Egypt, for each bey strove to cultivate allies at the imperial court in Istanbul in order to acquire lucrative tax farms (s. *iltizam*) and offices while avoiding hostile Ottoman governors. This intra-Qasimi struggle created a dilemma for the Ottoman government, which traditionally had played the Faqari and Qasimi factions off against each other. Now, it had to shift its support among an ever-growing collection of independently operating households. Complicating matters was the web of competing interests at the imperial center itself; the grand vezir, to take a typical example, sometimes might compete with and at other times might ally with the sultan's mother (*Valide Sultan*) and the Chief Black Eunuch of the imperial harem (*Kızlar Ağası* or *Darüssaade Ağası*).[3]

The divisions at both the center and the periphery during the 1720s manifested themselves in the imperial orders, or *fermans*, dispatched from Istanbul to Cairo and recorded in the *Mühimme-i Mısır*. These orders referred to whichever party had fallen out of favor with the dominant party at court as *şaki*, which may be translated as "brigand," "bandit," or "rebel." Yet the definition of brigandry or rebellion seems to have been quite malleable. Failing to remit the annual tribute to Istanbul rendered a grandee a *şaki*, as did neglecting to send the requisite money and grains to the poor of the Holy Cities of Mecca and Medina, or withholding provisions earmarked for the imperial pantry. Ignoring any sultanic decree or duty to the sultan did constitute rebellion, but such infractions seemed to be adduced only when the shifting balance of power in Istanbul had thrown one or another Egyptian grandee and his household out of favor. Such a grandee could then take measures to restore his standing at court. The experience of Osman Bey Zülfikar in the mid-1740s demonstrates the point. Driven from Cairo by a hostile grandee, Osman Bey fled to Istanbul. As the *fermans* recorded in the *mühimme* attest, after two years of lobbying and the payment of a hefty "pardon tax" (*bedel-i 'afv*), Osman Bey had reclaimed all his personal holdings in Egypt and been appointed *sancak beyi* of Edirne.[4] Likewise, although the *fermans* of the 1720s apply the term *şaki*, in turn, to Çerkes Mehmed and Ibn Ivaz,[5] these grandees needed only the right connections at court and, of course, the right amount of money to remove the label. Çerkes Mehmed Bey himself, early in his career, had received a pardon that allowed him to pay a fee to recover his confiscated village tax farms.[6]

---

of the School of Oriental and African Studies 15 (1953): 457-58.
3. On this phenomenon, see İ.H. Uzunçarşılı, *Osmanlı Devletinin Saray Teşkilatı* (Ankara, 1945, 1984, 1988), pp. 175-77.
4. Istanbul, Başbakanlık Osmanlı Arşivi, *Mühimme-i Mısır*, vol. VI, nos. 15, 16, 88, 89, 93, 94, 113, 114, 126, 127, 140, 141, 143, 144, 147, 166 (all 1157/1744-45); nos. 200-203, 255 (all 1158/1745-46); no. 298 (1159/1746). His pardon and the pardon tax are specifically mentioned in *Mühimme-i Mısır*, vol. VI, nos. 327 (1159/1746) and 373 (1161/1748). See also Jane Hathaway, *The Politics of Households in Ottoman Egypt: The Rise of the Qazdağlıs* (Cambridge, 1997), pp. 89-90.
5. For example, *Mühimme-i Mısır*, vol. III, nos. 30, 44, 45 (1131/1718-19); 137, 146-148, 150-52, 157-161, 163, 168 (1132/1719-20).
6. *Mühimme-i Mısır*, vol. III, no. 166 (1132/1719-20).

In the late 1720s, however, the equation in Egypt changed. In 1724, the popular Ibn Ivaz Bey was assassinated by Zülfikar Bey, the patron of Osman Bey Zülfikar, in complicity with Çerkes Mehmed Bey.[7] As a result, Çerkes Mehmed assumed sole leadership of what remained of the Qasimi faction, and the elimination of Ibn Ivaz reignited the old Faqari-Qasimi antagonism, pitting Çerkes Mehmed against his recent accomplice Zülfikar in a struggle to the death. As the tension between the two beys escalated, each undertook more and more dangerous feats of self-assertion.

Imperial *fermans* dispatched after Çerkes Mehmed Bey's death report that he had adopted the unauthorized title of *şeyh ül-beled*,[8] previously relegated to Arab village headmen.[9] Çerkes Mehmed, who enjoyed close ties to certain of Egypt's bedouin groups, had evidently asserted his primacy in Cairo by adopting this title. *Şeyh ül-beled* did not belong to the Ottoman hierarchy of offices, according to which the Ottoman governor was the dominant figure in Cairo. The chief posts filled by local grandees were those of *emīr ül-hācc*, or pilgrimage commander; *defterdar*, or financial director; ağa of the Janissaries; and *kaymakam*, or stand-in for an absent governor.[10] The *fermans* declare in no uncertain terms that Çerkes Mehmed's use of the illegitimate title is an act of rebellion against Ottoman authority--something rather more serious than neglecting to remit revenues.

The testimony of the *fermans* is itself revelatory, given the debate among scholars over the initial appearance of the title *şeyh ül-beled*. As Peter Holt pointed out over thirty years ago, the title first appears in the well-known chronicle of Abd al-Rahman al-Jabarti in reference to a client of Ibrahim Kâhya al-Qazdağlı in the 1750s. Stanford Shaw countered, on the basis of the *mühimme*, that Çerkes Mehmed was the first to hold the title.[11] A rereading of the *mühimme* in the context of the Ottoman court's reaction to Çerkes Mehmed's other provocative actions suggests, however, that the Ottoman central authority regarded the assumption of the title *şeyh ül-beled* as part and parcel of Çerkebi Mehmed's pattern of rebellion. The title, then, is linked inextricably to him.

Within fifteen years of the indignant *fermans*, the Ottoman court had fully

---

7. Ahmed Kethüda Azeban al-Damurdashi, *Al-Durra al-musāna fī akhbār al-Kināna*, British Museum, MS Or. 1073-4, pp. 263-64; Ahmed Çelebi b. Abd al-Ghani, *Awdah al-ishārat fī man tawalla Mısr al-Qāhira min al-wuzarā' wa'l-bāshāt*, ed. A.A. Abd al-Rahim (Cairo, 1978), pp. 384-85.
8. *Mühimme-i Mısır*, vol. IV, nos. 334, 336 (1143/1730-31).
9. See, for example, Abdülkerim b. Abdurrahman, *Tārīh-i Mısır*, Istanbul, Süleymaniye Library, MS Hekimoğlu Ali Paşa 705, fol. 75v.
10. See "Mısır Kanunnâmesi," in Ömer Lutfi Barkan, ed., *XV ve XVIıncı Asırlarda Osmanlı İmparatorluğunda Ziraî Ekonominin Hukukî ve Malî Esasları*, İstanbul Üniversitesi Edebiyat Fakültesi Yayınlarından No. 256 (Istanbul, 1943), vol. I, chapter 105.
11. P.M. Holt, *Egypt and the Fertile Crescent, 1516-1922: A Political History* (Ithaca and London, 1966), p. 92, n. 1; Stanford J. Shaw, ed. and trans., *Ottoman Egypt in the Age of the French Revolution*, by Hüseyin Efendi (Cambridge, MA, 1964), p. 11, n. 1. In al-Damurdashi's chronicle, the title is first applied to the Faqari grandee Mehmed Bey Qatamish, who was prominent in the 1720s and early 1730s. See *Durra*, p. 414.

accepted *şeyh ül-beled* as the title of Cairo's preeminent grandee. Consequently an order of 1746 refers to Osman Bey Zülfikar as *şeyh ül-beled* almost as a matter of course.[12] Although the court clearly considered Osman Bey a *şaki* at the time of his eviction from Cairo in 1744,[13] the post of *şeyh ül-beled* was no longer in dispute. In fact, the *şeyh ül-beled* was now formally invested by the Ottoman center after winning the consent of Cairo's dominant household. The dialogue-cum-negotiation between center and province that produced this compromise reflects the government's extraordinary ability to absorb defiant or threatening innovations and institutionalize them as part of the Ottoman system, a key strategy of Ottoman provincial rule.

In the late 1720s the atmosphere in Egypt was still highly unstable, as Çerkes Mehmed Bey and Zülfikar Bey embarked on their epic struggle. In these changeable circumstances, Çerkes Mehmed Bey ascended to a new level of rebelliousness. Driven out of Cairo by the forces of Zülfikar Bey, he chose not to strike out for Istanbul to lobby his case at court but made his way along the Mediterranean coast to Algeria.[14] There, he surely was aided by the quasi-autonomous dey of Algiers, although we know regrettably little about relations between Algeria's and Egypt's grandees during this period.[15] From Algiers, Çerkes Mehmed took ship across the Mediterranean and landed in Trieste, the Habsburg Empire's principal Mediterranean port, and quickly made his way to Vienna, where he petitioned for the support of the Austrian emperor Charles VI (r. 1711-40). According to the *mühimme*, Çerkes Mehmed sought shelter in both Austria (*Gyâh-i Nemçe*) and France (*Gyâh-i Farânca*). After a strongly worded letter from the sultan to the Habsburg emperor prompted the bey's flight from Vienna to Libyan Tripoli, he plotted his return to Egypt, where he intended to build up a huge army of bedouins to defeat the forces of Zülfikar Bey.[16]

Çerkes Mehmed Bey could hardly have chosen a course of action that would be viewed more negatively in Istanbul. Although the Roman Catholic Habsburg Empire had begun to yield pride of place to an expansionist Russia, it had been the Ottomans' chief European enemy since the early fifteenth century. The Ottomans had recently suffered through a series of costly wars against the Habsburgs, losing the critical fortress of Belgrade, which they would not regain until 1739, through a combination of battlefield prowess and skillful negotiation.[17]

---

12. *Mühimme-i Mısır*, vol. VI, no. 279 (1159/1746).
13. Hathaway, *Politics of Households*, pp. 89-90.
14. *Mühimme-i Mısır*, vol. IV, nos. 61, 72 (1140/1727-28); 127, 146 (1141/1728-29). See also Ahmed Çelebi, *Awdah*, pp. 478, 493, 498.
15. On Ottoman Algeria, see, for example, Tal Shuval, *La ville d'Algers vers la fin du XVIIIe siècle: cadre urbain et classe militaire* (Paris, 1998); Mahfoud Kaddache, *L'Algérie durant la periode ottomane* (Algiers, 1998); John Baptist Wolf, *The Barbary Coast: Algiers under the Turks, 1500-1830* (New York, 1979); Nasir al-Din Saīduni, *Dirāsāt wa-abhāth fī ta'rīkh al-Jazā'ir: Al-'ahd al-'Uthmānī* (Algiers, 1984).
16. *Mühimme-i Mısır*, vol. IV, no. 169 (1141/1728-29); nos. 231, 246, 247, 295, 296 (1142/1729-30); no. 337 (1143/1730-31). See also Ahmed Çelebi, *Awdah*, pp. 500, 534.
17. For a summary of these events, see Virginia H. Aksan, *An Ottoman Statesman in War and*

It is hardly surprising that the Ottoman court regarded Çerkes Mehmed Bey as far worse than a mere *şaki*, or "rebel". A *şaki* was someone who had neglected, deliberately or otherwise, to perform his duty to the sultan; his status could be reversed without unimaginable difficulty. Because Çerkes Mehmed had taken refuge with the Ottoman Empire's infidel archenemy, the *fermans* dealing with his case label him not *şaki* but *hain*, or "traitor," to the entire *Dārül'islâm*. He thus presumably had betrayed, besides the Ottoman Empire, Morocco, the sub-Saharan Islamic kingdoms of Africa, India, and even Iran, which, after the collapse of the Shi'ite Safavid dynasty, was now under the rather tenuous rule of Sunni Afghans. The orders are, moreover, quite insistent that if Çerkes Mehmed were caught trying to enter any Muslim territory, he was to be turned over to the authorities for execution.[18]

Despite the strident all-points bulletins, Çerkes Mehmed Bey did manage in 1730 to re-enter Egypt, raise a large bedouin army and advance against Zülfikar Bey. The Arabophone chronicler al-Damurdashi's account of the dénouement reads almost like a parable. Çerkes Mehmed Bey, who had escaped death so many times, drowned in the mud of the Nile as he was fleeing the forces of Zülfikar's ally Ali Bey Qatamish.[19] Two peasants stripped the bey's corpse, floated it down the Nile on a passing fishing boat, and ultimately delivered it up to Ali Bey Qatamish. Ali Bey cut off Çerkes Mehmed's head and had it flayed, then buried his body. In this fashion, al-Damurdashi notes with a hint of irony, Çerkes Mehmed fulfilled his vow to be buried only in the earth of Egypt. Ali Bey Qatamish and the surviving Zülfikarite leaders marched triumphantly into Cairo bearing Çerkes Mehmed's head, dressed in chain mail, on a golden platter, and presented it to the Ottoman governor.[20] Zülfikar Bey, however, did not live to see this victory, having been assassinated by a hostile grandee only five days earlier.[21]

A traitor to the Ottoman sultan who had accepted aid and comfort from the Christian enemy thus met the deserved end of the *hain*. Although the *şaki*, a fairly common figure in Ottoman political life, could still participate in a dialogue with the Ottoman center and be rehabilitated as a result, the *hain* had, by acting to undermine the Ottoman state, removed himself from any relationship with the Ottoman center. It is worth noting that the classical Islamic term for rebellion against the Muslim community, *baghi*, which contains an implication of sin,[22] was seldom used in

---

Peace: Ahmed Resmî Efendi (1700-1783) (Leiden, 1995), pp. 8-9, 18-19, 100 n. 2, 117, 196.
18. *Mühimme-i Mısır*, vol. IV, nos. 169, 231, 246. See also Ahmed Çelebi, *Awdah*, p. 542.
19. Ali Bey was the *mamlūk* of Mehmed Bey Qatamish, whom al-Damurdashi depicts as the first grandee to hold the title *şeyh ül-beled* (see n. 11).
20. Al-Damūrdāshī, *Durra*, pp. 384-89. See also Ahmed Çelebi, *Awdah*, pp. 567-68, a less dramatic account featuring, however, fifty-five heads and a brass platter. See also *Mühimme-i Mısır*, vol. IV, no. 303 (1142/1729-30).
21. Al-Damūrdāshī, *Durra*, p. 380. See also Ahmed Çelebi, *Awdah*, pp. 564-65, 567.
22. Joseph Schacht, *An Introduction to Islamic Law* (Oxford, 1964, 1998), p. 187; Fazlur Rahman, "The Law of Rebellion in Islam," in Fazlur Rahman, *et al.*, *Islam in the Modern World: 1983 Paine Lectures in Religion*, ed. Jill Raitt (Columbia, MO, 1984), pp. 1-10; Joel L. Kraemer, "Apostates, Rebels, and Brigands," *Israel Oriental Studies* 10 (1980): 35-73;

Ottoman discourse. In the case of Çerkes Mehmed, both *baghi* and terms indicating widespread social unrest or upheaval, such as *fitne, fesad,* or *isyan,* which occur frequently in Ottoman discourse, were similarly avoided.

The story of Çerkes Mehmed Bey, when viewed in its wider imperial context, illustrates more than the distinction that the Ottomans made between rebellion and treason. The Ottoman Empire, in the early eighteenth century, conducted a series of draining wars against the Habsburgs in the west, the Russians in the north, and the waning Safavids and Afghan conquerors of Iran in the east. As Virginia Aksan notes in her contribution to this volume, this three-front milieu led to a massive movement of recruits from all corners of the empire, so that Albanians fought in the Caucasus while Kurds and Abkhazians fought on the Danube. The resulting territorial and ethnic dislocations seem to have produced an atmosphere in which ethnic and regional boundaries blurred: a Circassian grandee in Egypt, whose own homeland was being defended from the Russians by Albanian troops, felt perfectly justified in approaching the Austrian emperor for help in besting an opponent back in Egypt. Tellingly, he reached Vienna with the help of grandees in other Ottoman provinces. His mutiny was thus an entirely provincial operation, with a narrowly circumscribed provincial goal, that partook of the chaotic mobility of an empire perpetually at war.

It is a measure of the Ottoman Empire's ethnic fluidity that Çerkes Mehmed's arch-enemies in Egypt were largely fellow Circassians. Ivaz Bey, the father of the charismatic Ismail, had been a Circassian *mamluk,* as had many of the leading grandees of Egypt during the seventeenth century.[23] The importation of Circassian *mamluk*s into Egypt may, in fact, have been carried on continuously since the later Mamluk sultanate. By the 1660s, at any rate, the Ottoman traveler Evliya Çelebi reported large numbers of Circassians in Egypt.[24] In Evliya's account of his travels in the Caucasus, the slave trade was omnipresent, both as a form of tribute to the Ottoman sultan and the Giray khans of the Crimea and as a result of opportunistic child-snatching among the Circassians, Abkhazians, and other populations of the region.[25] By 1730, however, the Circassians' pride of place in Egypt had been diluted, ironically, by influxes of eastern Anatolians, Abkhazians, and, above all,

---

M.J. Kister, "... *Illā bi-haqqihi*...: A Study of an Early *Hadīth,*" *Jerusalem Studies in Arabic and Islam* 5 (1984): 33-52.
23. On this point, see Jane Hathaway, "Egypt in the Seventeenth Century," in Martin W. Daly, ed., *The Cambridge History of Egypt,* vol. 2: *Modern Egypt from 1517 to the End of the Twentieth Century* (Cambridge, 1998), pp. 36-38, 46-48; idem, *Politics of Households,* pp. 44-46; P.M. Holt, "The Exalted Lineage of Ridwan Bey: Some Observations on a Seventeenth Century Mamluk Genealogy," *Bulletin of the School of Oriental and African Studies* 22 (1959): 221-30.
24. Evliya Çelebi, *Evliya Çelebi Seyahatnamesi,* ed. Ahmed Cevdet (Istanbul, 1888-1938), VII: 723.
25. See, for example, Mehmet Güneş, *Evliya Çelebi ve Haşim Efendinin Çerkezistan Notları* (Istanbul, 1969), pp. 8-95 *passim.*; Evliya Çelebi, *Narrative of Travels in Europe, Asia, and Africa,* trans. Josef von Hammer-Purgstall, 2 vols. in 1 (London, 1834), Part 3, pp. 52, 55, 56, 64, 174, 196.

Georgians.²⁶

Çerkes Mehmed's experience typifies the broader trend of increasing Ottoman reliance on geographically marginal populations during the seventeenth and eighteenth centuries. Like the Albanians, the Circassians and Abkhazians were problematic "mountain people" who proved either formidable fighters for the empire or troublesome rebels against it.²⁷ The stereotypical image of the treacherous Abaza perhaps had been forged in the days of Erzurum governor Abaza Mehmed Paşa's rebellion to avenge the murder of Osman II (1622-23),²⁸ and Aleppo governor Abaza Hasan Paşa's rebellion against grand vezir Köprülü Mehmed Paşa (1657).²⁹ In the late eighteenth century, the peripatetic *kadı* and chronicler Şemdanizade Fındıklılı Süleyman Efendi still invoked the same stereotype in denouncing the Egyptian grandee Bulut Kapan Ali Bey.³⁰ Meanwhile, the Circassians, dubbed *Çerakise-i nakise* ("dirty Circassians") by pro-Ottoman chroniclers of the conquest of Egypt from the Circassian Mamluk sultans, were in Evliya Çelebi's day renowned (or infamous) for their warlike ferocity and stubbornness.³¹ Even today, *Çerkes* is an insult, not unlike "jerk," in Farsi. Yet the Ottoman Empire in the seventeenth and eighteenth centuries could hardly have done without the Circassians or, for that matter, without the Albanians or Georgians.

While the ongoing wars at the peripheries of the empire surely contributed to the strident Ottoman response to Çerkes Mehmed's rebellion, significant tumultuous events also took place in Istanbul shortly before the bey's flight to Vienna. In Patrona Halil's rebellion of 1730, a naval mercenary officer led a massive mutiny that resulted in the deposition of Sultan Ahmed III (r. 1703-30).³² Although this mutiny did not involve an enemy power, it was regarded as such a threat to the Ottoman state that participants who had fled to Egypt were hunted down and summarily executed a number of years later. Al-Damurdashi claims that a grand vezir even executed the son of one of Patrona's supporters who had arrived at the imperial court from Egypt with a delegation wishing to depose the governor.³³ In this atmosphere, Çerkes Mehmed Bey elicited the extreme response of an empire

---

26. Hathaway, *Politics of Households*, pp. 43-46, 57, 61-64, 71, 101-06.
27. See Virginia Aksan's essay in this volume.
28. See Gabriel Piterberg's and Baki Tezcan's essays in this volume.
29. See, for example, Holt, *Egypt and the Fertile Crescent*, p. 105.
30. Şemdanizade Fındıklılı Süleyman Efendi, *Şemdanizade Fındıklılı Süleyman Efendi Tarihi*, ed. M. Münir Aktepe (Istanbul, 1976), III: 99. As Virginia Aksan notes in her contribution to this volume, Şemdanizade also witnessed the Ottoman defense of the Black Sea fortress of Ochakov against the Russians in 1771.
31. See, for example, Keşfî Mehmed, *Selimname*, Süleymaniye Library, MS Esad Efendi 2147, fol. 69r; Güneş, *Cerkezistan Notları*, pp. 25-27, 30, 37, 46, 52, 55, 59, 62-64. Evliya describes Seyyidi Ahmed Paşa as displaying "all the obstinacy of a Circassian." *Narrative of Travels*, Part 3, p. 194.
32. M. Münir Aktepe, *Patrona İsyanı, 1730*, İstanbul Üniversitesi Edebiyat Fakültesi Yayınlarından No. 808 (Istanbul, 1958). See also *Encyclopaedia of Islam*, 2nd ed., s.v. "Ahmad III," by Harold Bowen.
33. Al-Damūrdāshī, *Durra*, pp. 471-72.

embattled from both within and without.

Çerkes Mehmed Bey's rebellion is distinguished by the intervention of a hostile foreign power, a motif that resonates through the Arabic chronicles despite their varying versions of which foreign enemy Çerkes Mehmed enlisted. Certain manuscripts of the Damurdashi chronicle duplicate the *mühimme*'s account of the bey's flight into Habsburg territory, but the British Museum manuscript (MS Or. 1073-1074) has Çerkes Mehmed fleeing to Russia. In Moscow, he and his henchmen have an audience with the Russian "king" (*kral*, misrendered *kval* in the manuscript), presumably Tsar Peter II (1727-30), who promises to provide Çerkes Mehmed funds and a vessel in which to return to Egypt. From Moscow, Çerkes Mehmed and company proceed to Malta, which at the time was the seat of the Roman Catholic Knights of St. John and by no means under the control of the Orthodox Russian tsar.[34] There, nonetheless, Çerkes Mehmed supervises the construction of a *şayka*, a keelless boat effective in both oceans and rivers, in which he and his comrades journey back to the Nile.[35]

Even if the story gives a false account of Çerkes Mehmed Bey's movements, al-Damurdashi may have based it on some popular tradition of a rebel who sought the aid of the Russian tsar. The flight of a rebel leader or defeated prince to enemy territory was a familiar theme during the early years of the eighteenth century, when numerous Eurasian empires suffered political upheaval and chaotic territorial shifts. For instance, Ahmed Çelebi reported that the son of the last Safavid shah, fleeing from the invading Afghans, landed in Moscow in 1722.[36] In 1715, the Ottomans themselves had given shelter to a rebel against the Habsburgs, the Transylvanian prince Ferenc II Rákóczi (1676-1735), whose eight-year (1703-11) insurrection was finally crushed by Habsburg armies. After fleeing initially to France, Rákóczi spent the last twenty years of his life in the Thracian town of Tekirdağ.[37] In fact, Çerkes' tale, apart from his return to Egypt, constitutes a veritable mirror image of Rákóczi's and may have been framed as such, even in an "official" source such as the *mühimme*.[38] In 1711, meanwhile, Ottoman armies surrounded Tsar Peter the Great on the Pruth River and might have ended Peter's westernizing experiments

---

34. See Roderick Cavaliero, *The Last of the Crusaders: The Knights of St. John and Malta in the Eighteenth Century* (London, 1960); H.J.A. Sire, *The Knights of Malta* (New Haven, 1994), especially chapter 6.
35. Al-Damūrdāshī, *Durra*, pp. 350-57.
36. See *Awdah*, p. 410.
37. See *EI²*, s.v. "Erdel," by A. Decei; Kelemen Mikes (1690-1761), *Letters from Turkey*, trans. Bernard Adams (New York, 1998); Ladislas, baron Hengelmüller von Hengervár, *Hungary's Fight for National Existence, or, the History of the Great Uprising led by Francis Rákóczi II, 1703-11* (London, 1913); William B. Slottman, *Ferenc II Rákóczi and the Great Powers* (New York, 1997). I am grateful to Gábor Ágoston for drawing the Rákóczi affair to my attention.
38. On the subject of "chronicle-esque" *mühimme*s, see Jane Hathaway, "Sultans, Pashas, Taqwīms, and Mühimmes: A Reconsideration of Chronicle-Writing in Eighteenth-Century Egypt," in Daniel N. Crecelius, ed., *Eighteenth Century Egypt: The Arabic Manuscript Sources* (Claremont, CA, 1990), pp. 75-76.

prematurely had they not, for reasons that remain unclear, allowed him to escape after ceding the critical Black Sea port of Azov.[39]

In any case, the war-torn, three-front milieu was the inescapable backdrop to Çerkes' rebellion and to the military revolts that broke out in other provinces during the same period. At what other period was it plausible that a rebellious grandee could approach *either* the Russian tsar *or* the Habsburg emperor? Just fifteen years earlier or later, Çerkes Mehmed could have approached the Safavid shah, as well, although the Afghans had temporarily precluded that option.

In later decades, when the tale of Çerkes was being recounted through the haze of intervening years, the tsar would have seemed the more logical ruler for the bey to have approached. Over time, the Russian Empire, far more than the Habsburg Empire, came to regard Egypt as a linchpin of its geopolitical struggle with the Ottomans, particularly in the eastern Mediterranean. By the late eighteenth century, Russian envoys were actively wooing Egypt's grandees. As a result, in 1786, the Ottomans had to launch a naval expedition under the admiral Cezayırlı Hasan Paşa to oust Ibrahim and Murad, Georgian beys who seemed to be getting too cozy with the Russians.[40]

What the Ottomans had faced in 1730 was a challenge to their imperial system from among their own subjects. The severity of the Ottoman response to the challenges by Patrona Halil and Çerkes Mehmed Bey is indicative of the severe stress of the times in which they occurred. Compared to Patrona Halil's mutiny, of course, Çerkes Mehmed Bey's rebellion seems fairly minor: the bey was a single provincial grandee locked in a petty struggle with a local rival. Nevertheless, he obviously sensed that recourse to a foreign power was an option open to him, perhaps because he knew just how unstable the imperial center was. The Ottoman center could not entertain even the remotest threat of French or Habsburg interference in Egypt at that juncture, so it responded with the rhetoric of *cihad*, arguably giving Çerkes Mehmed's rebellion a significance it did not actually possess. This rhetoric, however, was highly effective among the sultan's servants in Egypt who remained loyal and delivered the traitor's head. They may occasionally have been *eşkıya*, after all, but *they* were not *huvvân*.

Ohio State University

---

39. See, for example, *EI²*, s.v. "Ahmad III," by Harold Bowen; Benedict Humphrey Sumner, *Peter the Great and the Ottoman Empire* (Oxford, 1949).
40. Abd al-Rahman b. Hasan al-Jabarti, '*Ajā' ib al-athār fī'l-tarājim wa'l-akhbār* (Cairo, 1958-67), III: 343ff. On the beys' relations with Russia, see Daniel N. Crecelius, "Russia's Relations with the Mamluk Beys of Egypt in the Eighteenth Century," in Farhad Kazemi and R.D. McChesney, eds., *A Way Prepared: Essays on Islamic Culture in Honor of Richard Bayly Winder* (New York, 1988).

Judith Mendelsohn Rood

MEHMED ALI AS MUTINOUS KHEDIVE: THE ROOTS OF REBELLION[*]

Mehmed Ali's rebellion in 1831 against the Ottoman sultan Mahmud II (1808-39) marked a fundamental turning point in the legitimization of rule in the Middle East. From the very beginning of his rule in Egypt, Mehmed Ali sought to change the political culture of the Ottoman Empire. As a result, the Islamic court records contain numerous government decrees that distinguish his rebellion from those of other provincial magnates who had mutinied against the Ottoman Porte.

This essay discusses the changing nature of law and political culture in the Ottoman Empire during the period of Mehmed Ali's rebellion. By placing Mehmed Ali in the context of Ottoman legal history and provincial administration, it identifies the reasons for his mutiny and for the resulting rebellions against him. Highlighted here is the significance of the Ottomans' decisions to recognize Mehmed Ali as Egypt's governor for life and, ultimately, to recognize his dynasty in perpetuity. They were decisions made to ensure that the extremely profitable province of Egypt would not be lost to the empire during an age when it was losing territory on all fronts. Also considered, is the way Mehmed Ali used Islam to legitimize the policies he devised to shake off Ottoman control of Egyptian--and Syrian--resources.[1]

Recent literature on nineteenth-century Egyptian history has drawn attention to the epistemological framework of nineteenth-century positivist social science. "Dependent upon a notion of universals, which was based on an understanding of human society as comparable to a biological system," positivist social science has been applied to government in Europe and in the realm of western colonialism.[2] In this vein, for example, Khaled Fahmy relies on Timothy Mitchell's *Colonising*

---

[*] A prior version of this paper was delivered at the 1996 Middle East Studies Association conference in Providence, Rhode Island, as part of the panel entitled "Mutiny: Idea, Narrative, and Event in Ottoman Contexts, Sixteenth-Nineteenth Centuries." I would like to thank Halil İnalcık for sharing his insights into Mehmed Ali's origins and relationship with Hüsrev Paşa, Palmira Brummett for organizing the panel, and John F. Guilmartin for his comments.
1. My doctoral dissertation, "Sacred Law in the Holy City: A Study in the Theory and Practice of Islamic Government in Jerusalem" (University of Chicago, 1993) is based primarily upon a close reading of all the Islamic court registers of Jerusalem for the years 1829-42. For a broader view of the issue of provincial notables, see Bruce McGowan, "The Age of the Ayans, 1699-1812," in Halil İnalcık, ed., with Donald Quataert, *An Economic and Social History of the Ottoman Empire, 1300-1914* (Cambridge, 1994), pp. 637-758.
2. Bernard S. Cohn, *Colonialism and Its Forms of Knowledge* (Princeton, 1996), p. 3.

Egypt, in his interpretation of Mehmed Ali. Mitchell analyzes power through the lenses of Jacques Derrida and Michel Foucault, to show that it is not only represented by but also achieved through spectacle and exhibition. He uses the concept of "enframing" to move the understanding of "modernization" in Egypt away both from a Weberian approach to the rationalization of power through codification, bureaucratization, and institution-building in society and from a Marxist concern for class struggle and economic determinism. Instead, Mitchell emphasizes the modernizers' plans to use "spectacle" as a means to power, and Fahmy discusses how--and how effectively--these plans were implemented.[3]

For both authors, the "show" put on by those in power as they extended their control over their subjects is the phenomenon of interest. The nature of the show was western, imposing its own categories and aesthetics of control through Orientalist notions of what the subjugated East should appear to be. The underlying discourse of this perspective is focused on an expansionist, colonializing West that is preoccupied with "rationality": science and routinization, objectification, transformation of the East into the West. By contrast, those subjugated--in this case, the Egyptians--are caught and controlled; they are not sentient beings with political rights, although Fahmy's and Mitchell's works share an implicit concern for the victims of western domination.

Equipped with a compelling paradigm and concentrating on the development of the Egyptian army, Fahmy examines not only the subjector but also the response of the subjects, the *fellahīn* (peasants) of nineteenth-century Egypt. He believes that the conflict between Mehmed Ali and the sultan must be understood within the Ottoman context, and he notes the use of law--including the Law of Cultivation (*Qānūn al-Filāha*)--in Mehmed Ali's extension of his personal control over the lives of his subjects. Fahmy's study and his postmodernist paradigm, however, ignore the classical issues of Islamic and western political philosophy--the nature of authority, the nature and role of law--that are critical to understanding Ottoman rule and the Muslim response to Mehmed Ali's policies.

In general, the postmodernist approach to world history ignores the development of constitutionalism--the articulation of the relationship between government and individual, with its focus on civil rights, political liberty, property rights, the rule of law, and due process. To neglect that fundamental aspect of the history of the state in studying the Middle East is an especially grave mistake, for it perpetuates the ideas that Islam is somehow exceptional and that it is improper to apply to non-Christians the standards governing the rule of law and human rights that evolved in the West. Because such an essentialist view robs meaning from Middle Eastern history, it is imperative to bring Harold J. Berman's path-breaking paradigm for the interpretation of legal history into the study of Islamic legal history. Specifically, applying it to the emergence of the successor states of the Ottoman Empire would allow comparison of different regions with varied cultural,

---

3. Khaled Fahmy, *All the Pasha's Men: Mehmed Ali, His Army, and the Making of Modern Egypt* (Cambridge, 1997); Timothy Mitchell, *Colonising Egypt* (Cambridge, 1988).

political, economic, and religious contexts.[4]

Both the western and the Islamic traditions of political philosophy have a common sense that justice is governed by the universal laws of a just God who seeks to ensure the common good through wise government. Only in the late twentieth and early twenty-first centuries, however, have scholars attempted to understand these common conceptions in order to reconsider the existence of universal laws governing human rights. The theory of a universally applicable law has its roots in monotheism and in the Roman law of nations, but it is the position of non-Christian minorities in Europe that has enabled scholars to understand the emergence of the concept of universal civil and human rights.[5] As a result, Berman and R. Po-Chia Hsia have developed new approaches that see the law not as immutable and rigid, but as dynamic and flexible. According to Berman:

> [A] social theory of law should stress the interaction of spirit and matter, of ideas and experience, in its definition and analysis of law. It should bring the three traditional schools of [western] jurisprudence--the political school (positivism), the moral school (natural-law theory), and the historical school (historical jurisprudence)--together in an integrative jurisprudence.[6]

In addition, Berman calls for the adoption of "a historiography that is appropriate to legal history, rather than a historiography that is derived principally from economic history, the history of philosophy, or other kinds of history."[7] The task is to integrate normative with practical law and to put that into a comparative framework based on a universal paradigm, untethered to a particular type of law or region.

---

4. Harold J. Berman, *Law and Revolution: The Formation of the Western Legal Tradition* (Cambridge, 1983); see also R. Po-chia Hsia, *The Myth of Ritual Murder: Jews and Magic in Reformation Germany* (New Haven, 1988).
5. See Judith Mandalsohn (sic) Rood, "Government, Law, and Family: Muhammad Ali, Marriage, and Procreation in Syria, 1835," *Archiv Orientalni: Quarterly Journal of African and Asian Studies (Czech Republic), Supplementa VIII: Proceedings of the XII Congress of CIEPO, 1996* (1998): 317-30, for analysis of the legal aspects of Mehmed Ali's rebellion; see also Abdullahi Ahmed an-Na'im, *Toward an Islamic Reformation: Civil Liberties, Human Rights, and International Law* (Syracuse, 1990) on current work on modern Islamic judicial theory; Amira El-Azhary Sonbol, "Questioning Exceptionalism: *Sharī'a* Law," *Arab Studies Journal* (1998): 76-86, on the reasons why both the academy and the ulema have treated Muslims and Islamic law as essentially different.
6. Berman, *Law and Revolution*, p. 44. To do so, he analyzes the first modern western legal system, the canon law of the Roman Catholic Church, which he characterizes as "having many characteristics in common with what contemporary social theorists call the secular, rational, materialistic, individualistic legal systems of liberal capitalist society."
7. Ibid.

The administrative law of the Ottoman Empire was embedded in the divinely revealed Islamic law, as it had been interpreted by Sunni legal traditions dating back to the Ayyubid period (1171-1250 C.E.). The sultan, as sovereign, possessed the authority to interpret this law in order to provide justice to his subjects. The sovereign was understood to represent divine authority through his adherence to the *şeriat*; he governed his people using the administrative law codified in the sixteenth century by Sultan Süleyman I. Any representative of the sovereign would be accepted by the people so long as he was perceived as being obedient to the sultan's will and thus to the *şeriat*. If a provincial governor were to rebel against the sultan, then justice could no longer be provided. Because the sultan, as the final arbiter of justice, had the prerogative to impose the death sentence for political offenses not stipulated in the *şeriat*, he could put to death anyone who rebelled against him. The sultan was the law to his subjects so long as he acted within it.

As imperialism began to drive western relations with the Ottoman Empire, the long history underpinning civil political life in Europe was discarded. The mentality of Holy War that had dominated the Crusades pervaded European thought long after the Middle Ages; initially both the Napoleonic regime and the British Foreign Office claimed to have a civilizing mission.[8] The imperialist project began with "scientific" studies of the societies over which Europeans aspired to rule and of subjects who were believed not capable of possessing the same inherent human civil, legal, and political rights as Europeans. While some romantic nationalists championed Greek nationalism, most nineteenth-century politicians dismissed the possibility of immediately extending political rights to peoples who were seen as ill-equipped to rule themselves until liberated or converted from Islam. This bias prevented the politicians from discerning the changes taking place in the political culture of the Ottoman Empire.

To understand the changes and the meaning of Mehmed Ali's actions in an Ottoman context, we must delve into the history of the political and legal institutions of the Ottoman Empire.[9] At the same time, we must consider Mehmed Ali's own

---

8. Suffice it to say that there still were significant differences in the history of the regions under their respective rules.

9. Halil İnalcık, "The Nature of Traditional Society: Turkey," in İnalcık, *The Ottoman Empire: Conquest, Organization, and Economy* (London, 1978), p. 54. For literature covering the subject of notables, see also Albert Hourani, "Ottoman Reform and the Politics of Notables," in Hourani, *The Emergence of the Modern Middle East* (Berkeley, 1981), p. 166; Abraham Marcus, *The Middle East on the Eve of Modernity: Aleppo in the Eighteenth Century* (New York, 1989); Bruce Masters, *The Origins of Western Economic Dominance in the Middle East: Mercantilism and the Islamic Economy of Aleppo, 1600-1750* (New York, 1988); idem, "The 1850 Events in Aleppo: An Aftershock of Syria's Incorporation into the Capitalist World System," *International Journal of Middle East Studies* 22 (1990): 3-20; Deena A. Sadat, "Rumeli Ayanları: The Eighteenth Century," *Journal of Modern History*, 59 (1987): 346-63; Ruth Roded, "The Syrian Urban Notables: Elite, Estates, Class?" *Asian and African Studies*, 20 (1986): 375-84; Kenneth M. Cuno, "Egypt's Wealthy Peasantry, 1740-1820: A Study of the Region of al-Mansura," in Tarif Khalidi, ed., *Land Tenure and Social Transformation in the Middle East* (Beirut, 1984); Linda Schatkowski Schilcher, *Families in*

political and socioeconomic origins.

Growing up in the Balkans in the 1780s, Mehmed Ali absorbed a Napoleonic attitude toward modernization and the uses of political and religious rhetoric. His early years coincided with the political upheaval in the Balkans that followed the Napoleonic invasions of southern Europe, well before Bonaparte invaded Egypt. Rebellions and revolts in the European provinces of the Ottoman Empire resulted in great shifts of populations as refugees from the fighting between the Ottomans and the Europeans redrew political boundaries. During this time, many Muslim Albanians moved from the Balkans to Egypt and Anatolia, where they joined the Ottoman armies. Under these changing circumstances, Mehmed Ali emerged as a leader.

A keen observer, Mehmed Ali had imbibed the lessons of European balance-of-power politics and the promises of mercantilism. He derived his own new approach to the issue of reform in the Ottoman Empire from the promulgations and decrees of the Napoleonic regimes in southern Europe, French and British gunboat diplomacy, and Russian expansionism. It was easy, he concluded, to don new trappings of power and to adopt a positivist technological epistemology to underpin measures of control and rule.

In the Ottoman Empire, political thought had turned to nationalism and the political rights of Ottoman subjects with the outbreak of the Greek and Serbian rebellions. Many western observers attributed interest in these issues to the influx of western nationalist ideas into the empire. Questions of legitimacy and power, however, were deeply embedded in the Sunni Islamic political theory of the just ruler, which already had found its best expression in the fourteenth century, during another time of great instability, despotism, and rapid change. Long familiar with the Circle of Equity or Circle of Justice that had been absorbed into the classic Sunni theory of just rule, Ottoman intellectuals concurred that only obedience to Islamic law ensured justice and tranquility--the common good. The North African historian and political theorist Ibn Khaldun, among others, articulated this concept in his

---

Politics: Damascene Factions and Estates of the Eighteenth and Nineteenth Centuries (Stuttgart, 1985); Judith E. Tucker, *Women in Nineteenth-Century Egypt* (Cambridge, 1985); 'Adel Manna', "The Sancak of Jerusalem between Two Invasions, 1798-1831," unpublished Ph.D. thesis, Hebrew University of Jerusalem, 1986; Haim Gerber, "*Sharī'a, Kanun*, and Custom in the Ottoman Law: The Court Records of Seventeenth-Century Bursa," *International Journal of Turkish Studies* 2:1 (1981): 131-47; idem, *Ottoman Rule in Jerusalem: 1890-1914* (Berlin, 1985); idem, *Social Origins of the Middle East* (Boulder, CO, 1987); Amnon Cohen, *Jewish Life under Islam: Jerusalem in the Sixteenth Century* (Cambridge, MA, 1984); Leila Tarazi Fawaz, *Merchants and Migrants in Nineteenth-Century Beirut* (Cambridge, MA, 1983); Ehud Toledano, *State and Society in Mid-Nineteenth Century Egypt* (Cambridge, 1990); Amy Singer, *Palestinian Peasants and Ottoman Officials: Rural Administration around Sixteenth-Century Jerusalem* (Cambridge, 1994) (see also my review of this book in *Journal of Near Eastern Studies* 59 (2000): 61-63); Jane Hathaway, *The Politics of Households in Ottoman Egypt: The Rise of the Qazdağlıs* (Cambridge, 1997); Dina Rizk Khoury, *State and Provincial Society in the Ottoman Empire: Mosul, 1540-1834* (Cambridge, 1997).

Muqaddima, using al-Mas'udi's story of the Persian King Bahram bin Bahram to make his point. The King's chief religious advisor admonished his sovereign:

> O King, the might of royal authority materializes only through the religious law, obedience toward God, and compliance with His commands and prohibitions. The religious law persists only through royal authority. Mighty royal authority is achieved only through men. Men persist only with the help of property. The only way to property is through cultivation. The only way to cultivation is through justice. Justice is a balance set up among mankind. The Lord set it up and appointed an overseer of it, and that is the ruler.[10]

The lesson of the story, according to Ibn Khaldun, "is that injustice ruins civilizations."[11] The classic conception of just rule in Sunni Islamic political theory traces the connections among power, universal law, and justice. Consequently, when the ruler no longer rules justly--when he lets good lands lie uncultivated, imposes unjust taxes, confiscates property, imposes forced labor or other illegal duties--the subjects of the kingdom will flee, as is their right when faced with injustice. There will be no money to pay the soldiers needed for defense, and neighboring rulers will attack, unseating the king and killing his subjects.

During the seventeenth and eighteenth centuries, the Ottoman Empire had become increasingly decentralized. The Porte had managed its extensive realms by allowing provincial magnates (the *ayan*) great autonomy, but in the eighteenth century, these provincial grandees had became tyrants, oppressing Ottoman taxpayers (the *reaya*) and forging alliances with enemies of the Porte in order to win their own independence. From the disastrous Russo-Ottoman War of 1768-74 through the Napoleonic invasion of Egypt and Syria in 1798-99, the Ottomans struggled to find new approaches to defending the empire. The destruction of the Janissaries in 1826 and the abolition of the *timar* system signaled the end of the classical Ottoman military system by which the empire had been ruled since the sixteenth century.

The destruction of the Janissaries left the question of legitimacy wide open. As provincial militia-based households led by members of the tax-paying classes struggled to find their place in the emerging political and military culture, the Porte and the provinces contended with internal and external pressures, beginning a process that led to the Tanzimat. In these fluid times, the Sunni political system articulated by the Ottomans was challenged by increasing demands from provincial elites to share in political legitimacy.[12]

---

10. Ibn Khaldun, *The Muqaddimah: An Introduction to History*, trans. Franz Rosenthal (Princeton, 1967), II: 104-10.
11. Ibid.
12. I have dealt with this aspect of the issue in "The Beginning of the End of Sunni

Mehmed Ali's mutinies must be viewed against the larger background of center-periphery relations within the empire. Mahmud II attempted to end the decentralization that had allowed for the emergence of autonomous provincial leadership in Anatolia, the Balkans, and the Middle East, starting to suppress the regional notables (*ayan*) in 1812. He began with the *derebeys* in the provinces--the paşas of Diyarbakır, Urfa, Mardin, Mosul, Baghdad, and Bosnia, as well as Scutari in Albania--and ultimately turned to Ali Paşa of Janina. An Albanian like Mehmed Ali, in his day Ali Paşa was a man of great fame, admired by Europeans such as Victor Hugo and Lord Byron, and his struggles with the Porte were a *cause célèbre* in Europe.[13]

Ali Paşa, born in Tepelene in 1740, was appointed governor of Janina, the old Epirus, in 1788. In his youth, he was a brigand, and for some twenty years he led a band of robbers in the vicinity of Thessaly and southern Albania. When he consented to help the Porte suppress his former comrades-in-arms, he was named paşa of Trikkala. In 1788, he conquered the rebellious town of Janina for the Porte. At the time, with a population estimated at 30,000, it was the most important town in Albania, if not in the whole greater region, including modern-day Greece. Under Ali Paşa, the regions of southern Albania and western Greece flourished commercially, as did the Galilee under another *ayan* leader, Zahir al-'Umar, at approximately the same time.

In 1797, Napoleon was expanding French control over Dalmatia and southern Italy and began stirring up trouble in the Balkans by occupying the Ionian Islands. The Ottomans allied themselves with England and Russia, declaring war on France, but Ali Paşa never reached an understanding with the Russians, who, during this war, fomented rebellion among the Suliot people of Albania, a large, independent Christian tribe. After Ali Paşa wiped out the Suliots in a merciless six-year campaign, the Ottomans dubbed him *arslan*, or "lion". The defeat of the Suliots was so complete that it climaxed with the act that ended the entire tragedy: the surviving

---

Preeminence: Muhammad Ali and Jerusalem, 1834," *Arab Studies Journal* 4 (1996): 86-95.
13. I am indebted to Miranda Vickers' excellent work *The Albanians: A Modern History* (New York, 1997), pp. 18-24, for information on Ali Paşa. However, in her rendition of Ottoman history in Albania, Vickers mistakenly writes that in 1757, the feudal lord Mehmed Bey Bushati, the father of Kara Mahmud, "inspired by the achievements of the Albanian founder of modern Egypt, Muhammad Ali Pasha," appointed himself overlord of the region of Shkoder. This is clearly impossible. Vickers probably had in mind Bulut Kapan Ali Bey al-Kabīr, who dominated Egypt during the 1760s and rebelled against the sultan in 1768, minting his own coins and having the *hutbe* said in his name--although Ali Bey was not Albanian but Georgian or Abkhazian. Indeed, Ali Bey is often named as another precursor to Mehmed Ali. Still, the date 1757 remains problematic. For information on Bulut Kapan Ali Bey and military households in Ottoman-Egyptian history, see Hathaway, *Politics of Households*, esp. pp. 47-48; I concur with Hathaway that Bulut Kapan Ali Bey was not a precursor of Mehmed Ali Paşa. See also Lord Byron's famous poem "Childe Harold's Pilgrimage," which has been published in many editions. Also recommended for the history of the Balkans during the last years of Ottoman rule is William Miller, *The Ottoman Empire and Its Successors, 1801-1922* (Cambridge, 1923).

Suliot women hurled first their children and then themselves over a precipice in the Zalongue mountains rather than be taken hostage.

Now considered the strongest man in southern Albania and Greece, if not in all the Balkans, in 1805, Ali Paşa sought an alliance with the English against the Russians. The Russians were determined to maintain their support for the Orthodox Christians and the Slavs, and in the same year the Treaty of Pressburg gave them this right in the Balkans. The Ottomans, meanwhile, appointed Ali Paşa's sons to the governorates of the Morea and Lepanto. By 1809, the Paşa was emboldened to seize the "granary of Albania" and its fortress city Berat, putting his son in charge, and in the following year, he occupied other adjoining districts.

According to Miranda Vickers, as he neared the peak of his powers, Ali Paşa became a member of the Bektaşi sufi order. The same order to which the Janissaries belonged, it was considered by the Ottomans to have heretical Shi'ite leanings.[14] By 1820, Ali Paşa was firmly in control of the entire region and began to endow mosques and churches, build fortifications, and finance other improvements to ready the region for conflict against the Ottomans.

After the Porte summarily dismissed Ali Paşa from his office, he came out in support of Greek independence. He used the Greek revolutionary group Philiki Etairia to rally men and local support, and by 1821 as many as 7,000 Greek fighters had named him their leader. When these same men surrendered, they left him besieged at his palatial garrison in Janina, where he was killed and beheaded. His severed head, along with those of his sons, was displayed in Istanbul. Victor Hugo lamented him as the "only colossus and man of genius of his time, worthy to be compared with Napoleon."[15]

Mehmed Ali Paşa, better than anyone, could understand the internal and international significance of Ali Paşa's achievements and his devastating end. Ironically, Mahmud II ordered Mehmed Ali to suppress the Greek rebellion following the execution of Ali Paşa, little realizing the lessons his commander had learned.

Mehmed Ali had a long, complex, and difficult relationship with the Ottoman Porte before he mutinied. Perhaps the venom in this relationship can be traced back to Mehmed Ali's earliest victory in Egypt. His Albanian irregulars had combined with the Mamluks of Egypt to defeat the Ottoman governor of Cairo, Hüsrev Paşa. Despite this loss, Hüsrev, a product of the imperial palace school and thus a member of the classical institution of imperial servants, eventually would become grand vezir after the death of Mahmud II. In 1826, he was charged with the reorganization of the Ottoman armies following the liquidation of the Janissaries. But resentment of his rival Hüsrev was not the only source of Mehmed Ali's problems with the Porte.[16]

---

14. Vickers, *The Albanians*, p. 22.
15. Ibid., pp. 21, 23.
16. Henry Dodwell, *The Founder of Modern Egypt: A Study of Muhammad Ali* (Cambridge, 1931), pp. 9-15; İnalcık, "The Nature of Traditional Society," p. 54; idem, "Hüsrev Paşa," *İslam Ansiklopedisi*, V: 609-16; Fahmy, *All the Pasha's Men*, pp. 41, 56-57, 66, 79-81, 272-

Mehmed Ali understood that as he was not a part of the ruling class, he would always be inferior to the *kapı kulları*, the sultan's servants. His rise to power within the Ottoman system was rooted in the tradition of *reaya* who had entered the military establishment as members of military households. Belonging to the social category of provincial magnates, like Abdullah Paşa and two recent Ottoman governors of Acre, Süleyman Paşa and Cezzar Ahmed Paşa, Mehmed Ali was not a product of the palace schools. He was the son of the commander of a governor's small militia in the little Macedonian seaport of Kavala, so his education was limited, though he was experienced in trade, shipping, and the practicalities of military life. He started out as just another of the many young Albanian mercenaries who joined the Ottoman army during the Napoleonic wars, but Mehmed Ali became one of the shrewdest, most innovative paşas in the history of the Ottoman Empire.

In 1828 Sultan Mahmud II faced three grave threats. The first and most immediate was Russia, the second was the French encroachment in North Africa, and the third was that of Mehmed Ali, who had risen to power in Egypt by helping to expel Bonaparte. The Porte subsequently had depended upon his abilities to subdue the Wahhabis and then the Greeks, enabling him to build both a powerful navy and an experienced army. Now it could not afford to unseat the ambitious governor of Cairo.

Mehmed Ali had officially voiced an interest in governing the Syrian provinces as early as his successes in the Hijaz in 1822. In return for his service to the Porte in Greece from 1825-27, he again requested the governorship of Syria but received only that of Crete. After the naval rout of the Ottoman forces at Navarino (20 October 1827), Mehmed Ali was finally convinced that even his military effectiveness could not transcend the fact that he was an upstart. He also realized that the sultan's new westernized armies, equipment, and advisors still would not be enough to overcome the Russian threat or to oust him from Cairo. Mehmed Ali's son Ibrahim Paşa had lost fifty-three ships and 6,000 men in the battle of Navarino. In complete dismay, Mehmed Ali ordered the withdrawal of his own forces from the Morea on 9 August 1828. On that day, father and son mutinied against the sultan's orders and became rebels.

With the disastrous Ottoman defeat at Navarino, Russian pressures on Istanbul intensified. The previous year, Russia had compelled the Ottomans to accept the Convention of Akkerman, which confirmed the provisions of the Treaty of Bucharest (1812) establishing the Russo-Ottoman border at the Pruth River and ceding to St. Petersburg Bessarabia, with its access to the mouth of the Danube. In addition, the Porte now had to give up some Asiatic fortresses and grant autonomy to the Serbs, who had won the right to hereditary rule in 1826, the Moldavians, and

---

73, 285-90, 300-01, 304. According to Dror Ze'evi, Hüsrev Paşa's active involvement during the Tanzimat period with the abolition of slavery can be seen as the logical culmination of the contradiction between the military *kul* and the military *reaya* personified respectively by Hüsrev Paşa and Mehmed Ali Paşa. *Proceedings of the XII Congress of CIEPO, 1996* (1998): 411-16. See also Ehud Toledano, *Slavery and Abolition in the Ottoman Middle East* (Seattle, 1998); Y. Hakan Erdem, *Slavery in the Ottoman Empire and Its Demise* (New York, 1996).

the Wallachians. Because the loss of the Ottoman fleet at Navarino left Russia the only naval power in the Black Sea, the sultan decided not to wait for the inevitable Russian assault and declared war on Russia in the winter of 1828. Plagued with poor military intelligence, treacherous commanders, and bad judgment, Mahmud II was forced to negotiate the Treaty of Adrianople in the autumn of 1829.

One year after confirming Mehmed Ali Paşa's government in Cairo, Sultan Selim III (1789-1807) had attempted to transfer him to Salonika, about 150 miles away from his hometown of Kavala. Mehmed Ali stayed in Cairo, declining the assignment. Mehmed Ali's acrimonious relationship with Istanbul continued throughout his years of service to the sultan. In 1805, as governor of Egypt, with his son Ibrahim Paşa as his commander-in-chief, Mehmed Ali had defeated the Wahhabis in Medina and restored Mecca to Ottoman control. As a result, Muslim pilgrims could once again undertake the *hacc*. This victory fueled Mehmed Ali's ambitions and increased his importance as a leader in the eyes of the Muslim community.

The sultan, who may have scorned Mehmed Ali's social origins, showed no compunction about putting his remarkable military abilities to use. This contradictory policy made Mehmed Ali a unique supra-regional member of the *ayan* class. He consequently was able to transfer his military power away from his local base to a different part of the empire, a great provincial capital with the resources that could serve as the foundation for a dynasty. From Cairo, Mehmed Ali embarked upon his ultimately successful mission to gain for himself and his progeny permanent recognition from the Porte as legitimate members of the ruling class.

When Mehmed Ali invaded Syria, Abdullah Paşa, governor of the provinces of Sidon and Tripoli and the districts of Jerusalem and Nablus, summed up the Ottoman perception of the threat. In a letter assuring the district governor in Jerusalem that the Ottoman navy was en route to the defense of Acre and the sultan's domains in Syria, Abdullah Paşa condemned Mehmed Ali in the strongest possible terms: the evil one (*al-khabūth*), the rebel (*al-khāraj*), the depraved villain (*al-shaqī al-khāsir*), and the devil (*al-la'īn*), as well as "the enemy of God" and "the enemy of the sultan." The promised help from the Ottoman admiral and the governor of Damascus, however, failed to arrive.[17]

Following Mehmed Ali's victory at the Battle of Konya and the capture of the Ottoman grand vezir Reşid Paşa on 21 December 1832, Ibrahim Paşa threatened to enter Istanbul. He treated Reşid Paşa as an honored guest, hoping to convince him to march to Istanbul at the head of the Egyptian army, depose Mahmud II, and replace him with the sultan's young son Abdülmecid. Ibrahim awaited only his father's orders before pressing on.

As a part of a long effort to find *ulema* who would justify Mehmed Ali's policies in Islamic terms, Ibrahim obtained a *fetva* in 1833. To the question, "If the *imam* of the Muslims oppressed (*jāra 'ala*) the *umma*, is it legal to depose him?" the answer was, "It is, on condition that the *umma* is composed of 12,000 men who are

---

17. *Law Court Register of Jerusalem* (*LCRJ*), defter 315, nos. 121-22 (14 Cemaziyül'evvel 1247).

all in agreement."[18] Because this number was the symbolic size of the Ottoman army sent against Mehmed Ali and defeated by him, Reşid Paşa would have fulfilled the terms of the *fetva* by agreeing to Ibrahim's scheme and leading his troops against the sultan. From this beginning, Mehmed Ali's use of Islamic law to legitimize his political aspirations became a part of the legal reforms that he initiated in the Arab provinces during the occupation of Syria.

Not only did Mehmed Ali rebel against the sultan, engaging him in warfare, occupying his lands, and seeking autonomy, but he also began to legislate new codes of law in the conquered territories. He based this law on his own political and economic policies rather than on the judicial practices and structures of the Ottoman state. In addition, he extended his personal control over endowed properties (*evkaf*) administered for the state by the local Muslim authorities.

Mehmed Ali's actions threatened the very basis of the state: its claim to legitimacy as an Islamic government. The offense to the Muslim community at first was not understood as the Syrian inhabitants perceived Mehmed Ali as just another rebellious governor. When he began to implement his policies in Syria, however, the enormity of his intentions stunned the Muslim establishment. The "spectacle" that he produced in his attempt to use western military and economic methods was clear evidence to the Muslims of Syria of the type of rule that he represented. In Islamic political philosophy the term for it was *mulk*--naked power, divorced from Divine Law.

The decrees and policies that Mehmed Ali enacted were self-consciously styled as the laws of a new polity. Initially it was called "The Just Egyptian State" (*al-dawla al-Misriyya al-'ādila*) or "The Just State" (*al-dawla al-'ādila*), but he soon referred to it as "khedival." The occupation of Syria, the rebellion that ensued, and the promulgation of a new corpus of law all marked the fundamental challenge to the Ottomans that characterized Mehmed Ali's regime in *Bilād al-Shām*.[19]

Mehmed Ali's choice of a derivative of the title khedive (Arabic, *khidīw*, Turkish *hıdiv*) for his regime in *Bilad al-Sham* is significant. From a Persian word meaning prince or lord, it was not a title used by the Ottomans for provincial governors. This member of the *ayan* was struggling to change the nature of rule in

---

18. Afaf Lutfi al-Sayyid Marsot, *Egypt in the Reign of Muhammad Ali* (New York, 1984), pp. 224-25.
19. *LCRJ*, defter 317, nos. 39, 49, 60; defter 318, nos. 70, 110; defter 320, nos. 34-35, 82, 171; defter 321, no. 234; defter 323, no. 33, spanning the years 1832-39. Sonbol lists other codes that were promulgated by Mehmed Ali in Egypt, in addition to the *Qānūn al-Filāha* (1830): the rules governing the *Majlis al-'Alī* (Supreme Council, 1825) and *Majlis al-Khāqāniyya* (Imperial Council, 1839), and two codes after winning dynastic legitimacy: *Majlis al-Tujjār* (Council of Merchants, 1846) and *Majlis al-Akām* (Council of Statutes/Legislative Assembly, 1850): Sonbol, "Questioning Exceptionalism," pp. 79-80. See also Raouf Abbas Hamed, "The *Siyasatname* and the Institutionalization of Central Administration under Muhammad Ali," in Nelly Hanna, ed., *The State and Its Servants: Administration in Egypt from Ottoman Times to the Present* (Cairo, 1995), pp. 75-86. There is still a lacuna in the history of the role of the French in legislating these codes although their influence is widely assumed in the literature.

the Ottoman Empire, to win legitimacy for an independent territory, as had the Serbs, and to establish a hereditary dynasty that would create a new form of government within the empire. Mehmed Ali, therefore, chose a title for himself and his government that would underscore both innovation and royalty. To call his khedival regime Egyptian incorrectly conveys the notion of a nation-state in Egypt during this period. The Porte did not officially confer the title khedive on the rulers of Egypt until 1867, preferring the old title of *vali*. Use of the term ended in 1914 with the end of Ottoman rule over Egypt.[20]

Mehmed Ali's invasion and occupation of Syria (1831-40) elicited two distinct responses among the Muslim inhabitants, especially those who served the Ottoman state as judicial authorities and administrators. At first, they welcomed Mehmed Ali because they disliked Abdullah Paşa and thought Mehmed Ali was just another typical Ottoman governor. By 1834, though, the Muslim elite, the nomadic tribes, and the tax-paying peasantry had realized that they were dealing with a completely different kind of despot. Western reports on the rebellions of 1834 in Jerusalem and throughout Syria were articulated in terms of political rights and sound as though they were written by English-speaking revolutionaries. Actually, the Muslims were responding to contraventions of Ottoman law and practice.

Mehmed Ali meant to control Egypt and to protect his family and its wealth. He shrewdly applied the economic and political lessons he had learned in the Balkans at the time of the Napoleonic invasions in southern Europe. The Serbian revolution of 1804 had ended with independence; the Greek rebellion had culminated in the execution of Ali Paşa. For Mehmed Ali, there was no political process that would allow him to secure his position for life. Nor was there any option but violence for the Porte to rein in the ambitions of the rebellious provincial governor. Mehmed Ali had no alternative to mutiny if he wanted to survive. Then, only victory in war and the support of European diplomats could secure his aims. He took the risk that international political competition in the Near East would work in his favor. Because it did, he was able to secure his aim: Ottoman legitimization of his dynastic rule of the Ottoman province of Egypt.

The roots of Mehmed Ali's rebellion lie deep in the political and legal history of the Ottoman Empire. A long period of administrative transformation throughout the empire culminated in the early nineteenth century; the next stage was the age of reform. The pressures exerted on the Ottoman provincial administration by the *ayan* required enactment of a new administrative order to harness the ambitions and abilities of those powerful provincial elites. In her model of Ottoman mutiny,

---

20. Sir John Bowring, *Report on the Commercial Statistics of Syria* (London, 1840); J.N. Spyridon, ed., *Annals of Palestine: 1821-1841--A Manuscript by the Monk Neophytus of Cyprus* (Jerusalem, 1938); J.C.B. Richmond, *Egypt, 1798-1952: Her Advance towards a Modern Identity* (New York, 1977), pp. 31-70; Robert Hunter, *Egypt under the Khedives, 1805-1879* (Pittsburgh, 1984). On Mehmed Ali's efforts to find support among the ulema, see Daniel N. Crecelius and Hamza Abd al-Aziz Badr, *Ta'rīkh al-wazīr Muhammad 'Alī Bāshā li-Shaykh Khalīl ibn Ahmad al-Rajabī* (Cairo, 1996) and idem, "*Ta'rīkh al-wazīr Muhammad 'Alī Bāshā*," in *Proceedings of the XII Congress of CIEPO, 1996* (1998): 101-10.

Palmira Brummett emphasizes that mutineers were members of the military-administrative classes, including provincial governors. They rebelled against the authority of the sultan primarily "to advance their positions and augment their wealth and power." Although the punishment for such rebellion was death, Brummett finds that often the process of mutiny began with a series of complaints and threats and concluded with "negotiation and compromise rather than punishment."[21]

Mehmed Ali was brought back into the Ottoman fold precisely through negotiation and compromise after the British sided with the Ottomans and threatened him with naval attack. His decision to use force against the sultan enabled him to push the Porte into accepting his autonomy, but he gave up his aspirations for an enlarged Egyptian state upon the death of Mahmud II and the ascension of Abdülmecid. Mehmed Ali accepted his duties to the new sultan once the Porte recognized his role as the Ottoman governor of Egypt and his right to pass that office on to his sons. This signified the creation of a new kind of authority in the Middle East and the vindication of the entire political class of the *ayan*.

The Khedive's tomb is in the Alabaster Mosque in Cairo, which demonstrates Mehmed Ali's unique relationship to both Islam and Europe more vividly than any other lasting monument. The mosque is Ottoman in architectural style but European in decoration. It is unheard of for a Muslim to be buried inside a mosque, while it is quite usual for European kings to be entombed in cathedrals. That statement sums up Mehmed Ali's complex relationship to both Islam and the West.

The pressures for change within the political culture of the Ottoman Empire were even stronger than the pressures from the West for legal reform in the empire. In the provinces, a long period of administrative change rooted in the eighteenth century and the emergence of provincial notables produced tension between the center and periphery of the empire. These provincial magnates never formed a conscious political class, but they took part in the processes that governed their rise and fall.

Mehmed Ali is the epitome of the provincial *ayan* in Ottoman history. An individual who straddled the early modern and modern periods, he rose to leadership through traditional service in the provincial militias, then manipulated the system to achieve his own ends. In contrast to other *ayan* leaders, he asserted his power in the occupied territories by promulgating a distinctive administrative law code that was sanctioned by the rhetoric of Islamic law and meant to supersede the code of the Ottomans.

---

21. Palmira Brummett, "Classifying Ottoman Mutiny: The Act and Vision of Rebellion," *Turkish Studies Association Bulletin* 22:1 (1998): 91-107. Karen Barkey, *Bandits and Bureaucrats: The Ottoman Route to State Centralization* (Ithaca and London, 1994), has shown how the Ottoman state dealt with autonomous "bandits" in a flexible way in order to make use of their abilities and resources to carry out state policies in the sixteenth and seventeenth centuries. While Mehmed Ali was a different sort of autonomous leader, the way that the Porte dealt with him was similar in many respects to the way it had dealt with some of the Celali leaders described by Barkey.

By placing discussion of Mehmed Ali's rebellion in the context of legal history, we can understand the reason for it: the culmination of the centuries-long political struggle of the tax-paying class--the *reaya*--to gain political legitimacy in the Ottoman Empire. By treating Islamic law and politics as flexible, evolving, and creative, we move farther away from the constraints of Middle Eastern or Islamic exceptionalism. The mutiny and rebellion in Syria during the 1830s were not limited to resisting authority or exerting control. Rather, they tested the limits of legitimacy and identity, of belonging and rule. This successful provincial rebellion thus marks the beginning of a modern struggle over authority and legitimacy in the Arab provinces of the Ottoman Empire.

William Tyndale College

Khaled Fahmy

MUTINY IN MEHMED ALI'S NEW *NIZAMÎ* ARMY, APRIL-MAY 1824

In April 1824, shortly after introducing conscription to round up men for his new army, Mehmed Ali, governor of Egypt for over eighteen years, faced a momentous challenge to his authority. A huge rebellion erupted in Upper Egypt and soon engulfed all villages and towns between Qus and Isne. It was led by the apparently charismatic Şeyh Ahmed, who is reported to have succeeded in rallying nearly 30,000 men and women around him in clear and daring defiance of Mehmed Ali's authority. The şeyh revealed himself to be the long-awaited *Mehdi*, declared that Mehmed Ali was an infidel, and urged his mostly peasant followers to attack the Paşa's provincial officials. Looting and arson on a large scale ensued, and in numerous towns, peasants marched into the residences of local officials, set fire to public buildings, and occasionally took officials prisoner.[1]

After a couple of weeks the rebellion showed no signs of abating. When it threatened to spread to villages in Middle Egypt to the north, Mehmed Ali finally decided to send some of his newly formed troops to deal decisively with the danger. This was a very serious decision, indeed, as most of the troops had been conscripted from the same villages in which they were now sent to fight. As it happened, the troops managed to quell the uprising at an enormous cost. Four thousand people were reported to have been killed in the month-long revolt that spread to the army itself, requiring severe action to stop it from engulfing more units. What follows is an investigation of this particular "mutiny" aspect of the rebellion.

Mehmed Ali, in dealing with the unprecedented challenge to his authority, evidently decided to differentiate between the peasants and the soldiers who took part in the disturbances. The peasants were seen as rebels and were punished with an equal measure of intimidation and terror, but there was an attempt to deal with the officers and soldiers who had sided with the peasants as military men who defied military authority and, therefore, had to be court-martialed.

We will trace the series of events that led to the mass rebellion in our effort to understand its causes and to see the options available to Mehmed Ali. Because the sources used below are necessarily those of Mehmed Ali and his military machine, this paper raises the methodological question of whether it is possible to "salvage" the voice of the peasant-soldier. "Can the subaltern speak?" thus is a question to be

---

1. Ma'iyya Saniyya-Turkī: S/1/48/1, letter no. 236, 7 Şaban 1239/7 April 1824. This letter and, unless stated otherwise, all subsequent archival material are from Dār al-Wathā'iq al-Qawmiyya (the Egyptian National Archives), Cairo. *Ma'iyya Saniyya*, literally "exalted entourage," refers to Mehmed Ali's cabinet.

taken literally in order to avoid viewing events from the perspective of the commanding general and inevitably reproducing his logic.

It must be stated at the outset that Mehmed Ali had faced a previous significant threat from his military forces. In August 1815, before he had begun conscripting Arabic-speaking peasants, he was confronted with a rebellion by his Albanian troops, who constituted the backbone of his military strength. Counting nearly as mercenaries within the larger Ottoman contingents that had brought them and Mehmed Ali to Egypt in 1801, the Arnavuts, as they were known, were not a very orderly body of troops. They often revolted in small uprisings in the streets of Cairo, claiming their delayed pay and demanding to be returned home. They also retained their tribal structure and recognized Mehmed Ali only as a "first among equals," resisting all his attempts to impose discipline.

In August 1815 the Paşa decided to impose order on the troops and "to put their pay and expenses under an organized principle" (*rābıta ve nizām*).[2] Influenced by Ibrahim Ağa, who had recently arrived from Istanbul,[3] the Paşa gathered his Albanian soldiers in Maydan al-Rumayla at the foot of the Citadel for target exercises. For over three hours, the soldiers fired their guns in "successive volleys, making a thundery noise like the French." The following day, it was rumored that the Paşa wanted to take a count of the soldiers and "to train them according to *al-nizām al-jadīd*, copying the positions of the French. He wanted them to put on tight clothes and to change their appearance (*ughayyir shaklahum*)."[4]

The attempt was a complete disaster. The soldiers reluctantly complied with the Paşa's orders on the first day, only to conspire to kill him on the following night. The Paşa was informed of the plot in time to escape, but when the rebels realized that their conspiracy had been foiled, they rampaged through the streets of Cairo, looting markets and damaging property. Mehmed Ali was able to placate the merchants and the populace only by returning their stolen property or compensating them for the damages.[5]

As for the Albanian soldiers, Mehmed Ali decided to get rid of them, but not by massacre, the method he had used against the Mamluks four years earlier. Instead, when Sultan Mahmud II (1808-39) ordered him to fight the Wahhabis in Arabia, Mehmed Ali saw a golden opportunity to get rid of many troublesome groups, foremost among them the Albanians. During the seven-year conflict against the Wahhabis, he consequently sent wave after wave of Albanians to face their destiny in the barren deserts of Arabia.[6]

---

2. Bahr Barra, box no. 4, document no. 149, 30 Ramazan 1230/5 September 1815.
3. P.M. Hamont, *L'Égypte sous Méhémet-Ali* (Paris, 1843), II: 4.
4. 'Abd al-Rahman al-Jabarti, *'Ajā'ib al-athār fī'l-tarājim wa'l-akhbār* (Cairo, 1880), IV: 222 (events of Şaban 1230).
5. Dhawāt, box no. 1, document no. 76, 1 Ramazan 1230/7 August 1815; al-Jabarti, *'Ajā'ib al-athār*, IV: 223-25; Félix Mengin, *Histoire de l'Égypte sous le gouvernement de Mohammed-Aly* (Paris, 1823), II: 49-50; J.J. Halls, *The Life and Correspondence of Henry Salt* (London, 1834), I: 445.
6. J. Heyworth-Dunne, *An Introduction to the History of Education in Modern Egypt* (London, 1938), p. 111; 'Abd al-Rahman al-Rafi'i, *'Asr Muhammad 'Alī* (Cairo, 1989), p.

Having managed to escape the Albanians' challenge by the skin of his teeth, Mehmed Ali became even more aware of how precarious his situation in Egypt was. He could not forget that he had been appointed to the lucrative *vilâyet* against the wish of Ottoman Sultan Selim III (1789-1807), who even tried to dislodge him by offering him the *vilâyet* of Salonika in 1806, only one year after his investiture as *vali* of Egypt. Nor could he forget that Mahmud II shared Selim's view that Mehmed Ali was a strong *vali* who had to be constrained if not removed. The *ferman* for Mehmed Ali to settle the menacing Wahhabi threat in Arabia, which Mahmud issued soon after his accession, was a clear attempt to embroil the *vali* in the quagmire and drain him of strength. Instead of weakening him, however, the Arabian campaign increased the fame of Mehmed Ali in the Ottoman Empire.

After capturing the Holy Cities of Mecca and Medina in January-February 1813, Mehmed Ali successfully restarted the pilgrimage, which had been suspended for a number of years. A few months later he sent a certain Latif Ağa to Istanbul to present the keys of the Holy Cities to the sultan in a clear gesture of obedience and submission, but Mahmud was not taken in. On the contrary, it was rumored that the sultan attempted to stage a palace coup to get rid of Mehmed Ali, not only giving Latif the title of paşa but also encouraging him to rebel against his master in Egypt. When Latif returned to Cairo, there were rumors that he intended to replace Mehmed Ali as *vali* of Egypt. Although the news of the conspiracy soon reached Mehmed Ali in Arabia, where he had taken personal command of his troops, he was not able to rush back because of pressing military matters. It was left to his trusted deputy Mehmed Lazoğlu (known in Egypt as Lazughli) to take personal revenge against Latif and have him beheaded at the foot of the Citadel.[7] Meanwhile, the sultan's actions had made Mehmed Ali acutely aware that he needed a stronger and more loyal military force to withstand other attempts by Istanbul to dislodge him.

Wary of conscripting local Egyptian peasants, both because of their questionable loyalty to him and because of the negative impact conscription might have on agricultural production, the Paşa set his eye on the Sudan. In 1820, two large expeditions of nearly 4,000 troops each were dispatched to Dongola and Kurdufan, but both proved disastrous. Mehmed Ali's son Ismail, who headed one of the expeditions, was inexperienced, indecisive, stubborn, and uncharismatic. His troops deserted him in a steady stream until his brutality, rashness, and impetuous nature ultimately cost him his own life. Moreover, because of the improvised manner in which the campaign was conducted and the lack of effective transportation, thousands of slaves perished before ever reaching Egypt. Even more staggering was the fact that out of a total of 20,000 slaves who finally did make it to Aswan in 1824, only 3,000 survived; the rest perished "like sheep with the rot."[8]

Having lost his own son and failed to raise the men required for his intended

---

121.
7. Al-Jabarti, *'Ajā'ib al-athār*, IV: 181-83 (events of Zilhicce 1228); Sir John G. Wilkinson, *Modern Egypt and Thebes* (London, 1843), II: 534. Cf. al-Rafi'i, *'Asr Muhammad 'Alī*, pp. 138-40.
8. Henry Dodwell, *The Founder of Modern Egypt* (Cambridge, 1931), pp. 64-65.

new army, Mehmed Ali realized that the Sudan campaign was a complete failure when he was informed that a large number of his Turkish-speaking officers were about to desert the campaign and return *en masse* to Egypt. He then wrote to the governor of one of the Upper Egyptian provinces that "since the Turks are members of our race and since they must be spared the trouble of being sent to remote and dangerous areas, it has become necessary to conscript around 4,000 men from Upper Egypt [to replace them]." These troops, he explained, were to be drafted for a period of three years, after which they would be given stamped certificates and allowed to return to their villages.[9] This regiment from Upper Egypt formed the nucleus of Mehmed Ali's army, which, in little over ten years' time, would number an impressive 130,000 troops.

One important characteristic of the new army was its ethnic composition. Arabic-speaking peasants, the bulk of the soldiery, were forcibly rounded up from their villages along the Nile, but their commanders were entirely Turkish-speaking. Strict orders prohibited the Arabic-speaking peasants from ever being promoted above the rank of *yüzbaşı*, i.e., captain. This system had a double aim. First, it was intended to attract men from all over the Ottoman world to serve under Mehmed Ali and his expanding household. Through these positions and others in the rapidly expanding civilian bureaucracy a loyal elite was being cemented around the persons of the Paşa and his family. Second, it was also aimed at preventing leaders from among the Arabic-speaking masses from challenging the Paşa's rule.

The peasants were, by far, the overwhelming majority of the Arabic-speaking masses, so it was believed crucial to keep them meek and submissive. In addition to jeopardizing agricultural production by the displacement of thousands of men, however, conscription was arming the peasantry at a time when resentment of the government's harsh policies was at its peak. By the 1820s, the Paşa had extended his monopolies to most of the staple foodstuffs as well as to several cash crops that the peasants used to cultivate and trade. As a result, the peasants were often required to grow crops that could be sold only to government warehouses at prices fixed by the Paşa and then to buy back the very crops they had grown at considerably higher prices. This system was implemented with extreme severity and harshness. Furthermore, to undertake his numerous and often ambitious public works, the Paşa had a much wider recourse to *corvée*. Peasants were not only forced to work without pay on various public works projects for longer and longer periods each year, but they also were forced to work on projects outside their village holdings and often outside their provinces altogether. As if this were not enough, to finance his various projects, the Paşa had increased the land tax to such a degree that by the 1820s the countryside had reached its upper limit.

Because the countryside could not withstand yet more pressure, the decision to conscript the peasants had repercussions that threatened Mehmed Ali's authority. Immediately after he introduced conscription to Lower Egypt in 1823, a large revolt erupted in Minufiye province, northwest of Cairo. Although conscription seemingly

---

9. Ma'iyya Saniyya-Turkī: S/1/50/2, document no. 145, 25 Cemaziyül'evvel 1237/17 February 1822.

triggered the revolt, it was just the final straw on top of the excessively high taxes and the brutal manner in which they were collected. Reports from provincial governors warned the Paşa in Cairo of massive desertion of villages if the tax collectors proved to be as diligent in Lower Egypt as they had been in Upper Egypt. The governors suggested conscription be postponed until the harvest had been gathered, and recognizing the risks of coupling forced conscription with high taxation, the Paşa agreed.[10] In a further concession, twenty-two villages that were growing cotton in the Delta and all the villages that were growing rice in Mansure and Gharbiye provinces were to be exempted from conscription.[11]

The concessions came too late. When there were additional reports of trouble in Minufiye, where peasants were refusing to pay taxes and declaring revolt (*isyan*),[12] Mehmed Ali responded in a prompt and decisive manner. He summoned his leading generals to a "war council" at his palace in Shubra, at the time a northerly suburb of Cairo. Arming himself with six field cannons, he then marched on the villages and subdued the revolt in less than a week.[13] Soon thereafter, he issued firm orders for conscription to be resumed, and eventually 700 and 936 men were rounded up from the Lower Egyptian provinces of Minufiye and Mansure, respectively.[14]

The revolt in Minufiye showed the Paşa just how repulsive conscription was for the peasantry. In addition, it must have brought home how heavy were his demands on the country's manpower and the essential conflict between his desire to enhance the productive capacity of the agricultural sector and his desire to raise a conscript army. Nevertheless, his deeply felt insecurity in his tenure as *vali* of Egypt made these demands necessary; once the decision to conscript the peasants was taken, there was no turning back from it. Rather, the Minufiye uprising taught him that peasant resistance was inevitable and that it could be dealt with only through brute force.

If the Minufiye uprising taught Mehmed Ali not to be lenient, the events between that uprising and a second, major one in Upper Egypt less than a year later showed him that his newly formed troops could be relied upon to quell any further disturbances. Not long after dealing with the first uprising, the Paşa discovered that he had spread himself too thin. His troops in the Sudan were still having difficulties sending back the slaves they had captured; a new uprising had erupted in Asir against his government in Arabia; then the sultan issued a new *ferman* asking him for assistance in fighting the Greek "rebels" in the Morea. Moreover, on 22 March 1824, an explosion in a powder magazine inside the Citadel killed more than 4,000

---

10. Ibid.: S/1/50/4, documents no. 46, 8 Şaban 1238/20 April 1823; no. 55, 15 Şaban 1238/27 April 1823.
11. Ibid.: S/1/50/4, document no. 50, 13 Şaban 1238/25 April 1823.
12. Ibid.: S/1/50/4, documents no. 51, 13 Şaban 1238/25 April 1823; no. 63, 21 Şaban 1238/3 May 1823.
13. Ibid.: S/1/50/4, document no. 64, 21 Şaban 1238/3 May 1823.
14. Ibid.: S/1/50/4, documents no. 72, 27 Şaban 1238/9 May 1823; no. 91, 7 Ramazan 1238/18 May 1823.

people, generating rumors that it was the work of some old Albanian and Mamluk troops who were not pleased with the Paşa's introduction of the *nizamî* troops. Now the Paşa's dangerous position was being compared to that of Selim seventeen years earlier, when the sultan had attempted to get rid of the Janissaries.[15]

In dealing with all the challenges, the new troops emerged from their eighteen months' training to prove effective beyond all expectation.[16] In March 1824, there came news of an impressive victory over the Wahhabis in Asir, where a contingent of only 2,500 Egyptian infantry had defeated a Wahhabi force ten times its size.[17] Likewise, although the big explosion in the Citadel was regarded ominously by the French consul, a single battalion of the new troops rushed to the scene, isolated the powder magazine, and quickly brought the situation under control. Finally, the regiments dispatched to the Morea were so successful that they caused "as much alarm by defeating the Greeks as the Sultan had done by failing to do so."[18]

While the Paşa was receiving very encouraging news about the performance of his new troops, the event that would truly put the loyalty of those forces to the test also developed in March 1824, as a major uprising in Upper Egypt soon spread to the army itself. Like the earlier uprising in the Delta, this one was caused by excessive taxation and conscription. It might have been triggered as well by a new directive issued by the Paşa in November 1823, forbidding the new conscripts from living near their villages or engaging in any agricultural work.[19] Shortly afterward, conscription gangs were sent to the villages of Upper Egypt to gather the 12,000 men that Mehmed Ali and his staff officers had asked for.[20]

Late in March 1824, the first signs of revolt were detected near Asyut, where Şeyh Ahmed, claiming to be the *Mehdi*, surrounded himself with some 600 peasants and started attacking local officials and government storehouses. After it quickly became clear that the movement was gaining momentum, Mehmed Ali ordered one of his cavalry officers in Minye to join forces with the provincial governor of Asyut and to attack the rebels' stronghold.[21] Although he gave this provincial governor, Ahmed Paşa (Tahir?), *carte blanche* to deal with the rebels as he saw fit, Mehmed Ali added some general guidelines:

> Since these men have followed each other blindly and taken this hateful

---

15. Drovetti to Chateaubriand, 30 March 1824, in Eduard Driault, ed., *L'Expédition de Crète et de Morée (1823-1828)* (Cairo, 1930), pp. 11-12.
16. For the training of the troops, see Khaled Fahmy, *All the Pasha's Men: Mehmed Ali, His Army, and the Making of Modern Egypt* (Cambridge, 1997), pp. 92-97, 120-55.
17. Ma'iyya Saniyya-Turkī: S/1/50/4, document no. 327, 14 Receb 1239/15 March 1824; Driault, ed., *Expédition*, p. 10.
18. H.M.V. Temperley, *England and the Near East: The Crimea* (London, 1964), p. 53.
19. Ma'iyya Saniyya-Turkī: S/1/47/7, document no. 193, 21 Rebiülevvel 1239/25 November 1823.
20. Ibid.: S/1/48/1, document no 192, 25 Cemaziyü'l'ahır 1239/26 February 1824. Another 16,000 men were to be conscripted in Lower Egypt.
21. Ibid.: S/1/47/7, document no. 291, 24 Receb 1239/25 March 1824.

path [of rebellion], they certainly must be punished. This, however, is not to be done haphazardly, nor are they all to be punished severely. Rather, you have to conduct a thorough investigation in the villages of these brigands to identify the leaders of this insurrection and to hang at village entrances those who are too old to be of use in village work so that they be an example to others....As for those younger men who might be capable of bearing arms, those you should conscript....And as for the rest, they have to be warned not to follow this path in the future.[22]

The climactic confrontation with the şeyh and his followers was left to Osman Bey, the colonel of one of the earliest regiments originally ordered to go to the Sudan.[23] As he marched southward, Osman Bey confronted one of the rebel leaders, Şeyh Rıdvan, who was a follower of Şeyh Ahmed and who had with him 3,000 infantrymen and 500 cavalrymen. On 23 March, after a fierce battle, the rebels fled to the neighboring villages, followed by Osman Bey's troops. All in all, seven battles were fought during March and April between the regular troops under Osman Bey and the rebels.[24] In one battle, the number of men and women with the şeyh amounted to 20,000. When the rebellion finally started to abate and the şeyh had disappeared in the desert, a cannon was placed in every urban center between Isne and Jirja and manned by artillerymen conscripted from desert bedouin rather than from the neighboring villages.[25]

Occurring at a time when Mehmed Ali's troops were spread over various parts of the Ottoman Empire, in Arabia, the Sudan, and Morea, the uprising near Asyut was his most important challenge since securing the *vilâyet* of Egypt. Its scale alone made it impossible to deal with as he had with the Minufiye uprising a year earlier, i.e., by sending some cavalry troops and a number of artillery pieces. Subduing a revolt of some 20,000 men and women led by a man with obvious religious zeal and charisma required sending in well-trained troops under a loyal and competent commander. Complicating matters further, however, was the fact that the newly trained regular soldiers would have to be sent to their own villages to quell the uprising. But the gamble paid off in little less than a month. In one incident, a corporal ordered to deal with people from his own village met up with his own father. Having failed to convince his father to give himself up, the son shot and killed him. Mehmed Ali, upon learning of the case, issued an order to promote the corporal to sergeant.[26]

Nonetheless, fire smoldered beneath the ashes,[27] and the uprising spread to the

---

22. Ibid.: S/1/47/7, document no. 306, 13 Şaban 1239/13 April 1824.
23. He struck camp for his destination in early February. Ibid.: S/1/48/1, document no. 170, 4 Cemaziyül'ahır 1239/5 February 1824.
24. Ibid.: S/1/48/1, document no. 242, 13 Şaban 1239/13 April 1824.
25. Ibid.: S/1/48/1, document no. 255, 25 Şaban 1239/25 April 1824.
26. Ibid.: S/1/48/1, document no. 253, 25 Şaban 1239/25 April 1824.
27. Ibid.: S/1/48/1, documents no. 263, 2 Ramazan 1239/1 May 1824; no. 268, 7 Ramazan

army itself as the soldiers apparently buckled under the unaccustomed pressures and rigorous discipline of military life. Reasons for their mutiny included delayed pay and seeing their families and folk famished by the Paşa's heavy taxes, monopoly systems, and draconian police measures.[28] In one incident, 700 soldiers deserted their units and joined forces with Şeyh Ahmed. Lax discipline and probable connivance on the part of some officers were also suspected.

Mehmed Ali had to order an immediate investigation. Dispatching two of his senior officials, his *kapı kethüda* (his agent in Istanbul, who had been visiting Egypt at the time) and his *silahdar*, he issued them and Osman Bey, the colonel of the regiment in question, some general directives. The investigation had to be conducted in accordance with military law, and those found guilty among the non-commissioned officers with the ranks of *başçavuş*, *çavuş*, and *bölük-emini* were to be shot in plain view of their men. Privates who had mutinied should be literally decimated: they were to stand in file, and every tenth man was to step forward and be shot. The resulting gaps were to be filled by conscripting men from the villages that the regiment would pass through on its way to the Sudan.[29] As a result, forty-five officers were shot in front of their men.[30]

On reflection, Mehmed Ali could not find anyone to blame except Osman Bey himself and his Mamluk officers.

> [T]he soldiers of this regiment were the same soldiers who had endured earlier hardships in the Hijaz, during which time they set an example of discipline, obedience, and cleanliness. This was their state when they joined your regiment and...when they marched on the rebels and engaged with them in no fewer than six battles. This they did in spite of the fact that they had originally come from these same areas. Nevertheless, they did not hesitate to shoot at friends and family alike, and showed more signs of fortitude and bravery than could possibly be expected of them. But then they dared to go on a mutiny and to desert. They would not have ended in this situation if it were not for the temptations and intrigues [of the Mamluk officers] and your own laxity.[31]

Osman Bey was spared the worst of the Paşa's wrath. Instead, his deputy Ali Ağa was fired and replaced by an officer from another regiment. Osman Bey seems

---

1239/6 May 1824.
28. The point about pay is mentioned directly in only one letter, namely, ibid., S/1/48/1, document no. 421, 17 Şevval 1239/15 June 1824, in which Mehmed Ali summarizes the events of the whole dramatic month in a letter to Mehmed Bey the *defterdar*, who had been appointed governor-general of the Sudan. For how adequate the pay was and its role, if any, in earlier incidents of desertion, see Fahmy, *All the Pasha's Men*, p. 91.
29. Ma'iyya Saniyya-Turkī: S/1/48/1, document no. 273, 15 Ramazan 1239/14 May 1824.
30. Ibid.: S/1/47/7, document no. 331, 2 Ramazan 1239/1 May 1824.
31. Ibid.: S/1/48/1, document no. 277, 15 Ramazan 1239/14 May 1824.

to have received the warning, put his regiment in order, and eventually arrived at his final destination after losing some more of his men subduing yet another revolt in Halfa. Having succeeded Mehmed Bey the *defterdar* as governor-general of the Sudan, Osman Bey helped found the city of Khartoum, where he died and was buried in 1825.[32]

The above account has been pieced together entirely from the Ma'iyya Saniyya records housed in the Egyptian National Archives in Cairo. Of course, it would have been extremely unlikely that even one of the peasant-soldiers who were the true authors of the mutiny could read or write, let alone that his account of the dramatic events would find its way into the archives and be kept there. Moreover, the archives do not have any records of the courts-martial that we know were conducted to deal with the mutineers.[33] Rather, the records of the Ma'iyya Saniyya contain nothing but the letters and decrees issued from Cairo or Alexandria by Mehmed Ali himself, for the Ma'iyya was the "Exalted Viceregal Cabinet." Those documents, in turn, were based on reports forwarded to Mehmed Ali by different officers, provincial governors, and other officials. If we can judge by similar reports that the Paşa received on other occasions, the accounts of the mutiny-revolt likely were replete with expressions of appeasement, prostrations, and various attempts at twisting facts and covering up major mistakes in order to present a smooth and rosy picture of a messy situation.[34]

Bearing in mind that relying on the Paşa's letters and orders is problematic, we still can make two points about them. Upon first glance at their language, one is struck by the self-assured tone the Paşa assumed in dealing with the unprecedented challenge to his authority in Egypt. Mehmed Ali comes across as the confident, ever-present, omnipotent ruler he proved to be in later years. He may have been in Alexandria while the battles and insurrections were being fought out and quelled in Isne and Aswan, but it was enough for him to send dispatches via emissaries to Osman Bey. "We are sending our *silahdar* to guide you to the right path," he wrote, and, in the same breath, added, "However, we remain confident that you will look into this matter yourself and will deal with the situation according to the laws and regulations that you undoubtedly follow." The insinuations, the concealed threats, the words left unsaid would not have been lost on Osman Bey. The Paşa did not have to appear in person armed with six palace guns, as he had done when subduing the Minufiye uprising the year before; his letters, backed by the power he had recently found in his newly trained troops, now sufficed.

A self-assured tone might also have reflected the fact that Mehmed Ali was no stranger to mutiny. Indeed, his whole career might be regarded as a clever and successful mutiny against the Ottoman sultan. The Paşa was, moreover, well aware

---

32. Abdel-Rahman Zaki, "The Governors of the Sudan," *Al-Majalla al-ta'rīkhiyya al-Misriyya* (*The Egyptian Historical Review*) 1 (1948): 429.
33. The archives do contain records of later courts-martial, starting with the reign of Said Paşa (1854-63).
34. For an analysis of the functioning of the bureaucracy under Mehmed Ali, see Fahmy, *All the Pasha's Men*, chapter 4.

of the Janissary revolt that had deposed Sultan Selim III in 1807, and he had managed to suppress various mutinies of his own Albanian troops, including the significant one of 1815. So, in spite of the scale and alarming proportions of the mutiny of 1824, it was essentially nothing new to him. Furthermore, before he took the gamble to employ the newly trained troops to quell the initial uprising, evidence indicates, the Paşa had weighed the odds cleverly in reading the events of early 1824 to mean that the troops were reliable and trustworthy enough to withstand the pressures to which they were subjected.

The second point to be made is that the Paşa distinguished between the revolt of the peasants and the mutiny, or insurrection, among the soldiers. The term used was often the same--*isyan*--but the punishment meted out was obviously different. Peasants were to be hanged at village entrances or shot after a civilian investigation; soldiers and officers were to be decimated or shot after a court-martial in front of the battalion. As for the men themselves, who left no written records, a question remains as to which aspect of their hyphenated identity the peasant-soldiers were most likely to assume. The Paşa decided that since the men had put on his uniforms, they certainly were soldiers. One wonders, however, if putting on a military uniform would have transformed them into the obedient, docile soldiers who would not hesitate to kill their fathers when ordered to do so. It is more likely that they were Upper Egyptian peasants all the way through and that what appeared to the Paşa as an army mutiny was for them still a peasant revolt, dangerous and risky though this surely was.

New York University

SELECT BIBLIOGRAPHY

PRIMARY SOURCES

Abdülkerim b. Abdurrahman. *Tarih-i Mısır.* Istanbul, Süleymaniye Library, MS Hekimoğlu Ali Paşa 705.
Ahmed Çelebi b. Abd al-Ghani. *Awdah al-ishārāt fī man tawalla Misr al-Qāhira min al-wuzarā' wa'l-bāshāt,* ed. A.A. Abd al-Rahim. Cairo, 1978.
Ata'i, Nevizade. *Hadâik'ul-hakâik fî tekmîletişş-Şakâik.* Istanbul, 1268 A.H. Reprinted with an index by Abdülkadir Özcan, *Şakaik-ı Nu'maniye ve Zeyilleri.* 5 vols. Istanbul, 1989.
Ayvansarayi, Hafız Hüseyin. *Mecmua-i Tevarih,* ed. Fahri Ç. Derin and Vahid Çabuk. Istanbul, 1985.
Babur, Zahiruddin Muhammad. *The Baburnama: Memoirs of Babur, Prince and Emperor,* trans. Wheeler M. Thackston. New York, 1996.
Barkan, Ömer Lutfi, ed. *XV ve XVIıncı Asırlarda Osmanlı Imparatorluğunda Ziraî Ekonominin Hukukî ve Malî Esasları.* İstanbul Üniversitesi Edebiyat Fakültesi Yayınlarından No. 256. 2 vols. Istanbul, 1943.
Bostanzade Yahya. *Vak'a-ı Sultân Osmân Hân.* Bibliothèque nationale, MS Suppl. Turc. 1142. Istanbul, Süleymaniye Library, MS Halet Efendi 611. Istanbul, Topkapı Palace Library, MS Revan 1305.
Bowring, Sir John. *Report on the Commercial Statistics of Syria.* London, 1840.
Cevdet Paşa, Ahmed. *Tarih-i Cevdet.* Vol. 6. Istanbul, 1966.
Al-Damurdashi, Ahmed Kethüda Azeban. *Al-Durra al-musāna fī akhbār al-Kināna.* British Museum, MS Or. 1073-4.
Driault, Eduard, ed. *L'Expédition de Crète et de Morée (1823-1828).* Cairo, 1930.
Enverî, Sadullah. *Tarih.* Istanbul University Library, MS T. 5994.
Evliya Çelebi. *Evliya Çelebi Seyahatnamesi,* ed. Ahmed Cevdet. 10 vols. Istanbul, 1888-1938.
———. *The Intimate Life of an Ottoman Statesman: Melek Ahmed Pasha (1588-1662),* ed. and trans. Robert Dankoff. Albany, 1991.
———. *Narrative of Travels in Europe, Asia, and Africa,* trans. Josef von Hammer-Purgstall. 2 vols. in 1. London, 1834.
Faulkner, William. *As I Lay Dying.* New York, 1985. Originally published New York, 1930.
Gomez, Madeleine-Angélique de. *Histoire d'Osman, premier du nom, XIXe empereur des Turcs, et de l'impératrice Aphendina Ashada.* 2 vols. Paris, 1734.
———. *The Life of Osman the Great,* trans. John Williams. 2 vols. London, 1735.
Halisi, Mehmed. *Beşâretnâme-i Sultân Mustafâ Hân.* Austrian National Library, mixt. 21.
Hamont, P.M. *L'Égypte sous Méhémet-Ali.* 2 vols. Paris, 1843.
Hasanbeyzade Ahmed. *Hasanbeyzade Tarihi.* Austrian National Library, H.O. 19. Istanbul, Nuruosmaniye Library, MS 3134. Istanbul, Ragıp Paşa Library, MS 987.
Hüseyin Efendi. *Ottoman Egypt in the Age of the French Revolution,* ed. and trans.

Stanford J. Shaw. Cambridge, MA, 1964.
Ibn Khaldun, ᶜAbd al-Rahman Abu Zayd b. Muhammad. *The Muqaddimah: An Introduction to History*, trans. Franz Rosenthal. 2 vols. Princeton, 1967.
Ihchiev, D., compiler. *Turski D'rzhavni Dokumenti za Osman Pazvanoglu Vidinski (Turkish State Documents on Osman Pazvanoglu from Vidin)*. Sofia, 1909.
Al-Jabarti, ᶜAbd al-Rahman b. Hasan. *ᶜAjā̕ib al-athār fī'l-tarājim wa'l-akhbār*. Cairo, 1880.
_____. *ᶜAjā̕ib al-athār fī'l-tarājim wa'l-akhbār*. Cairo, 1958-67.
Karaçelebizade Abdülaziz. *Ravzatü'l-ebrâr*. Bulaq, 1248 A.H.
Kâtip Çelebi. *Fezleke-i Tarih*. 2 vols. Istanbul, 1286-87 A.H.
Keşfî Mehmed. *Selimname*. Istanbul, Süleymaniye Library, MS Esad Efendi 2147.
Marsigli, Luigi Ferdinando, Comte de. *Stato militare dell'Impèrio Ottomanno/ L'État militaire de l'Empire Ottoman*. 2 vols. in 1. Amsterdam and La Haye, 1732.
Mengin, Félix. *Histoire de l'Égypte sous le gouvernement de Mohammed-Aly*. 2 vols. Paris, 1823.
Mikes, Kelemen. *Letters from Turkey*, trans. Bernard Adams. New York, 1998.
Naima, Mustafa. *Annals of the Turkish Empire from 1591-1659 of the Christian Era*, trans. Charles Fraser. Vol. 1. London, 1832.
_____. *Tarih-i Naima*. Vol. 1. Istanbul, 1281-83 A.H.
Olivier, Guillaume Antoine. *Voyage dans L'empire Othoman, l'Égypte, et la Perse fait par ordre du Gouvernement, pendant les six premières anneés de la Republique*. Paris, 1801-1807.
Peçevi, Ibrahim. *Tarih-i Peçevi*. 2 vols. Istanbul, 1281-83 A.H.
_____. *Peçevi Tarihi*, ed. Bekir Baykal. 2 vols. Ankara, 1982.
Rajabi, Khalil b. Ahmad. *Ta̕rīkh al-wazīr Muhammad ᶜAlī Bāshā li-Shaykh Khalīl ibn Ahmad al-Rajabī*, ed. Daniel N. Crecelius and Hamza Abd al-Aziz Badr. Cairo, 1996.
Rashid al-Din. *The Successors of Genghis Khan, Translated from the Persian of Rashid al-Din*, ed. and trans. John Boyle. New York, 1971.
Roe, Sir Thomas. *The Negotiations of Sir Thomas Roe in His Embassy to the Ottoman Porte*. London, 1740.
Er-Rumi, Mehmed b. Mehmed. *Tarih*. Istanbul, Süleymaniye Library, MS Lala Ismail.
Rumiantsev, Piotr Aleksandrovich. *Sbornik documentov (Collected Documents)*. Moscow, 1953.
Rycaut, Paul. *The Present State of the Ottoman Empire*. London, 1668. Reprint New York, 1971.
Sabanović, Hazim, ed. *Turski Izvori o Srpskoj Revolutsiji, 1804 (Turkish Sources on the Serbian Revolution of 1804)*. Belgrade, 1956.
Şemdanizade Fındıklılı Süleyman Efendi. *Şemdanizade Fındıklılı Süleyman Efendi Tarihi: Mür̕i't- Tevârih*, ed. M. Münir Aktepe. 2 vols. in 3. Istanbul, 1980.
Şeyhî Mehmed Efendi. *Vakâyi'ül-fudalâ*. Istanbul, Beyazıt Library, MS Veliyüddin Efendi 2361-62.
Solakzade Mehmed Hemdemî Çelebi. *Tarih-i Solakzade*. Istanbul, 1298 A.H.
Spyridon, J.N., ed. *Annals of Palestine: 1821-1841--A Manuscript by the Monk Neophytus of Cyprus*. Jerusalem, 1938.

Süreyya, Mehmet. *Sicill-i Osmanî*. 4 vols. Istanbul, 1311/1893-94.
Tugi Çelebi, a.k.a. Hüseyin bin Sefer. *Tarih-i Tugi*. Austrian National Library, H.O. 74. University Library, Cambridge, MS Dd. 11.18.
Wilkinson, Sir John G. *Modern Egypt and Thebes*. 2 vols. London, 1843.
Yücel, Yaşar, ed. *Osmanlı Devlet Düzenin Ait Metinler I: Kitâb-ı Mustetâb*. Ankara, 1974.
_____, ed. *Osmanlı Devlet Düzenin Ait Metinler II: Kitâbu Mesâlihi'l-Müslimîn ve Menâfi'i'l-Mü'minîn, Tıpkıbasımı*. Ankara, 1980.
_____, ed. *Osmanlı Devlet Düzenin Ait Metinler III: Kitâbu Mesâlihi'l- Müslimîn ve Menâfi'i'l-Mü'minîn, Metnin Türk Harflerine Çevirisi ve Değerlendirmesi*. Ankara, 1981.
_____, ed. *Osmanlı Devlet Düzenine Ait Metinler VI: II. Osman Adına Yazılmış Zafernâme*. Ankara, 1983.
_____, ed. *Osmanlı Devlet Teşkilatına Dair Kaynaklar: Kitâb-ı Müstetâb, Kitabu Mesâlihi'l-Müslimîn ve Menâfi'i'l-Mü'minîn, Hırzü'l-Mülûk*. Ankara, 1988.

SECONDARY SOURCES

Abou-el-Haj, Rifaat A. "The Ottoman Vezir and Paşa Households, 1683-1703: A Preliminary Report." *Journal of the American Oriental Society* 94 (1974): 438-47.
_____. *The 1703 Rebellion and the Structure of Ottoman Politics*. Istanbul, 1984.
Ahmad, Feroz. "Rıdâ Nûr." *Encyclopaedia of Islam*, 2nd ed. (hereafter EI^2).
Akdağ, Mustafa. *Celali İsyanları*. Ankara, 1963.
_____. "Djalālī." EI^2
Aksan, Virginia H. "Mutiny and the Eighteenth-Century Ottoman Army." *Turkish Studies Association Bulletin* 22.1 (1998): 116-25.
_____. *An Ottoman Statesman in War and Peace: Ahmed Resmî Efendi (1700-1783)*. Leiden, 1995.
_____. "Whatever Happened to the Janissaries?" *War in History* 5 (1998): 23-36.
Aktepe, M. Münir. *Patrona İsyanı (1730)*. İstanbul Üniversitesi Edebiyat Fakültesi Yayınlarından No. 808. Istanbul, 1958.
Arıcanlı, Tosun, and Mara Thomas. "Sidestepping Capitalism: On the Ottoman Road to Elsewhere." *Journal of Historical Sociology* 7.1 (1994): 25-48.
Atanasov, Shteryu. *Selskite V'staniya v B'lgaria k'm Kraya na XVIII vek i nachaloto na XIX vek i S'zdavaneto na B'lgarskata Zemska Voiska (Rural Revolts in Bulgaria at the End of the Eighteenth and the Beginning of the Nineteenth Century, and the Creation of the Bulgarian Rural Army)*. Sofia, 1952.
Ayalon, David. *L'esclavage du mamelouk*. Jerusalem, 1951.
_____. "Studies on the Structure of the Mamluk Army," Part 2. *Bulletin of the School of Oriental and African Studies* 15 (1953): 448-76.
Aykut, Nezihi, ed. *Hasan Bey-zâde Tarihi*. 3 vols. Ph.D. dissertation, Istanbul University, 1980.
Babinger, Franz. *Die Geschichtsschreiber der Osmanen und Ihre Werke*. Leipzig, 1927.
Baer, Gabriel. "Popular Revolt in Ottoman Cairo." *Der Islam* 54 (1977): 213-42.

Barkey, Karen. *Bandits and Bureaucrats: The Ottoman Route to State Centralization*. Ithaca and London, 1994.
Baysun, M. Cavid. "Hasan-beyzade Ahmet Paşa." *Türkiyat Mecmuası* 10 (1951-53): 321-40.
_____. "Reis'ül-Küttab Küçük Hasan Bey." *İstanbul Üniversitesi Edebiyat Fakültesi Tarih Dergisi* 2.3-4 (1950-51): 97-102.
Berman, Harold J. *Law and Revolution: The Formation of the Western Legal Tradition*. Cambridge, 1983.
Boppe, Auguste. "La Mission de l'adjudant-commandant Mériage à Widin en 1807-1809." *Annales de l'École Libre des Sciences Politiques* 1.3 (1886): 259-93.
Bowen, Harold. "Ahmad III." EI^2.
Brummett, Palmira. "Classifying Ottoman Mutiny: The Act and Vision of Rebellion." *Turkish Studies Association Bulletin* 22.1 (1998): 91-107.
_____. "Subordination and Its Discontents: Ottoman Campaign, 1578-1580." In Caesar Farah, ed., *Decision-Making and Change in the Ottoman Empire*. Kirksville, MO, 1993.
Cahen, Claude. "À propos des Shuhūd." *Studia Islamica* 31 (1970): 71-79.
Çarıcı, Mustafa. "Bostanzade Yahya Efendi." *Tarih Diyanet Vakfı İslam Ansiklopedisi*.
Cassels, Lavender. *The Struggle for the Ottoman Empire, 1717-1740*. London, 1966.
Cavaliero, Roderick. *The Last of the Crusaders: The Knights of St. John and Malta in the Eighteenth Century*. London, 1960.
Cezar, Mustafa. *Osmanlı Tarihinde Levendler*. Istanbul, 1965.
Cohen, Amnon. *Jewish Life under Islam: Jerusalem in the Sixteenth Century*. Cambridge, MA, 1984.
_____. *Palestine in the Eighteenth Century: Patterns of Government and Administration*. Jerusalem, 1973.
Cohn, Bernard S. *Colonialism and Its Forms of Knowledge*. Princeton, 1996.
Creasy, Edward S. *History of the Ottoman Empire*. London, 1878.
Crecelius, Daniel N. *The Roots of Modern Egypt: A Study of the Regimes of Ali Bey al-Kabir and Muhammad Bey Abu al-Dhahab, 1760-1775*. Minneapolis and Chicago, 1981.
_____. "Russia's Relations with the Mamluk Beys of Egypt in the Eighteenth Century." In Farhad Kazemi and R.D. McChesney, eds., *A Way Prepared: Essays on Islamic Culture in Honor of Richard Bayly Winder*. New York, 1988.
_____, and Hamza Abd al-Aziz Badr. "Ta'rīkh al-wazīr Muhammad ʿAlī Bāshā." In *Archiv Orientalni: Quarterly Journal of African and Asian Studies (Czech Republic), Supplementa VIII: Proceedings of the XII Congress of CIEPO, 1996* (1998): 101-10.
Cuno, Kenneth M. "Egypt's Wealthy Peasantry, 1740-1820: A Study of the Region of al-Mansura." In Tarif Khalidi, ed., *Land Tenure and Social Transformation in the Middle East*. Beirut, 1984.
Cvetkova, Bistra. "Recherches sur le système d'affermage (*iltizam*) dans l'Empire Ottoman au cours du XVIe-XVIIIe s. par rapport aux contrées Bulgares." *Rocznik Orientalistyczny* 27.2 (1964): 111-32.
Danişmend, İsmail Hami. *İzahlı Osmanlı Tarihi Kronolojisi*. 4 vols. Istanbul, 1947-55.
Darling, Linda T. *Revenue-Raising and Legitimacy: Tax Collection and Finance*

Administration in the Ottoman Empire, 1560-1660. Leiden, 1996.
Decei, A. "Erdel." *EI²*.
Dodwell, Henry. *The Founder of Modern Egypt.* Cambridge, 1931.
Erbakan, Cevat. *1736-1739 Osmanlı-Rus ve Avusturya Savaşları.* Istanbul, 1938.
Erdem, Y. Hakan. *Slavery in the Ottoman Empire and Its Demise.* New York, 1996.
Fahmy, Khaled. *All the Pasha's Men: Mehmed Ali, His Army, and the Making of Modern Egypt.* Cambridge, 1997.
Faroqhi, Suraiya. "Crisis and Change, 1590-1699." Part 2 of Halil İnalcık, ed., with Donald Quataert, *An Economic and Social History of the Ottoman Empire.* Cambridge, 1994.
Fawaz, Leila Tarazi. *Merchants and Migrants in Nineteenth-Century Beirut.* Cambridge, MA, 1983.
Finkel, Caroline. *The Administration of Warfare: The Ottoman Military Campaigns in Hungary, 1593-1606.* 2 vols. Vienna, 1988.
Fleischer, Cornell H. "Royal Authority, Dynastic Cyclism, and 'Ibn Khaldunism' in Sixteenth-Century Ottoman Letters." *Journal of Asian and African Studies* 18 (1983): 198-220.
Forst, H. "Der türkische Gesandte in Prag, 1620, und der Briefwechsel des Winterkönigs mit Sultan Osman II." *Mitteilungen des Instituts für Österreichische Geschichtsforschung* 16 (1895): 566-81.
Gerber, Haim. *Ottoman Rule in Jerusalem: 1890-1914.* Berlin, 1985.
_____. "*Sharī'a, Kanun*, and Custom in the Ottoman Law: The Court Records of Seventeenth-Century Bursa." *International Journal of Turkish Studies* 2 (1981): 131-47.
_____. *Social Origins of the Middle East.* Boulder, CO, 1987.
Gökyay, Orhan Şaik. "II. Sultan Osman'ın Şehadeti." In Erol Güngör, *et al.*, eds., *Atsız Armağanı.* Istanbul, 1976.
_____. "Kâtip Çelebi: Hayatı, Şahsiyeti, Eserleri." In *Kâtip Çelebi: Hayatı ve Eserleri hakkında İncelemeler.* Türk Tarih Kurumu Yayınlarından series 7, no. 33. Ankara, 1957.
Göyünç, Nejat. "Kara-çelebi-zâde." *EI²*.
Griswold, William. *The Great Anatolian Rebellion, 1591-1611.* Berlin, 1983.
Günay, Vehbi. "H. 1159 (M. 1746) Tarihli Karaferye Kazası Şer'iye Sicili (Transkripsiyon ve Değerlendirme)." Master's thesis, Eğe Üniversitesi, Izmir, 1993.
Güneş, Mehmet. *Evliya Çelebi ve Haşim Efendinin Çerkezistan Notları.* Istanbul, 1969.
Halls, J.J. *The Life and Correspondence of Henry Salt.* 2 vols. London, 1834.
Hamed, Raouf Abbas. "The *Siyasatname* and the Institutionalization of Central Administration under Muhammad Ali." In Nelly Hanna, ed., *The State and Its Servants: Administration in Egypt from Ottoman Times to the Present.* Cairo, 1995.
Hammer-Purgstall, Josef von. *Geschichte des osmanischen Reiches.* 10 vols. Pest, 1827-35.
Hathaway, Jane. "Egypt in the Seventeenth Century." In Martin W. Daly, ed., *The Cambridge History of Egypt.* Vol. 2: *Modern Egypt from 1517 to the End of the Twentieth Century* Cambridge, 1998.

_____. "The Military Household in Ottoman Egypt." *International Journal of Middle East Studies* 27 (1995): 39-52.
_____. *The Politics of Households in Ottoman Egypt: The Rise of the Qazdağlıs.* Cambridge, 1997.
_____. "Problems of Periodization in Ottoman History: The Fifteenth through the Eighteenth Centuries." *Turkish Studies Association Bulletin* 20.2 (1996): 25-31.
_____. "The Role of the Ulema in Social Protest in Late Eighteenth-Century Cairo." M.A. thesis, University of Texas at Austin, 1986.
_____. "Sultans, Pashas, *Taqwīms*, and *Mühimmes*: A Reconsideration of Chronicle-Writing in Eighteenth-Century Egypt." In Daniel N. Crecelius, ed., *Eighteenth Century Egypt: The Arabic Manuscript Sources.* Claremont, CA, 1990.
Heinisch, Reinhard Rudolf. "Habsburg, die Pforte und der Böhmische Aufstand (1618-1620)." *Südost-Forschungen* 33 (1974): 125-65, 34 (1975): 79-124.
Heyworth-Dunne, J. *An Introduction to the History of Education in Modern Egypt.* London, 1938.
Holt, P.M. "The Career of Kuchuk Muhammad (1676-94)." *Bulletin of the School of Oriental and African Studies* 26 (1963): 269-87.
_____. *Egypt and the Fertile Crescent, 1516-1922: A Political History.* Ithaca and London, 1966.
_____. "The Exalted Lineage of Ridwan Bey: Some Observations on a Seventeenth Century Mamluk Genealogy." *Bulletin of the School of Oriental and African Studies* 22 (1959): 221-30.
Hourani, Albert. "Ottoman Reform and the Politics of Notables." In William R. Polk and Richard L. Chambers, eds., *The Beginnings of Modernization in the Middle East: The Nineteenth Century.* Chicago, 1968. Reprint in Hourani, *The Emergence of the Modern Middle East.* Berkeley, 1981. Reprint in Hourani, Philip S. Khoury, and Mary C. Wilson, eds., *The Modern Middle East: A Reader.* London, 1993.
Howard, Douglas A. "Ottoman Historiography and the Literature of 'Decline' of the Sixteenth and Seventeenth Centuries." *Journal of Asian History* 22 (1988): 52-77.
Hunter, Robert. *Egypt under the Khedives, 1805-1879.* Pittsburgh, 1984.
İnalcık, Halil. "Adâletnâmeler." *Belgeler* 2.3-4(1965): 49-142.
_____. "Centralization and Decentralization in Ottoman Administration." In Thomas Naff and Roger Owen, eds., *Studies in Eighteenth-Century Islamic History.* Carbondale and Edwardsville, IL, 1977.
_____. "Hüsrev Paşa." *İslam Ansiklopedisi.*
_____. "Military and Fiscal Transformation in the Ottoman Empire, 1600-1700." *Archivum Ottomanicum* 6 (1980): 304-11.
_____. "The Nature of Traditional Society: Turkey." In Robert E. Ward and Dankwart A. Rostow, eds., *Political Modernization in Japan and Turkey.* Studies in Political Development 3. Princeton, 1964.
_____. "The Socio-Political Effects of the Diffusion of Fire-Arms in the Middle East." In V.J. Parry and Malcolm Yapp, eds., *War, Technology, and Society in the Middle East* London, 1975.
Itzkowitz, Norman. "Men and Ideas in the Eighteenth-Century Ottoman Empire." In Thomas Naff and Roger Owen, eds., *Studies in Eighteenth-Century Islamic History.*

Carbondale and Edwardsville, IL, 1977.
Jakšić, Grgur (Grégoire Yakichitch). "Documents et Mémoires: Notes sur Passvan Oglou, 1758-1807." *La Revue slave* 5.1 (1906): 261-79, 418-29; 5.2 (1906): 139-44, 436-88; 5.3 (1907): 138-44, 278-88.
_____. *L'Europe et la résurrection de la Serbie, 1804-1854*. Paris, 1917.
Kaddache, Mahfoud. *L'Algérie durant la periode ottomane*. Algiers, 1998.
Kaldy-Nagy, Gyula. "The `Strangers' (*Ecnebiler*) in the Sixteenth-Century Ottoman Military Organization." In Gyula Kara, ed., *Between the Danube and the Caucasus*. Budapest, 1987.
Keralio, Louis Feliz. *Histoire de la guerre des russes et des impériaux contre les Turcs en 1736, 1737, 1738 & 1739 & de la paix de Belgrade qui la termina*. Paris, 1780.
Khoury, Dina Rizk. *State and Provincial Society in the Ottoman Empire: Mosul, 1540-1834*. Cambridge, 1997.
Kister, M.J. "... *Illā bi-haqqihi...*: A Study of an Early *Hadīth*." *Jerusalem Studies in Arabic and Islam* 5 (1984): 33-52.
Kraemer, Joel L. "Apostates, Rebels, and Brigands." *Israel Oriental Studies* 10 (1980): 35-73.
Kunt, Metin. "Ethnic-Regional (*Cins*) Solidarity in the Seventeenth-Century Ottoman Establishment." *International Journal of Middle East Studies* 5 (1974): 233-39.
_____. *The Sultan's Servants: The Transformation of Ottoman Provincial Government, 1550-1650*. New York, 1983.
Ladislas, Baron Hengelmüller von Hengervár. *Hungary's Fight for National Existence, or, the History of the Great Uprising led by Francis Rákóczi II, 1703-11*. London, 1913.
Lascaris, M. *Salonique à la fin du XVIIIe siècle d'après les rapports consulaires français* Athens, 1939.
Livingston, John W. "The Rise of Shaykh al-Balad ᶜAli Bey al-Kabir: A Study in the Accuracy of the Chronicle of al-Jabarti." *Bulletin of the School of Oriental and African Studies* 33 (1970): 283-94.
Lynn, John A. "The Evolution of Army Style in the Modern West, 800-2000," *International History Review* 18.3 (1996): 505-45.
Madariaga, Isabel de. *Russia in the Age of Catherine the Great*. London, 1981.
Mannaᶜ, ᶜAdel. "The Sancak of Jerusalem between Two Invasions, 1798-1831." Ph.D. dissertation, Hebrew University of Jerusalem, 1986.
Marcus, Abraham. *The Middle East on the Eve of Modernity: Aleppo in the Eighteenth Century* New York, 1989.
Marsot, Afaf Lutfi al-Sayyid. *Egypt in the Reign of Muhammad Ali*. New York, 1984.
_____. "The Ulama of Cairo in the Eighteenth and Nineteenth Centuries." In Nikki R. Keddie, ed., *Scholars, Saints, and Sufis: Muslim Religious Institutions since 1500*. Berkeley and Los Angeles, 1972.
Masters, Bruce. "The 1850 Events in Aleppo: An Aftershock of Syria's Incorporation into the Capitalist World System." *International Journal of Middle East Studies* 22 (1990): 3-20.
_____. *The Origins of Western Economic Dominance in the Middle East: Mercantilism and the Islamic Economy of Aleppo, 1600-1750*. New York, 1988.

McGowan, Bruce. "The Age of the Ayans, 1699-1812." Part 3 of Halil İnalcık, ed., with Donald Quataert, *An Economic and Social History of the Ottoman Empire, 1300-1914*. Cambridge, 1994.
Mehmed Murad (Mizancı Mehmed). *Ta'rîh-i Ebû'l-Fârûk: Ta'rîh-i Osmânîde Siyâset ve Medeniyet İ'tibâriyle Hikmet-i Asliye Taharrîsine Teşebbüs*. 7 vols. Istanbul, 1325-32 A.H.
Mertzios, K. "Sympleroma eis ta `Mnemeia Makedonikes Historias.'" *Eis Mnemen K.I. Amantou*. Athens, 1960.
Meservey, Sabra F. "Feyzullah Efendi: An Ottoman Şeyhülislâm." Ph.D. dissertation, Princeton University, 1965.
Miller, William. *The Ottoman Empire and Its Successors, 1801-1922*. Cambridge, 1923.
Mitchell, Timothy. *Colonising Egypt*. Cambridge, 1988.
Mutafčieva, Vera. "L'institution de l'*ayanlık* pendant les dernières décennies du XVIIIe siècle." *Études Balkaniques* 2-3 (1965): 233-47.
Nagata, Yuzo. *Muhsin-zâde Mehmed Paşa ve Ayânlık Müessesesi*. Tokyo, 1976.
Na'im, Abdullahi Ahmed an-. *Toward an Islamic Reformation: Civil Liberties, Human Rights, and International Law*. Syracuse, 1990.
Nenadović, Mateja. *Prota Matija Nenadović*. Belgrade, 1978.
Noradounghian, Gabriel. *Recueil d'actes internationaux de l'Empire Ottoman*. Vol. 2. Paris, 1900.
Nur, Rıza. *Türk Tarihi*. 12 vols. Istanbul, 1924-26.
Osmanlı Ansiklopedisi: Tarih--Medeniyet--Kültür 7 vols. Istanbul, 1993.
Özkaya, Yücel. *Osmanlı İmparatorluğunda Dağlı İsyanları, 1791-1808*. Ankara, 1983.
Pamuk, Şevket. *A Monetary History of the Ottoman Empire*. Cambridge, 2000.
Pantelić, Dušan. *Beogradski Pašaluk: Pred Prvi Srpski Ustanak, 1794-1804* (*Belgrade Pashalik: Prior to the First Serbian Uprising*). Belgrade, 1949.
Peirce, Leslie P. *The Imperial Harem: Women and Sovereignty in the Ottoman Empire*. New York and Oxford, 1993.
Piterberg, Gabriel. "Speech Acts and Written Texts: A Reading of a Seventeenth-Century Ottoman Historiographic Episode." *Poetics Today* 14.2 (1993): 387-418.
_____. "A Study of Ottoman Historiography in the Seventeenth Century." Ph.D. dissertation, Oxford University, 1992.
Pocock, J.G.A. *The Ancient Constitution and the Feudal Law: A Study of English Historical Thought in the Seventeenth Century--A Reissue with a Retrospect*. Cambridge, 1987. 1st ed. 1957.
Rafeq, Abdul-Karim. *The Province of Damascus, 1723-1783*. Beirut, 1966.
Rafiʿi, ʿAbd al-Rahman al-. *ʿAsr Muhammad ʿAlī*. Cairo, 1989.
Rahman, Fazlur. "The Law of Rebellion in Islam." In Fazlur Rahman, *et al.*, *Islam in the Modern World: 1983 Paine Lectures in Religion*, ed. Jill Raitt. Columbia, MO, 1984.
Ranke, Leopold von. *The History of Servia, and the Servian Revolution*, trans. Mrs. Alexander Kerr. London: Henry G. Bohn, 1853.
Raymond, André. "Une `Révolution' au Caire sous les Mamelouks: La Crise de

1123/1711." *Annales Islamologiques* 1 (1966): 95-120.
Refik, Ahmed. "Devşirme Usulı, Acemi Oğlanlar." *Edebiyat Fakültesi Mecmuası* 15 (1927): 1-14.
Richmond, J.C.B. *Egypt, 1798-1952: Her Advance towards a Modern Identity.* New York, 1977.
Roded, Ruth. "The Syrian Urban Notables: Elite, Estates, Class?" *Asian and African Studies* 20 (1986): 375-84.
Roider, Karl A. *The Reluctant Ally: Austria's Policy in the Austro-Turkish War, 1737-1739.* Baton Rouge, LA, 1972.
Rood, Judith Mendelsohn. "The Beginning of the End of Sunni Preeminence: Muhammad Ali and Jerusalem, 1834." *Arab Studies Journal* 4 (1996): 86-95.
_____. "Government, Law, and Family: Muhammad Ali, Marriage, and Procreation in Syria, 1835." *Archiv Orientalni: Quarterly Journal of African and Asian Studies (Czech Republic), Supplementa VIII: Proceedings of the XII Congress of CIEPO, 1996* (1998): 317-30.
Sadat, Deena A. "Rumeli Ayanları: The Eighteenth Century." *Journal of Modern History* 59 (1987): 346-63.
Saiduni, Nasir al-Din. *Dirāsāt wa-abhāth fī ta'rīkh al-Jazā'ir: Al-ᶜahd al-ᶜUthmānī.* Algiers, 1984.
Sakaoğlu, Necdet, ed. *Duru Tarih.* Istanbul, 1978.
Schacht, Joseph. *An Introduction to Islamic Law.* Oxford, 1964. 2nd ed. 1998.
Schilcher, Linda Schatkowski. *Families in Politics: Damascene Factions and Estates of the Eighteenth and Nineteenth Centuries.* Stuttgart, 1985.
Şeref, Abdurrahman. *Tarih-i Devlet-i Osmaniye.* 2 vols. Istanbul, ?-1312 A.H. 2nd imprint 1315-18.
Shaw, Stanford J. *Between Old and New: The Ottoman Empire under Sultan Selim III, 1789-1807.* Cambridge, MA, 1971.
_____. *History of the Ottoman Empire and Modern Turkey.* Vol. 1: *Empire of the Gazis: The Rise and Decline of the Ottoman Empire, 1280-1808.* Cambridge, 1976.
Shmuelovitz, Aryeh. "MS Pococke No. 31 as a Source for the Events in Istanbul in the Years 1622-1624." *International Journal of Turkish Studies* 3.2 (1985-86): 107-21.
_____. "MS Pococke No. 31 as a Source for the Events in the Years 1622-24 in Istanbul." In Graciela de la Lama, ed., *Thirtieth International Congress of Human Sciences in Asia and North Africa (Mexico City, 1976): Middle East I.* Mexico City, 1982.
Shuval, Tal. *La ville d'Algers vers la fin du XVIIIe siècle: Cadre urbain et classe militaire* Paris, 1998.
Singer, Amy. *Palestinian Peasants and Ottoman Officials: Rural Administration around Sixteenth-Century Jerusalem.* Cambridge, 1994.
Sire, H.J.A. *The Knights of Malta.* New Haven, CT, 1994.
Slottman, William B. *Ferenc II Rákóczi and the Great Powers.* New York, 1997.
Sonbol, Amira El-Azhary. "Questioning Exceptionalism: *Sharīᶜa* Law." *Arab Studies Journal* (1998): 76-86.
Sumner, Benedict Humphrey. *Peter the Great and the Ottoman Empire.* Oxford, 1949.
Svoronos, Nikos G. *Le Commerce de Salonique au XVIIIe siècle.* Paris, 1956.

Temperley, H.M.V. *England and the Near East: The Crimea*. London, 1964.
Teofilova, Maria. *Bunt't na Pazvanoglu i Negovoto Znachenie za B'lgarskoto Osvoboditelno Dvizhenie v XIX vek* (*Pazvanoğlu's Rebellion and Its Meaning for the Bulgarian Liberation Movement in the Nineteenth Century*). Sofia, 1932.
Tezcan, Baki. "Tarih ile Tarihyazımı İlişkisi Ekseninden *Tugi Tarihi* Metinleri üzerinde bir Deneme." Paper presented to the Kuruluşunun 700. Yıldönümünde Bütün Yönleriyle Osmanlı Devleti Uluslararası Kongresi, Selçuk University, Konya, Turkey, April 1999.
_____. "*Zafername* Müellifi Halisi'nin Bilinmeyen bir Eseri Münasebetiyle." *Osmanlı Araştırmaları/The Journal of Ottoman Studies* 19 (1999): 83-98.
Toledano, Ehud R. *Slavery and Abolition in the Ottoman Middle East*. Seattle, 1998.
_____. *State and Society in Mid-Nineteenth Century Egypt*. Cambridge, 1990.
Tucker, Judith E. *Women in Nineteenth-Century Egypt*. Cambridge, 1985.
Turan, Şerafeddin. "Peçevî." *İslam Ansiklopedisi*.
Ursinus, Michael. "Mîzândjı Mehmed Murâd." *EI²*.
Uzunçarşılı, İ.H. *Osmanlı Devletinin Saray Teşkilatı*. Ankara, 1945, 1984, 1988.
_____. "Vezir Hakkı Mehmed Paşa, 1747-1811." *Türkiyat Mecmuası* 6 (1936-1939): 177-284.
Vasdravelles, I. *Historika Archeia Makedonias, B'Archeion Veroias-Naouses, 1598-1886*. Thessaloniki, 1954.
Vickers, Miranda. *The Albanians: A Modern History*. New York, 1997.
Wolf, John Baptist. *The Barbary Coast: Algiers under the Turks, 1500-1830*. New York, 1979.
Yazıcı, Betül. "Bostan-zâde Yahyâ Efendi ve *Vakʿa-ı Sultân Osmân* Adlı Eseri." Senior thesis, Istanbul University, 1959.
Zaki, Abdel-Rahman. "The Governors of the Sudan." *Al-Majalla al-taʾrīkhiyya al-Mis riyya* (*The Egyptian Historical Review*) 1 (1948): 428-43.
Zeʾevi, Dror. "The Abolition of Slavery and *Kul* Identity." *Archiv Orientalni: Quarterly Journal of African and Asian Studies (Czech Republic), Supplementa VIII: Proceedings of the XII Congress of CIEPO, 1996* (1998): 411-16.

INDEX

Abdi Paşa, governor of Köstendil 75, 78-79, 80, 81, 82, 84, 85 n.47, 86
Abdullah Paşa, governor of Sidon and Tripoli 123, 124, 126
Abdullah Paşa, Karasu *mutasarrıfı* 68
Abdullah Paşa, Muhsinzade 65
Abdülmecid I (1839-61), Sultan 124, 127
Abdurrahman Ağa, *ayan* of Salonika 80, 81, 82
Abkhazians (Abazas) 8, 9, 10, 71, 72, 110, 111, 121 n.13
Acre 123, 124
Afghans 109, 110, 112, 113
Agra 59
Ahmed I (1603-17), Sultan 14, 15, 22, 25, 29 n.21, 30 n.23, 32 n.38, 34 n.56
Ahmed III (1703-30), Sultan 1, 111
Ahmed, Kara, Karaferye *ayan* 74, 75, 76, 77, 78, 79, 80, 82, 83, 86, 87, 88
Ahmed, Şeyh, Egyptian messianic figure 129, 134, 135, 136
Ahmed Çelebi b. ʿAbd al-Ghani 107 n.7, 108 nn.14, 16, 109 nn.18, 20, 21, 112
Ahmed Paşa, Tahir 134
Ahmed Paşa of Srebrenica, muhafız of Vidin 96, 97
Akkerman 61, 123
Alasonya (Elassona) 75, 76
Albania, Albanians 2, 3, 5, 9, 10, 54, 65, 70, 71, 72, 76, 78, 79, 83, 84, 86, 88, 91, 94, 101, 102, 103, 110, 111, 119, 121-22, 123, 130, 131, 134, 138
Aleppo 111, 118 n.9
Alexandria 36, 62, 137
Algeria, Algiers 12, 102, 108, 123
Ali Bey, Bulut Kapan 1 n.4, 9, 111, 121 n.13
Ali Bey Qatamish 109

Ali Paşa, Canbuladoğlu 22
Ali Paşa, Tepedelenli, of Janina (Epirus) 89, 97-98, 99, 121-22, 126
Alo Paşa, muhafız of Vidin 92
Anatolia 1, 8, 14, 15, 16, 18, 19, 22, 23, 27, 28, 29 n.21, 34 n.56, 39, 40, 69 n.19, 71, 78 n.17, 110, 119, 121
Ankara 38, 40
Arabs 8, 41, 107, 125, 128, 130, 132 See also bedouin.
artillery 49, 53, 65, 66, 135
As I Lay Dying 45-46, 49, 55, 57, 58
Asir 133, 134
Aswan 62, 131, 137
Asyut 62, 134, 135
At Meydanı See Hippodrome.
Atatürk, Mustafa Kemal 25, 38, 40
Austrians See Habsburgs.
ayan 115 n.1, 127; Albanian, 3, 84; Balkan, 86, 93, 97, 99, 103 n.72; Circassian, 110; in Algeria, 108; in Anatolia, 16; in Egypt, 105, 106, 107, 108, 109, 110, 111, 113; in Karaferye and vicinity, 73-78, 80, 82, 83, 85, 87, 88; in Salonika, 80; in Vidin, 92; Mehmed Ali as, 2, 9, 124, 125, 127; of Rusçuk, 94; provincial, 120; rebellious, 4-5, 6, 113; studies on, 118-19 n.9; vs. central government, 89, 90, 121, 126
Ayntab See Gaziantep.
Azov 63, 113

Babadağı 69
Babur, Muhammad Zahiruddin, Mughal emperor 48, 58-60
Baghdad 12, 17, 121
baghi 96, 109-110
Baki Paşa 32, 33
Balkans 8, 50, 86, 89, 90, 91 n.11, 93, 94, 96, 97, 98, 99, 100, 103, 119, 121, 122, 126

bandits 21-22, 23, 64, 127 n.21 See also *eşkiya*.
banishment See exile.
bedouin 107, 108, 109, 135
Bektaşis 122
Belgrade 12, 28, 53, 61, 63, 66, 78 n.17, 89, 90, 91, 94, 95, 96, 97, 98, 100, 101, 102, 103, 108
Bender 61, 65, 68 n.14, 71
Berman, Harold J. 116-17
Bessarabia 63, 66, 123
Black Sea 2, 12, 61, 63, 66, 70, 111 n.30, 113, 124
boats 13, 46, 47, 48, 49, 50, 53, 58, 69, 70, 109, 112, 119, 123
Bonaparte See Napoleon.
Bosnia, Bosnians 3, 15, 32, 50, 65, 70, 78 n.17, 90, 94, 99, 100, 101, 102, 121
Bostanzade Yahya 29-30, 34, 35
bridges 48, 49, 50, 51, 52, 53, 54, 57, 58
brigands See *eşkiya*.
British 9 n.17, 53, 103 n.72, 112, 118, 119, 121, 122, 127
Bucharest, Treaty of (1812) 63, 123
Buda 53, 61
Bug River 61, 63, 67
Bulgaria, Bulgarians 74 n.4, 90 n.2, 91 n.9, 94, 98
Bundren family 46, 49, 52, 55, 57, 58
Burgos 61, 70
Bursa 14, 29 n.21, 40, 61, 119 n.9
buyruldu 77, 78, 79, 80, 82, 83, 84, 86, 91 n.10, 98 n.50, 99 nn.55, 56
Byron, Lord (George Gordon) 121

Cairo 1 n.4, 3-4 n.7, 6, 12, 14, 62, 106, 107, 108, 109, 122, 123, 124, 127, 130, 131, 132, 133, 137
cannon 51, 52, 69, 133, 135
capitalism 20, 117 n.6, 118 n.9
Catholics 26, 108, 112, 117 n.6
Caucasus 8, 72, 110
*celali*s 1, 15, 22, 23, 28, 127 n.21

centralization 1 n.3, 7, 8, 22, 75 n.7, 89-90, 93, 127 n.21
Charles VI, Habsburg emperor 108
Chief Black Eunuch 14, 26 n.2, 106
Christians 8, 28, 31, 35, 37, 41, 48 n.7, 51, 53, 54, 55, 65, 70, 71, 77, 79, 82, 83, 85, 109, 116, 117, 121-22
*çiftlik*s 74 n.6, 79, 93, 94, 97
Circassians 3, 10, 105, 110, 111
citadel of Cairo 130, 131, 133, 134
cizye 76, 78, 85 n.46, 91
Committee of Union and Progress 36
conscripts, conscription 129, 130, 131, 132, 133, 134, 135, 136
contract between ruler and subjects 4, 65, 116
Cossacks 27, 65, 66 n.8, 67
court-martial 6, 129, 137, 138
Crete 96, 123, 134 n.15
Crimea 66, 71, 72, 110, 134 n.18
Croatia 50, 54

Damascus 1 n.4, 12, 14, 119 n.9, 124
Damurdashi, Ahmed Kâhya ᶜAzeban al- 6, 107 nn.7, 11, 109, 111, 112
Danişmend, İsmail Hami 39, 40
Danube River 8 n.16, 9, 12, 48, 49, 50, 51, 61, 63, 65, 66, 67, 69, 70, 71, 72, 90, 94, 99, 103, 110, 123
Darüssaade Ağası See Chief Black Eunuch.
Davud Paşa, Kara, grand vezir 14, 27, 28, 30, 32
dayı (dey) 102, 108
decentralization 7, 8, 75 n.7, 120, 121
decline paradigm 7, 20, 23, 40 n.85
defterdar 18, 107, 136 n.28, 137
Delta, Nile 133, 134
Derviş Bey, son of Haci Mustafa Paşa 101-102
Derviş Efendi 76
desertion 4 n.12, 60, 64, 66, 67, 70, 99, 131, 132, 133, 136
devşirme 8, 27-28, 40, 41 n.92
disease 46, 53, 59, 64, 66

Diyarbakır 8, 12, 18, 19, 33, 121
Dnieper River 9, 12, 63
drowning 49, 50, 51, 53, 55, 57, 59, 60, 109

Ebu Bekir Paşa, muhafız of Belgrade, vali of Bosnia 91, 94, 95 n.27, 102
ecnebi 8, 37 n.74, 38
Edirne 27, 29 n.21, 34 n.57, 61.75, 94, 106, 124
Edirne vakʿası (1703) 1, 3
Erzurum 8, 12, 14, 16, 17, 18, 31, 111
eşkiya 3, 18, 64, 74, 76, 77, 78, 82, 83, 84, 85, 90, 91, 92, 93, 95, 96, 97, 98, 99 n.57, 100, 101, 102, 106, 108, 109, 113, 121, 124, 135
Evliya Çelebi 110, 111
execution 5, 14, 15, 19, 22, 27, 30, 31, 32 n.41, 37, 42, 53, 71, 79, 80, 91, 92, 96, 102, 103, 109, 111, 118, 122, 126, 131, 135, 136, 138
exile 5, 36, 38, 78, 79, 80, 82, 84, 85, 87, 92, 96, 101, 108

Famagusta See Mağusa.
Faqari faction 105, 106, 107
Faulkner, William 45, 46, 47, 48, 49, 51, 55, 56, 57, 58
fellāhīn See peasants.
*ferman*s 5, 6, 76, 77, 78, 80 n.24, 81, 82, 83, 84, 85, 86, 91, 92, 93 n.19, 94, 97, 98, 99 nn.52, 56, 101, 102, 103, 106, 107, 109, 131, 133
*fetva*s 96, 101, 124-25
Fezleke-i Tarih 15, 16, 34 n.61, 41 n.92, 42 n.95
fitne 3, 18, 33 n.49, 64, 76
fitne ü fesad 3, 17, 18, 33, 34, 74 n.3, 110
floods 46, 47, 49, 50, 52, 53, 54, 55, 57, 58
food 4, 46 n.1, 50, 52 n.20, 53, 59, 60, 65, 66, 69, 99, 106, 132
foreign See *ecnebi*.

French 36, 40, 84 nn.41, 44, 99, 103 n.72, 107 n.11; 108, 113, 119, 121, 123, 125 n.19, 130, 134

Gábor, Bethlen, prince of Transylvania 26
Ganges River 46, 58
Gaziantep 17
Georgians 9, 96, 111, 113, 121 n.13
Gharbiye province 62, 133
grandees See *ayan*.
Greece, Greeks 3, 40, 70, 89, 94 n.25, 118, 119, 121-22, 123, 126, 133, 134
guilds 3, 85, 86, 88
guns 1 n.3, 67, 70, 79, 93 n.21, 96, 100, 102, 119, 130, 137
Gurgan River 58

Habsburgs 3, 10, 26 n.5, 48, 50, 66 n.9, 89, 91, 93, 95, 102, 103, 104, 108, 110, 112, 113
hacc 14, 27, 33, 107, 124, 131
Hafız Ahmed Paşa, governor of Diyarbakır 8, 18, 19, 33
Haile-i Osmaniye (Ottoman Tragedy) 13, 14, 15, 16
hain 96, 109, 113
Halil Ağa, Koşancalı (Gushanatz Ali) 102, 103
Halil Paşa, kapudan paşa, grand vezir 22, 23
harem 7 n.15, 14, 26 nn.2, 4
Hasan Ağa, Arnavud, of Katerin 74 n.6, 84, 85
Hasan Paşa, Abaza, governor of Aleppo 111
Hasan Paşa, Cezayırlı, kapudan paşa 113
Hasan Paşa, governor of Bosnia 50-51, 52
Hasanbeyzade Ahmed 15, 31-32, 33, 34, 35
Hijaz 123, 136
Hippodrome 14

horses 46, 49, 51, 54, 55, 57, 58, 72, 95
households 4, 5, 9, 18, 22, 69, 72, 106, 108, 110 n.23, 111 n.26, 119 n.9, 120, 121 n.13, 123, 132
hüccet 77, 78, 82, 83, 84, 91 n.7, 93 n.20
Hugo, Victor 121, 122
Hungary, Hungarians 8, 26, 48, 54, 59, 112 n.37
hunger See food.
Husayn Mirza, Sultan 58
Hüseyin b. Sefer See Tugi Çelebi.
Hüseyin Paşa, *kâhya bey* of Haci Mustafa Paşa 96-97
Hüsrev Paşa, governor of Cairo 115 author's note, 122
Hüsrev Paşa, grand vezir 15

Ibn Khaldun 74 n.4, 119-20
Ibrahim Ağa 130
Ibrahim Ağa, Seyyid 80, 81
Ibrahim Bey Abu Shanab 105
Ibrahim Efendi, *vekil* of Abdurrahman Ağa 81
Ibrahim Paşa, son of Mehmed Ali 123, 124-25
Idris Ağa, Molla, protégé of Pasvanoğlu 98 n.51, 99 n.58, 103
iltizām See tax farm.
imperialism 118
India (Hindustan) 9 n.17, 47, 58, 59, 60, 109
Indus River 58, 59
İnebahtı See Lepanto.
Ionian Islands 121
Iran 8, 28, 109, 110
Islam 8, 20, 28, 37 n.74, 41 n.88, 73, 77 n.12, 79, 96, 109, 115, 116, 117, 118, 119, 120, 124-25, 127, 128
Ismail, son of Mehmed Ali Paşa 131
Ismail, town on Danube 61, 67
Ismail Ağa, Terseniklioğlu, *ayan* of Ruşçuk 94, 97, 98, 99, 103
Ismail Bey b. Ivaz 105, 106, 107, 110

Ismail Paşa, governor of Temeşvar 53
Isne 62, 129, 135, 137
Istanbul 12, 61; army in, 25, 27; as capital, 1, 5, 7, 16-17, 26, 29 n.21, 30, 31, 55, 56, 64 n.2, 79, 85, 87, 92, 93, 95, 99 n.58, 122, 131; as city, 14, 33, 36; as *kul* center, 8, 18, 19, 40; as power center, 65, 76; flight to, 102, 106, 108; gifts from, 98; Janissaries from, 68; judgeship of, 34 n.56; Mehmed Ali's agent in, 136; military threat to, 124; moving capital from, 38, 39; orders from, 9, 17, 80, 106; Ottoman court in, 106; Patrona Halil revolt in, 111; ships leaving, 69; sultan in, 15, 51, 131; synonym for government, 87, 123, 124; tax-farmers in, 80
isyan, âsi 3, 16, 17, 18, 23, 64, 91 n.11, 94 n.23, 98 n.51, 99 n.53, 110, 133, 138

Jabarti, ʿAbd al-Rahman al- 1 n.4, 107, 113 n.40, 130 nn.4, 5, 131 n.7
Janina 61, 121, 122
Janissary, Janissaries aga, 17, 49, 107; and Abaza Mehmed Paşa, 16, 17, 18, 19, 22, 31; at Ochakov, 67-70; at Pruth, 48 n.6; attack commander, 53; barracks, 17; Bektaşis and, 122; "bosses," 4; cross Raab, 54; destruction of, 17, 30, 120, 122; dispossessed by war, 93; fixed salaries of, 4; in Belgrade, 94, 95, 96, 101-102; in guilds, 3; in Istanbul, 5, 16, 17; in Karaferye and vicinity, 73 n.2, 79 n.20, 83; in Vidin, 91, 92, 100; non- 65; numbers, 42, 63, 68-69; of Porte, 80; oppose Nizam-i Cedid, 90, 97; oppose Osman II, 8, 14, 28; overturn soup kettles, 6; Republican historians and, 36-38; Selim III and, 134, 138; Tugi as, 28, 34, 35

Jassy, Treaty of (1792) 63
Jerusalem 6, 12, 115 n.1, 119 n.9, 121 n.12, 124, 126
Jirja 62, 135
justice 17, 56, 64, 65, 74 n.4, 87, 117, 118, 119-20, 125

kabadayı 102
kadı 6, 17, 68, 73, 76, 79, 80, 81, 85, 86, 90 n.4, 111
kâhya See *kethüda*.
kapı kulları 123
Karaçelebizade Abdülaziz 34, 35
Karasu 68
Katerin 84
Kâtip Çelebi 14, 15, 16, 19, 34-35, 41, 42 n.95 See also *Fezleke-i Tarih*.
Kautiliya 47, 52
Kavala 61, 75, 76, 82, 123, 124
kaymakam 26 n.2, 84, 98, 107
Kemal, Mustafa See Atatürk.
Kerment 54
kethüda 78, 79, 81, 84 n.44, 95, 96, 107, 136
Khartoum 137
khedive 115, 125-26, 127
Khwaja Khan 59
Kilburun 66, 67, 71
Kızlar Ağası See Chief Black Eunuch.
knezes 94, 95 n.27, 97, 100, 101, 102
Knights of St. John 112
Köprülüs 19
Kösem Sultan 14, 22, 27
Kosovo 61, 90
Köstence 69
Köstendil 61, 70, 75, 78, 80 n.26
Kraina 94, 99, 100
Kritopoulos 85, 88
Kublai Khan 46-47, 49
Küçük Kaynarca, Treaty of 71
kullar 8, 14, 15, 16, 17, 18, 19, 23, 24, 28 n.11, 42, 123 n.16
Kupa River 50
Kurds 3, 9, 41, 65, 72, 110

Latif Ağa 131
law 19, 27, 28, 38, 39, 42, 56, 75, 81, 87, 91, 92, 93, 100, 101, 109 n.22, 115, 116, 117, 118, 119-20, 124-25, 126, 127, 128, 136, 137
Lazarević, Ranko 100
Lazoğlu (Lazughli), Mehmed 131
Lepanto (İnebahtı, Naupactos) 61, 84, 122
levends 68, 69, 70
Lower Egypt 132, 133, 134 n.20

Macedonia 70, 75, 84, 88, 123
Mağusa (Famagusta) 75, 78
Mahmud II (1808-39), Sultan 2, 37, 39, 115, 121, 122, 123, 124, 125, 127, 130, 131
Ma'iyya Saniyya 129 n.1, 132 n.9, 133 nn.10-14, 134 nn.17, 19-21, 135 nn.22-27, 136 nn.28-31, 137
malikâne See tax farm.
Malta 112
Maltepe 33
mamluks 1 n.4, 8, 9 n.18, 105, 109 n.19, 110, 111, 113 n.40, 122, 130, 131, 133, 134, 136
Mansure province 62, 118 n.9, 133
Marxism 20, 21, 116
Mecca 12, 27, 106, 124, 131
Medina 12, 106, 124, 131
Mediterranean Sea 12, 61, 62, 108, 113
medrese 31, 34 n.57, 75
Mehdi 129, 134
Mehmed III (1595-1603), Sultan 29 n.21, 52
Mehmed IV (1648-87), Sultan 34 n.57, 54, 55, 56
Mehmed Ağa, Elhac, brother of Kara Ahmed 74 n.6, 75, 76, 77, 79
Mehmed Efendi, Ramiz, Karaferye *ayan* 74 n.6, 75, 77, 78, 79, 82, 86, 87
Mehmed Murad Bey See Mizancı Murad.

154 Index

Mehmed Paşa, Abaza, field commander at Ochakov 71
Mehmed Paşa, governor of Salonika 75
Mehmed Paşa, Gürcü, grand vezir 22, 23-24
Mehmed Paşa, Köprülü, grand vezir 111
Mehmed Paşa, muhafız of Vidin 93
Mehmed Paşa, Muhsinzade 65 n.6, 71, 88 n.58
Mehmed Paşa, Satırcı 52, 53
Mehmed Paşa, Silahdar, grand vezir 65
mercenaries 6 n.14, 8, 111, 123, 130
Michael, voyvoda of Wallachia 51, 53
Minufiye province 62, 132, 133, 135, 137
Minye province 62, 134
Mitchell, Timothy 21, 23, 115-16
Mizancı Murad (Mehmed Murad Bey) 36-38, 39
modernity 21, 42, 118 n.9
modernization 40, 116, 119
Moldavia, Moldavians 61, 67, 123
Mongols 49
Montecucoli, General Raimondo, Count of 54
Morea 96, 122, 123, 133, 134, 135
Moscow 112
Mosul 119 n.9, 121
mud 48, 53, 109
Mughals 48, 58
mühimme registers 6, 68 n.14, 106, 107, 108, 109 nn.18, 20, 112
mukataa See tax farm.
Münnich, Field Marshal Burkhard Christoph, Count von 65, 66 n.8
Murad IV (1623-40), Sultan 14, 15, 22, 29 n.21, 34 n.56
Murad Paşa, Kuyucu, grand vezir 15, 22
Mureş(ul) River 52, 61

Muslims 3, 4 n.7, 37 n.74, 41, 42, 51, 52, 55, 56, 64, 65, 68, 77, 79, 80, 82, 83, 89, 101, 109, 116, 117 n.5, 119, 124, 125, 126, 127
Mustafa I (1617, 1623), Sultan 14, 25, 27, 28, 29, 30 n.23, 31, 32 n.38, 38, 42
Mustafa, Molla, Karaferye *ayan* 74, 75, 76, 77, 78, 79, 80, 81, 82, 83, 84, 85, 86, 87, 88
Mustafa, Poriçeli Köse 96, 98
Mustafa Ağa, brother of Kara Ahmed of Karaferye 75, 76, 83
Mustafa Ağa, Çelebi 95, 96
Mustafa Paşa, Alemdar, of Rusçuk 103
Mustafa Paşa, Haci, muhafız of Belgrade, Rumeli vali 94, 95, 96, 97-98, 99, 100, 101, 102, 104
mutasarrıf 68, 69, 70, 98, 99
mutiny 1, 2, 3, 4, 5, 6, 7, 10, 45, 46, 49, 50, 52, 53, 55, 56, 57, 59, 60, 63, 64, 65, 67, 68, 70, 71, 110, 111, 113, 115, 121, 122, 123, 126-27, 128, 129, 136, 137, 138
Naima, Mustafa 13, 16, 19, 42 n.95, 48, 49, 50, 51, 52
Napoleon Bonaparte 103 n.72, 118, 119, 120, 121, 122, 123, 126
nationalism 3, 9, 37, 38, 39, 41, 90, 118, 119
Navarino 123, 124
Nenadović, Alexa 100, 101
Nicopolis (Niğbolu) 53, 61, 94, 96, 97, 99 n.57
Nile River 12, 62, 109, 112, 132
Niş 61, 101, 102
Nizām al-Jadīd, Mehmed Ali's 129, 130, 134
Nizam-i Cedid, Selim III's 5, 90, 97
non-Muslims See Christians, *zimmis*.
notables See *ayan*.
Nur, Riza 38, 39

Ömer, father of Pasvanoğlu Osman Paşa 90-91

Ömer Efendi, tutor of Osman II 26, 30, 32 n.40, 33, 34
Orientalism 20, 116
Osman, Elhac 80, 81
Osman II ("Genç Osman," 1618-22), Sultan 2, 4, 6, 7-8, 14, 15, 16, 17, 18, 19, 22, 25, 26, 27, 28, 29, 30, 31, 32, 33, 34, 35, 36, 37, 38, 39, 40, 41, 42, 111
Osman Ağa, Binbaşı 68
Osman Bey, officer of Mehmed Ali Paşa 135, 136-37
Osman Bey Zülfikar 106, 107, 108
Osman Paşa, Gürcü, Rumeli vali 96, 99
Oxus River 59
Özbeks 8, 58, 59

Passarowitz (Pozorofça) 61, 96, 98, 100
Patrona Halil rebellion 1, 4, 111, 113
pay 4, 50, 53, 63 n.1, 64, 65, 68, 69, 70, 100, 120, 130, 132, 136
peasants 5, 6, 37 n.74, 116, 118-19 n.9, 126, 129, 130, 131, 132, 133, 134, 137, 138 See also *reaya*.
Peçevi, Ibrahim 15, 16, 18, 19, 23, 26 n.2, 29 n.21, 32-33, 34, 35, 36, 42, 51 nn.14, 15, 52 n.20
Peloponnese 84
Peter I ("the Great"), tsar of Russia 112-13
Peter II, tsar of Russia 112
pilgrimage See *hacc*.
piyade 69
Plovdiv (Filibe) 61, 97
Polish campaign of 1621 14, 26-27, 29-30
Poriçe Island 98
Porte 26 n.5, 41 n.91, 76, 78, 79, 80, 81, 83 n.37, 85, 86, 87, 88, 95, 96, 97, 98 n.49, 99, 100, 101, 102, 103, 115, 120, 121, 122, 123, 124, 126, 127
Potemkin, Marshal Grigorii 63, 67

Pozorofça See Passarowitz.
Protestants 26
provisions See food.
Pruth River 48 n.6, 61, 112, 123

Qānūn al-Filāha (Law of Cultivation) 116, 125 n.19
Qasimi faction 105, 106, 107
Qazdağlıs 9, 105, 106 n.4, 107, 119 n.9
Qus 62, 129

Raab River 54, 56
rain 52, 54, 55, 58, 66
Rákóczi, Ferenc II 112
Ramiz Efendi See Mehmed Efendi, Ramiz.
Rashid al-Din 46-47, 49
reaya 1, 3, 8, 9, 74, 76, 78, 84, 88, 89, 91, 94, 97, 98, 100, 101, 120, 123, 128 See also peasants.
rebels 3, 6, 10, 16, 18, 19, 33, 36, 39, 41, 64, 71, 74, 75, 80, 87, 91, 92, 95, 96, 99, 101, 102, 106, 107, 108, 109, 110, 111, 112, 117 n.5, 118, 123, 124, 125, 126, 127, 128, 129, 130, 131, 133, 134, 135, 136
reform, reformers 3, 7, 25, 36, 37, 38, 39, 40, 41, 42, 43, 90, 93, 94, 97, 119, 125, 126, 127
Reşid Paşa, grand vezir 124-25
"rights" 65, 68, 116, 126
Romania 69
Romanovs 63
Rumiantsev, Field Marshal Piotr Aleksandrovich, Count 68 n.17, 71
Rumeli, Rumelia 19, 29 n.21, 30 n.23, 34 n.56, 74 n.4, 77, 78 n.17, 84, 85, 86, 91, 92 n.14, 93, 96, 97, 98, 99, 101, 102, 118 n.9
Rusçuk 94, 97
Russia, Russians 3, 9 n.18, 10, 36, 48 n.6, 63, 65, 66, 67, 70, 71, 93, 103, 104, 108, 110, 111 n.30, 112, 113, 119, 120, 121, 122, 123, 124
Rycaut, Sir Paul 53-55, 56

Safavids 8, 10, 28, 40 n.84, 109, 110, 112, 113
şaki See *eşkiya*.
Salonika 12, 61, 73, 75, 76, 78, 79, 80, 81, 82, 83 n.40, 84, 87 n.56, 124, 131
sancak 16, 17, 69, 73, 78, 82, 84, 90, 92, 94, 119 n.9
Sarıgöl (Ptolemais) 75, 77, 83, 85
Sava River 61, 100
Second Constitutional Period 35, 36
Segedin 53, 61
*sekban*s 14, 17, 18, 22, 23
Selim I (1512-20), Sultan 8
Selim III (1789-1807), Sultan 3, 4, 5, 37, 39, 89, 92, 94, 96, 97, 98 nn.46-48, 99, 100, 101, 102 n.68, 103, 104, 124, 131, 134, 138
Selva 98, 99
Şemdanizade Fındıklılı Süleyman Efendi 69 n.19, 70 n.26, 71, 111
Semendire 98, 100
Serbia, Serbs 3, 89, 90, 91, 92, 94, 95, 96 n.34, 97, 99 n.58, 100, 101, 102, 103, 104, 119, 123, 126
*serdengeçti*s 48 n.6, 69
Şeref, Abdurrahman 35-36
şeriat 6, 77, 90, 91 n.7, 93 n.19, 117 n.5, 118, 119 n.9
şeyh ül-beled 1 n.4, 107, 108, 109 n. 19
şeyhülislam 26 n.2, 29 n.21, 34 n.57, 78, 96
Shaw, Stanford J. 40, 89 n.1, 107
ships See boats.
*sicil*s 6, 19-20, 73, 74 n.5, 75, 77, 78, 79, 80 n.25, 83 nn.39, 40, 84, 86, 90 n.4, 115, 119 n.9
Sinan Paşa, grand vezir 51, 52
Sinop 71, 96
sipahis 5, 14, 30-31, 36, 68 n.17, 76, 77, 84, 98, 102
Siska 50, 61
Sistova 61, 97; Treaty of (1791), 91, 95 n.29

Sofia 61, 90 n.4, 98, 99
state, Ottoman: and Abaza Mehmed Paşa, 13; and ayan, 86 n.55; and bandits, 127 n.21; and Patrona Halil revolt, 111; and rebels, 6, 10, 80; and tax-farming, 81; centralizing, 90; Council of, 36; Egyptian, 127; intervention in Belgrade, 89, 91, 95 n.27; intervention in Karaferye, 73-76, 78, 81, 84 n.46, 85, 87, 88; intervention in provinces, 86 n.55, 87, 119 n.9; Osman II and, 15, 36; reformist, 40; synonym for government, 2, 5, 15, 16, 24, 34, 37, 38, 68, 71, 79, 80, 89, 90, 93, 97, 100, 101, 103, 109, 125, 126; theoretical issues, 13, 19-23, 116
Sudan 131, 132, 133, 135, 136, 137
Süleyman I (1520-66), Sultan 7, 8, 22, 29 n.21, 34 n.56, 40, 47 n.4, 56, 118
Süleyman Paşa, Canikli 67, 70
Suliots 121-22
Şumla (Şumnu, Shumen) 71, 97, 99
Suvorov, General Aleksandr Vasil'evich 66, 67
Syria 14, 19, 22, 39, 115, 117 n.5, 118 n.9, 120, 123, 124, 125, 126, 128

Tanzimat 7, 120, 123 n.16
Tarih-i Al-i Osman 15, 18
Tatars 48 n.6, 65, 66
tax farm, tax farmers 68, 74, 75, 76, 78, 80, 81, 84, 94, 106
taxes 3, 5, 7 n.15, 68, 76, 87, 89, 91, 93, 94, 97, 100, 102, 106, 120, 126, 128, 132, 133, 134, 136
Terseniklioğlu Ismail Ağa See Ismail Ağa, Terseniklioğlu.
Thessaly 84, 121
Thirty Years' War 26
timar 120
Tırnovo 97, 98
Tisza River 53, 61

Topkapı Palace 4, 5, 8, 14, 22, 24, 25, 26, 27, 29 n.20, 31, 34, 35, 37, 38, 40, 41 n.92, 72, 79, 122, 123, 131
Transylvania 26, 52, 53, 61, 112
treasury 27, 42, 49, 53, 77, 81, 82-3
Trieste 12, 61, 108
Tripoli, Lebanon 124
Tripoli, Libya 12, 108
Tugi Çelebi 15, 16, 17, 18, 19, 23, 27-28, 29, 30, 31, 32, 33 n.46, 34, 35, 42 n.95
Turks 32 n.40, 37, 38, 39, 40, 41, 42, 54, 55, 56, 66 n.10, 67, 83 n.39, 92, 94, 97, 108 n.15, 132

ulema 3, 4 n.7, 27, 28, 32, 34 n.57, 38, 39, 77, 78, 92, 93, 117 n.5, 124, 126
ümera 14, 15, 16, 18, 19, 23
Upper Egypt 129, 132, 133, 134, 138
Üsküdar 19
Uzbeks See Özbeks.

vakʿanüvis 16, 19, 35, 36
Varad 52, 53, 61
Varna 69, 99
Venetian consul in Salonika 73, 79, 80, 82, 83, 84 n.45

vezirs 5, 8, 38, 54, 78 n.17, 97 n.40, 99, 100, 126 n.20
Vidin 6, 61, 86, 89, 90, 91, 92, 93, 94, 96, 97, 98, 99, 100, 101, 102, 103
Vienna 48, 61, 108, 110, 111
voyvoda, voyvodalık 51, 74, 75, 76, 77, 78, 80, 81, 87, 96, 98, 99

wagons 49, 57
Wahhabis 123, 124, 130, 131, 134
Wallachia, Wallachians 51, 61, 90 n.4, 91, 92, 94, 95, 96, 97, 103, 124
Weber, Max 20, 116

Yahya, Bostanzade See Bostanzade Yahya.
Yahya Paşa, commander at Ochakov 65, 66
*yamak*s 67, 68, 69, 70, 91, 94, 100, 101, 103
Yangtze River 49
Yediküle 14
Yergögü 51, 52, 61
Young Turk Revolution 35, 36
Yücel, Yaşar 39-40

Zahir al-ʿUmar 86 n.55, 121
*zimmi*s 76, 78, 85, 89, 91
Zülfikar Bey 107, 108, 109

www.ingramcontent.com/pod-product-compliance
Lightning Source LLC
Chambersburg PA
CBHW070945230426
43666CB00011B/2562